# Dreamer

20 years of psychic dreams and
how they changed my life

# Dreamer

20 years of psychic dreams and
how they changed my life

Andrew J. Paquette

BOOKS

Winchester, UK
Washington, USA

First published by O-Books, 2011
O Books is an imprint of John Hunt Publishing Ltd., The Bothy, Deershot Lodge, Park Lane, Ropley,
Hants, SO24 0BE, UK
office1@o-books.net
www.o-books.com

For distributor details and how to order please visit the 'Ordering' section on our website.

Text copyright Andrew J. Paquette 2010

ISBN: 978 1 84694 502 1

A CIP catalogue record for this book is available from the British Library.

Design: Stuart Davies

Printed in the UK by CPI Antony Rowe
Printed in the USA by Offset Paperback Mfrs, Inc

We operate a distinctive and ethical publishing philosophy in all
areas of its business, from its global network of authors to
production and worldwide distribution.

# CONTENTS

# Acknowledgements

More people than I can name have contributed in some way to this book. Here are some of them: Nina, who sat outside in baking sun, or inside on rainy days, coming up with excellent questions for me to answer. Without her, the book wouldn't be the same. Kitty, who unfailingly spotted errors that I had to fix, and modestly made me aware of them. Dr. Gillian Holloway PhD, with whom I corresponded on subjects related to the book, reinvigorated my interest in the subject by helping me look at it in a new way. Dr. Richard Breedon PhD, whose friendship over the past twenty-two years has always been reliable, and whose unflinching honesty in the letters he has provided for this book will always be appreciated. Dr. David Ryback PhD, who a very long time ago told me this would make an interesting book.

My family and friends put up with numerous verification phone calls from me. Their cooperation is very much appreciated, especially from my skeptical Uncle Tom, who was a very good sport about my calls on paranormal topics.

This book is dedicated to my wife Kitty, who has put up with all my projects for the last twenty-six years, and has been unflagging in her support.

# Introduction

Dreams are memories. They are not simply "a series of thoughts, images, or emotions occurring during sleep," as Merriam-Webster's dictionary describes them. Those things may be involved, but that is just another way to describe how the various elements of a dream are remembered. What happened to you today? Was it a collection of thoughts, images, and emotions? No. What happened to you today were a series of events that you participated in, either passively or actively. Your memory of your day, however, can be described using the dictionary definition for "dream," apart from one thing: you weren't asleep.

Why is there a special word for memories that originate from sleep, when there is no special word for memories related to waking activity? Because it is not generally accepted in western cultures that anything real happens during sleep, therefore, they are not "memories," because there is nothing real to recall. Instead, the images themselves are the dream, like abstract paintings made by an artist without a model. This is like saying that the videotaped footage of a birthday party is the same as the party itself, except it denies the birthday party ever happened and accepts only the footage. From what is this footage supposedly created? According to Freud, repressed desires, combined with memories from our waking lives, are enough to fraudulently manufacture even the most vivid, magnificently detailed dream. More modern theories state that dreams are the by-product of chemical activity in the brain. It is wrong, but in academic circles, it is de rigueur to accept some permutation of this theory. Both of these ideas are dependent upon a wholly mechanical view of life, all of which is soulless, the random by-product of purely physical forces.

To prove this wrong, one needs only one "dream," one memory retained after sleep, that is demonstrably connected to something real but outside one's own experience. There are reports of many such dreams throughout history. They are mostly isolated incidents, occurring on only a handful of widely spaced occasions in any given person's life. Regardless of incidence, if any one of these are what they purport to be, then everything we've been told about dreams is wrong. In my own life, I have had hundreds of dreams that convincingly correspond with things that could not possibly be connected with anything I could be expected to know or imagine. These are dreams of future events, such as the 9/11 disaster, the Boxing Day tsunami, the Gulf War (both of them), of people at distant locations, friends, family, and strangers, people at the moment of death or severe distress, dreams of future *Time* magazine covers, and many more things. They are so numerous that to somehow retain a belief that dreams are literally some kind of accidental by-product of brain activity or repressed desire would make no sense. How does random brain activity or a repressed desire create a dream of a future plane crash?

Over the last twenty years, I have made an effort to record, analyze, and understand my dreams. This avocation of mine was inspired by the social friction I encountered every time my knowledge of what dreams truly are came into conflict with daily life. This happened far more often than one might think, because so many beliefs are dependent on other core beliefs. If a person does not believe in the existence of a soul, for instance, then their perspective on all things related to death will be affected by it. Beyond that, it can have a pronounced effect on other life decisions, such as divorce, money, and career. It can affect one's taste in poetry, music, film, and books. It touches so many aspects of one's life, that a difference of opinion may be noticed in myriad ways. I found myself constantly confronted with contrary attitudes on this subject, as well as great curiosity. It is for this reason that I have decided to put down on paper a description of my experiences, and an explanation of what they mean.

My records are extensive, and the wealth of information they contain has proven enough to suggest some very intriguing possibilities. At the very least, certain dreams completely destroy commonly held skeptical arguments against precognition, telepathy, and out-of-body-experiences, among other things. That is the small stuff, however. Our sleep memories are more than the occasional intersection of the supernatural with our physical environment. They are a continuum of shared experience, something we all participate in at some level, whether to a weak degree or strong. They are memories of our other life, lived in another place, and with each other. Our memories may be fragmentary and riddled with mistakes, but if you make the effort you will see that they are not just images, they are recollections. If you know this, you can begin to work on improving your memory, and then you too will see that a "dream" is not a dream, it is something much, much, more.

Andrew Paquette

*Part one:*

Earthbound

Mundus Limus

## Chapter One

# Amsterdam

Two people come up from behind me. One flanks me on the right, the other walks directly behind me. They want me to go into an alley with them, an alley I now see to be less than a hundred yards away. I want to cry out, to get the attention of some of the people I see crossing the street, but one look from the man on my right and I know I'd better not. They want my money, but want to take it in private. I can't run to the left because of a brick wall. I can't run to the right because I am flanked on that side. I can't stop walking because whoever is behind me keeps pushing me forward. Running forward would bring me to the alley. I decide that the situation is completely out of my hands. I will go in the alley, give them my money, and leave. With any luck, they'll let me keep my passport.

The alley is deeper than it looked from the street. Inside, it is nearly empty, almost clean. The man behind me comes around to my side and brandishes a pistol. He waves me to the back of the alley, well away from any prying eyes on the sidewalk outside. There is what at first looked like a pile of rags lying on the ground at the rear of the alley. Another look and I realize it is a person. A corpse. At that moment, I know these men in front of me are responsible. I lose all my strength then, my knees buckle, and I sink to the ground.

The two men pause for a moment and exchange a few phrases in Dutch. They seem to think I am funny, kneeling on the ground, terror stricken. The man with the gun doesn't pay attention to me for a moment. He holds the gun carelessly by his side, inches from my nose. I'm not going to get a better chance than this. I bring my hand to the gun as quietly as I can, intent on grabbing it. Neither man pays any attention to me. Emboldened, I feel the cool metal beneath my fingers when I touch the barrel. I am scared. I hesitate, and this is a mistake.

The gunman looks at me with sad, smirking eyes as if to say, "too bad," and shoots me in the neck. The pain is intense. Every nerve I have screams from the overload of sensation. I want to yell, but can't. My throat doesn't work. Warm blood washes down my neck and soaks my shirt. I know I am dying. I don't care about the muggers anymore. I forget they are there. I try to crawl to the street, but it is too far. Every beat of my heart pumps more of my blood into the alley, and with every beat the distance to the street seems to double. It takes an eternity to crawl ten feet. I am still an eternity away from safety and know I will die right there in that alley.

I feel my life slipping away. I grow faint to the point that I barely feel pain. I want to hold on, but can't. I think of my girlfriend, Kitty, in New York. I love her, and can't imagine leaving her this way. Even as I think all these things, I feel my spirit leave my body. My bloody, empty shell lies in the alley, fifteen feet from the sidewalk. Already the muggers are moving towards it to pull it back out of sight. I don't care anymore. I want to see Kitty.

Now I am looking down on Kitty in her mother's New York City apartment. I float near the ceiling. Kitty is alone. She sits at the kitchen table sipping tea. She hasn't heard of my death yet, and probably won't anytime soon. I want to scream at her, to tell her what has happened, that I am right there, that I am dead but not gone. She is completely oblivious. I know there is nothing I can do to attract her attention. I look at her mother's ceiling for a while and wonder. So this is what it is like to be dead. I can't believe it. I am really dead.

I have no idea what I should do next. I think about how I have died and how my spirit left my body. I realize then that it was thinking of Kitty that brought me to her. In this new state, I feel

7

more aware of my surroundings than I ever was when alive. There isn't much to do, but it is interesting that death is not only a rather peaceful event, but I feel more awake when outside of my body than in it.

Some colors on the ceiling attract my attention, pink and blue. I stare at them for what seems like a long time, but "time" doesn't exist any longer, not for me anyway. There is something about these colors that is familiar. They are like the colors of a neon sign outside my apartment window in Amsterdam. My gaze travels down the wall to a window, where I see the sign. This is my apartment! And then I have another shock: I am alive! I am sitting upright in my cot; with my eyes already wide open. I must have been looking at my own ceiling with my eyes open while convinced of my death, but it was all a dream.

Full of adrenalin, I got out of bed to call Kitty. It was four in the morning in Holland, but would be a slightly more reasonable nine P.M. in New York. She couldn't talk for long, but it was enough to work out the idea that it was time for me to return to the states. Clearly, the loneliness of living in a foreign country had taken a toll on me, or I wouldn't have had such a frightening dream.

Kitty and I made arrangements to share an apartment in New York. Two weeks after the call, I went to the Veringigde Spaarbank and closed out my account. I then walked over to the post office, called Kitty, and told her I would leave in twenty-four hours. My third stop was the travel agency in Amsterdam's diamond district. I picked up my one-way ticket to New York City, and turned south on the street for what I knew would be my last walk on these paving stones.

Overhead, the sky was a brilliant blue, just as it had been in my dream. It was then that I realized I was on the street from my dream. I had been on this street before, but it was months earlier. I was uneasy. I had fifteen hundred dollars in cash, a six hundred dollar one way ticket to New York City, and my US passport on me. I felt silly to be so unnerved by a dream, but I was worried anyway. I knew from earlier visits that there wasn't an alley on this street, but I walked faster nevertheless.

The people around me calmly went about their business. They were distributed on the street exactly the way they were in my dream. Or were they? I couldn't be sure; it had been a few weeks already. It seemed the same. And then a big, dark, muscular arm stretched out around my neck from behind.

"Hey man, it's good to see you again. How much money you got wit' you today?"

At the same time, another muscular man flanked me on my right.

"Is it in US dollars? Is yo' money in dollars, hey?"

The man behind me held my head in a viselike grip, but continued walking forward, forcing me to do the same.

In heavily accented English the man on the right continued with his banter, alternating between fake friendly comments about the weather and questions about the cash I had on my person. I couldn't get the dream out of my mind. I had never been mugged before, let alone in a manner so similar to my dream. They kept talking about my money, but I could focus on only one thing: was this my dream? It didn't make sense. It couldn't be, because I knew that this street didn't have an alley. The dream was similar, but it had to be a coincidence. Yet try as I might, this man kept my head in his unwanted grip, holding it so that passersby would think he was a friend with his arm around my shoulder, but for me it was a prison.

Then I saw the scaffolding neatly piled on the sidewalk about fifty feet in front of me. On every occasion I'd been here before, the scaffolding had been assembled into an impenetrable wall, no different from any of the other similar structures erected all over town as various old buildings had their facades worked on. I'd never paid much attention to it, other than to cross the street to avoid the construction mess. I couldn't take my eyes off it because I could see that all this time it had covered up an opening in the street, an alley.

At that moment I decided that nothing was going to get me into the alley. I didn't care if it was stupid, and I didn't care if I got hurt. All this time the two muggers were saying things to me in poor English, trying to make it look to others on the street as if we were old friends out for a stroll. But they didn't stop pushing me forward.

I didn't have the raw muscle power to fight them, but it occurred to me that the man behind me might relax if I could confuse him, and that would be my opportunity, if it worked. They thought of me as a tourist, not a local. I'd been living in Amsterdam for three months, long enough that I could speak some Dutch. Meanwhile, they weren't Dutch, as their accents proved. I decided to suddenly start speaking in Dutch and claim to be an Amsterdammer, a local.

"Ik ben Amsterdammer! Ik wonen in Amsterdam voor drie jaren! Mijn geld is guilders!"

("I'm an Amsterdammer! I've lived in Amsterdam for three years! My money is in guilders!")

It was bad Dutch, but it worked. Both men slowed momentarily, a puzzled look came over the face of the man on the right, and most importantly, the man behind me did relax his grip, exactly as I wanted. I pushed his arm from me and ran to the newsstand across the street. I yelled at the man behind the counter to get his attention. I told him two men had just tried to mug me. When I pointed to show him where they were, they had already turned tail and were running as fast as they could in the other direction. I stayed there abstractedly paging through Dutch magazines for a half hour, not wanting to leave the safety of this public place. My heart was pounding so loudly that I could barely hear anything else, and every beat felt like a huge machine trying to burst loose from my chest.

The first half of the dream matched the events I'd just experienced almost perfectly, but then the dream and the real mugging forked, exactly when I decided to change the outcome by doing something to free myself. If it had forked anywhere else, it would be easier to suggest that the differences between the dream and my encounter on the street indicated that they were not related. Because they did correspond perfectly up until then, an argument could be made that I had just avoided my fate by changing the future.

If it was a simple dream of the future, then it was in error because it didn't show the outcome of my decision to escape from the muggers. Instead, just like Scrooge's Ghost of Christmas Future vision in *A Christmas Carol*, I experienced a vivid possible future as a warning. I was given an opportunity to decide for myself whether I live or die, and the crux of that decision was my ability to recognize and act on the warning in this dream. But the decision didn't just save my life, it changed my life. At the time of the dream, I did not believe that a dream could predict the future. I was an atheist. I derided religious people for fun because of my low regard for their superstitious belief in the supernatural. When I decided to distract the muggers and make a run for it, I was, even if just for that moment, joining those people upon whom I had heaped so much scorn. For that moment, I was superstitious too.

This assumes that the men were prepared to kill me. Maybe they weren't. Maybe they were trying to borrow money in a particularly aggressive manner. Maybe they didn't intend to push me into the alley, but to go past it. I'll never know the answers to those questions, but what I do know is that because of my choice, for the first time in my life I was willing to dip my toe into the supernatural and to trust it, even if temporarily. As I calmed down in the newsstand and the adrenaline faded, I thought about other aspects of the dream, from the part that didn't happen.

For instance, when I was taken into the alley and shot in the throat, the pain and other associated sensations were specific to the injury in a way that I found difficult to imagine. I remember wondering what the warm sensation on my chest could be, then realizing it was my blood. I thought I would be able to yell, and was surprised that I couldn't. I wondered about it, and then understood the mechanical impossibility of speech or sound coming from my ruined throat. The pain was expected, but not the amount of it. It makes sense that my blood would be warm, that I wouldn't be able to talk, and that the pain would be beyond anything I'd ever experienced, but for all these sensations to arrive right on time without forethought on my part, and to be exactly appropriate didn't make sense to me. How did I know what it felt like to be shot in the neck? I remember feeling the exact shape of one edge of my torn throat as parts of it pressed against other anatomical features and stuck there because of fluid blood between them.

More disturbingly, as I died in the dream, I lost consciousness of my body and left it behind. I felt every phase of this in great detail, even though I didn't believe in the existence of a soul. Yet right there, whether I believed it or not, I clearly experienced my soul separating from my body. Because of my upbringing and personal aversion to the subject, I could not have known that what happened to me in the dream was exactly what some would expect, based on their religious or spiritual beliefs.

After being shot, I fully expected to be snuffed out like a candle, but then my soul left my body and I was still conscious. I was amazed because it was so unexpected. Just like the pain of my wounds, the process of leaving my body was realistic and natural. Previously, I imagined that a "soul" was an invention created by people frightened by death. When it happened in the dream, it was nothing of the sort. I wasn't hoping for an afterlife or thinking about it at all. As far as I was concerned, it was over, but then it wasn't.

Looking down on Kitty from her mother's ceiling had to be the strangest experience I'd had up to that point in my life. I was fully conscious that I had just died a violent unreported death several thousand miles away, yet managed to zero in on Kitty's exact location and travel there at the speed of thought. I had time to consider what had happened as I tried to find a way to communicate with Kitty. I thought about the mugging, the shooting, the pain, then the cessation of both pain and life and the continuation of my consciousness and identity. I reflected on how I slipped out of my body, like a hand from a glove, and then came to the apartment, all the while re-evaluating my beliefs about life and death. Mostly, I wondered what I was going to do next. I seemed completely helpless to do anything but observe, and that was boring. And then I was awake in bed.

When I first awoke from the dream, I was grateful to be alive, but I did not even consider the possibility that the dream might be a warning of some kind. As soon as I woke, I snapped out of it, like I'd been temporarily under the thrall of a very good hypnotist. Some hint of menace remained as a side effect, and the realism of the dream remained a curiosity, but both were soon absent from my thoughts. Later, after having just had a run-in with two would-be muggers on the same street as in the dream, I was thinking the thoughts that less prejudiced people might have had as soon as they woke from the dream. I wondered if the dream had been connected to the encounter with the two men a few weeks later. I decided it had to be a coincidence.

That decision was the sensible one to make, and I can hardly be blamed for evaluating it that way. It is exactly what would be expected of any intelligent, properly educated person; but was it correct?

*Chapter Two*

# By force of numbers

Although I have always remembered my dreams, I never saw a need to record them. Even after the Amsterdam dream, I would only mention a dream now and then to Kitty, and consign the rest to the delete pile in my memory. A series of events in 1988 and 1989 changed that.

June 20 1988, New York City
Suddenly, I know that I am dreaming. "This is a dream of the future!" I think, and simultaneously realize that I need only shift my attention from the ten losing lottery tickets in my right hand to the list of winning numbers in my left to use this dream to my advantage. The problem is, I can feel myself waking. I want more time, I keep looking at the wrong hand, I have to look at the list...why is it so hard? I just need to focus... Some of the tickets have winning numbers, but not enough...

Then I woke. I grabbed a pen and wrote down what I remembered: two definite winners: 6 and 44, and five others that I thought might be winners, but I wasn't sure. Kitty wanted me to run out and buy tickets, but I resisted. Not only did I not remember all the numbers, but I didn't believe it was possible to dream of the future. Kitty insisted, and I went.

I bought five games instead of ten. This was the first time I'd ever bought lottery tickets, and didn't want to waste ten dollars. This attitude was vindicated when the results came out and none of my tickets won. Then, Kitty surprised me and pulled out five tickets of her own.

"You had ten tickets in the dream, so I bought five more," she said. Hers were losers also, but my dream hadn't predicted anything different. My dream predicted I would have ten Lotto tickets (correct, despite my attempt to thwart this by purchasing five), we didn't win any money (correct), that I would have a ticket with three winning numbers (correct, 6,17, and 44), that 6 and 44 would definitely be winners (true), and that I had four winning numbers in my 'pool' of seven possibilities (also true; 6, 17, 23, and 44). The dream was correct on every point.

The Amsterdam dream is a warning because it showed me a negative outcome if I did nothing. This dream is an opportunity because it suggests a positive outcome if I do something. Ironically, the events in both dreams could not have happened without the dreams that preceded them. In Amsterdam, the dream frightened me into moving back to the US, thus putting me on the street in the dream. With the lottery, I would not have played without the encouragement of the dream.

Were these messages directed at me specifically? Or were they neutral, like passing features of a landscape seen through a car window, there for anyone to see? If neutral, then it is just a dumb feature of some unknown aspect of nature, but if it is directed, then communication is involved, and that implies the presence of another party.

It is easy to see how either event might have been neutral - if they are mere possibilities, two of many others, then there is no reason to suppose they are meant for any specific person. I do not, however, have multiple dreams of these events with variable outcomes. There are only these two dreams, and the dreams themselves are required in order to be realized. In other words, the communication of the information contained in the dream is a part of the event.

What is the point of communicating this information to me? Not to win the Lottery, or I would have won in the dream and after I woke. The dream did perform a job, though maybe not the one I would have liked at the time. Rather than putting money in my pocket, it directed my attention at an event that was plainly inexplicable.

Was that its purpose? Could it be as simple as that? I was sent a dream, a description of an opportunity, not to win money, but to see something I hadn't noticed before. And what did I do? Just like in Amsterdam, I acted on it.

One month later, I had this dream:

DB0/14, August, 1988

A man approaches me. He asks me to come with him. He has transportation ready, and I hop in. After a brief ride, we stop in the road and he points up in the air, indicating where I should look. Some jets roar by fast and low in front of us. The wing of one of the planes nicks another one, sending both planes spinning out of control. One explodes into a massive fireball and careens towards the ground. A huge crowd of people watches the event from the sidelines.

The wreckage of the plane flies straight towards this crowd in huge flaming chunks of twisted metal. It plows into them, killing hundreds and sending severed body parts flying through the air. It stops in a smoking heap of mangled metal, bone, and flesh.

On waking, I still feel the heat of burning fuel. Silhouettes of body parts against a backdrop of flame and sky flash through my mind. Kitty sleeps quietly beside me. I close my eyes and can see it all again. I tell Kitty about the dream, but she has to get to work, and leaves in a rush.

About two weeks later, on August 28, 1988, regular TV programming was interrupted for a breaking news bulletin. Earlier that day three Italian air force jets collided in midair, sending one of them hurtling into a crowd of spectators at Ramstein airbase in Germany. The footage clearly showed the collision, the fireball that erupted, and the wreckage plowing into people on the ground. The scene was identical to the one I dreamed of just a couple weeks earlier. Plane crashes are not so rare as to be unheard of, but planes crashing into crowds of spectators are much rarer, and this was the first time I'd ever heard of such an accident.

Unlike the previous two dreams, this dream is unquestionably a communication. A man comes to fetch me, and shows me an event from the future. He behaved something like a tour guide: "Come with me and I'll show you something interesting. Look over here, right there in the sky, and you'll see it," and then the disaster happens.

My grandfather did something almost exactly like it when I was six years old. We were driving along a dry city street in Kingman, Arizona, when he said "Hey Andy, lookit that car over there; you keep watching it, it's gonna crash" and then less than a minute later, it did. I was amazed that he could know such a thing before it happened, but as I found out later, the driver was drunk and slowly drifting towards a parked car. Almost any adult could have predicted that crash.

Unlike my grandfather, the man in the Ramstein dream was not observing a slow moving drunk. They both had something to show me, but my grandfather was guessing. The man in the dream *knew*. My grandfather made his prediction for fun, but there was no obvious motive for being shown the Ramstein disaster in advance. The man came to get me, like it was his job, showed me the scene, and it was over.

In the Amsterdam and lottery dreams, the future represented was changeable, but here, it isn't. There wasn't enough information to warn anyone or to change anything. Instead, I was shown just enough to recognize the event after the fact. Is it possible that I was given more information than I remember, and that the only reason I couldn't warn anyone is that I forgot some crucial detail? If I did forget any details, did I forget on my own, or, like the lottery dream, was I manipulated into remembering only what I was supposed to remember?

The result of this dream is that for the first time I was now completely convinced I had experienced a genuine dream of the future. From this point on, I knew that such things weren't just possible, they happened.

This next non-dream event started before the lottery dream, but ended some time afterwards.

1987-1988, New York City

As I held the doorknob on my side of the door, I knew for a fact that the woman on the other side would commit suicide. I didn't know her yet and had never seen her before, but I did know who she was. Sumi Koide was my new friend Richard's girlfriend. I'd met him at a yoga retreat in Woodbourne, New York a few weeks previously. Now, he was bringing Sumi to dinner to meet me and Kitty for the first time. I opened the door and they came in. My premonition faded immediately as I assumed my duties as host.

After they left, I helped Kitty do the dishes in the kitchen. She thought Sumi had been snobbish because she, Richard, and Kitty all had college degrees but I didn't. The way Kitty saw it, Sumi made an effort to cast critical remarks in my direction all night on the subject.

"You shouldn't talk that way about someone who is going to kill herself," I said.

"What! What are you talking about?" shot back Kitty with horror.

I realized then that when I'd had the feeling about Sumi earlier, I accepted it as an unremarkable true bit of information without bothering to question it. Later, I responded to Kitty the way I did because I had already assimilated the information as pure fact. After I explained this to Kitty, she calmed down, but still thought it was strange to say such a thing. So did I. It was the first time in my life that I'd ever said anything like it.

I considered mentioning it to Richard, but thought it would come across as peculiar, and might affect our friendship. Another concern was that I didn't want to put any ideas in Sumi's head. Over the next few months, we played chess often at Richard's apartment. Sumi usually worked on her homework in another room. After the first moment when I decided to say nothing to Richard, I rarely thought of it. Sumi seemed fine.

By September of the next year, Richard had earned his doctorate and gone to work for UC Davis as a research physicist. They sent him to Geneva to work at the CERN particle accelerator. Kitty and I moved downtown to Tribeca, just a few blocks from the World Trade Center. Sumi remained in their old apartment on York Avenue, across the street from Rockefeller University.

Sumi was on our minds because Richard had recently recommended I go see her to pick up a cane of his, to ease some serious back pain I'd incurred from a yoga related injury. Kitty thought it might be good for Sumi to have some company since Richard was away for a few months. I agreed she was right, but there was plenty of time, "We'll talk about it tomorrow."

When "tomorrow" came, I was working on a book jacket illustration for Houghton/Mifflin. Kitty was uptown on an assignment, so I had the apartment to myself. Suddenly, Kitty burst in with tears in her eyes, "She's dead!"

Kitty had been riding on the subway when she happened to look to her left at a man reading the Post. She recognized Sumi's photo on a page beside a full page story about her death. Kitty burst into tears and screamed, "I know her!" According to the story, Sumi, a promising medical student at Cornell, jumped from a window of the sixteenth floor apartment she had shared with Richard and died on a concrete overhang below.

Richard flew out and stayed with us that night. His sister came out the next day and picked him up at our place. Before they left, Richard sat on my red metal stool as his sister stood beside him in the large front room of the loft. Sun streamed in through four eight-foot tall windows. Traffic passed by outside. Kitty made breakfast in the kitchen. Richard looked at me and asked, "Did you know? Did you have a dream about her before it happened?"

This remains among the saddest of all my experiences, psychic or otherwise. It brings to mind a number of questions, like Richard's, none of them comfortable. With his, at least I knew the answer. There was no dream, but I did have a premonition. I knew, and had known for almost a year. Other questions, though more removed emotionally, were harder.

Was Sumi's suicide inevitable? Or did she have a fork not taken, like my dream in Amsterdam, that may have prolonged her life? Was my premonition meant to be a warning for her? If so, did I have a responsibility to pass it on?

I've thought about this last question often, and still do. My justifications for not saying anything at the time still make sense to me, hollow as that is. If I had told Richard, a skeptical physicist, of the premonition, he would have ignored it or been offended. At least, so I thought. If it had gotten to Sumi somehow and then she did commit suicide, my "warning" could have been interpreted as an incitement, and that would be worse.

An interesting aspect of this event is how quickly I accepted the idea that she would commit suicide. I didn't think about it at all. If anything, it bypassed my thought process altogether and landed in my data bank of done deals, like a memory of the future. Normally, if I saw or heard something unusual, I would question it. This time, I didn't. Why?

All day, every day, we have opportunities to check the credibility of information we receive. Not just important data, like whether a certain person was on a certain street when a crime was committed, but mundane things also, like, "Is this peach really ripe? Have I been here before? What is that?" We constantly ask ourselves questions to get our bearings. If I make any effort to recall this type of detail, I can usually bring up a fairly long list of these "credibility checks" from my day. But on the one occasion when I have a premonition of suicide, it is immediately deposited as fact. This is beyond just recognizing that something is credible, which only means that something is probably true. A fact is something that has happened, and yet here, it is something that had happened in the future. What does that mean?

First, it means that the premonition either bypassed the normal credibility check, or it was granted immediate access, like an FBI badge at a crime scene. If accepted on the latter basis, it came with authority, but on an unconscious level. This brings up another point, that I was willing to accept the authority and truth of this premonition without knowing its source. Not only that, but I accepted it without any contest or consideration because it was unremarkable. Why was it unremarkable? Because it had already happened. Part of the premonition was that it was done. That contributed to my lack of urgency at the time, and probably later as well. But how could it have already happened? Perhaps the only reason my dreams of Ramstein, Amsterdam, or the lottery were possible is the same, linear time is an illusion, just as mystics have been saying for thousands of years.

As for the source of the premonition and the reason I accepted it without question, maybe I did know the source, but interacted with it on an unconscious level, like a subroutine in a computer program. This interpretation is supported by the fact that I continued to accept the premonition while talking with Kitty in the kitchen. At that point, unlike the moment at the door, I was paying attention to the premonition, but I still didn't believe that any kind of paranormal event was possible. Despite this, *I still accepted it as true.*

In March of 1989, we moved to Vermont. There, the dreams and other unusual incidents continued.

DB0/15 app July 1, 1989, Putney, Vermont
I am a business passenger on a big airplane bound for some Midwest city. I sit in a window seat on the wing and look outside. We descend towards a highway between large cornfields. I think we are near Sioux City, Iowa but haven't reached it yet. We fly low over a highway, as if for a landing, but overshoot and fly over a cornfield to the side.

The plane tips its wings, and one of them makes contact with the ground. The plane immediately jerks and cartwheels across the field just as a powerful pulse of heat makes me turn. I look back to see a fountain of flame shooting up the fuselage straight for me. The heat is unbearable and I know I will be dead in a second, no more. Thousands of tiny flaming projectiles fill the air. They cut into me and everything else like so many thousands of molten bullets, but they are plastic forks, screws, bent hinges, metal rods, bits of broken chairs, and globs of burning plastic. It happens in less than a second.

This was like a replay of the Ramstein dream. For the first time in my life, I decided to record a dream, and did so with an old typewriter given to me by my stepmother.

About two weeks later, On July 19, United Airlines flight 232 left Denver, Colorado. During the flight, it lost all hydraulic power, making it impossible to control the rudder, flaps, and ailerons. By using the throttle, the crew could only make right turns. Using this method, they flew towards the nearest airport, in Sioux City, Iowa. They flew over a highway that had been cleared for them in the event they could not make it to the airport. Shifting winds blew the plane from side to side as it neared a runway. The crew manually dropped the landing gear, and then a wing was caught by the wind and the plane pitched to its side, causing the right wing to make contact with the ground. It broke loose, causing a fuel spill and explosion. Then the fuselage hit the ground, the left wing broke off, and the fuselage somersaulted in several distinct sections all over the airport and into a nearby field.

In this dream the outcome is fixed, but it provides more clues about the accident than the Ramstein dream. Here, I knew they were trying to land in Sioux City. What I didn't know is that they were not scheduled to land there. If I had tried to warn anyone based on that knowledge, it wouldn't have been effective because the plane was en route to Chicago, not Sioux City. Without more information, the dream cannot be a warning. My impression is that it was a dream about a certain man and his death. He died in a plane crash, but the dream was about him, not the crash.

Who was this man, and why did I think his experience was my own? It was as if his mind reached out to me in its panic, and brought me bodily into his moment of terror. For those few seconds, I was him, as if his spirit panicked and fled, leaving me to experience his last moments.

One night when Kitty and I were playing backgammon, I had a feeling similar to when I touched the doorknob and knew Sumi would commit suicide. It was nothing so dire, but was at least as strong; "Kitty," I said, "we are now going to roll matching descending doubles, from sixes to ones."

Kitty shook her cup and rolled double sixes. I rolled double sixes also. She rolled double fives and I matched them. She rolled double fours; I did likewise. She got double threes and I got double threes. She rolled a pair of twos, and I did the same. At this point, the staggering mathematical improbability of what I'd just seen hit me like a wave. I lost confidence and predicted we would not get the double ones. Kitty then rolled a pair of non-matching numbers.

For visualization, here is the sequence we rolled: 6,6,6,6,5,5,5,5,4,4,4,4,3,3,3,3,2,2,2,2

The odds of rolling a certain number on a six-sided die are one in six. The odds of rolling an exact twenty number sequence using six-sided dice as we had just done are one in 3,656,158,440,062,976. The odds of winning the Powerball lottery jackpot are one in 120,526,770.

In other words, a person is over thirty million times more likely to win the Powerball jackpot than to roll the dice Kitty and I rolled in the sequence we rolled them in. This does not factor in the prediction, only the rolls themselves.

After hearing about this, a mathematically gifted friend of mine once told me, "It didn't happen."

"What do you mean?" I asked.

"It is impossible. It couldn't happen, so it didn't."

"Are you kidding? I saw it, Kitty was there, she participated, we each had our own dice, and she remembers it too."

"I am just saying it is impossible, that is all. Therefore, it could not have happened."

Maybe I would have reacted the same way if I hadn't seen it myself, but as it is, I had no choice but to point out that, with all due respect, he was mistaken.

An odd thing about this incident is that it literally felt like someone else had softly made a kind of mental offer to me: "Say this, and it will happen." Curious, I gave it a try, and it worked. Did I have to make the prediction? Would it have happened without it? My impression was that it wouldn't have, but there is no way to know that for sure.

I did make the prediction, and the rolls came out as predicted, up until I balked. Remember that at the end, I lost confidence and said so before missing the last double one rolls? This "prediction" was not fixed in stone. It was contingent on something. At a minimum, willingness to suspend disbelief.

The issue, I think, comes down to confidence. I had to make the statement as a proof of confidence. As the rolls kept coming out the way they were supposed to, my confidence grew until the point when my reasoning abilities interfered and shattered my confidence. After this, the streak ended.

The source of the prediction felt external, but I don't know in what way. It felt like it was dropped into my ear in a compact bundle. It was an offer, waiting only for my answer. The offer itself was easy to remember. In only thirteen words, and one sentence, it laid out a complex prediction of a long sequence of numbers, twenty-four in all (twenty of which were realized before I lost confidence). This by itself suggests that the selection of this exact sequence may have had a purpose. The sequence, and the way it was described to me was about as compact as it could be for the complexity of the sequence described. There are many ways to have made the prediction, but like poetry, the expression that found its way to me was well organized.

My impression is that this event is not an example of telekinesis, as it first appears to be, at least, not telekinesis on my part. If anything, the dice were controlled by another agent, most probably the one that made the suggestion. The symmetry of the rolls, if nothing else, look anything but natural and that indicates some conscious control, but by whom is a mystery.

Something like this happened twice more while we lived in that house, both during Scrabble games. In the first, the announcement was, "I will now proceed to withdraw all eleven remaining 'E's' from the draw bag." I drew ten in a row before losing confidence, announcing it, and missing the last one. The second was, "You [Kitty] will play all seven tiles on each of the next three turns." And she did. In all three of these, the exact same pattern is evident: we are playing a game when a prediction is dropped in my head. "Say this, and it will happen." I make the prediction, and it happens as promised, no matter how improbable the prediction is. These are the only predictions of this type that I made.

When I was younger, I had a reputation for being bizarrely lucky when it came to board games. Back then, I attributed it to chance, luck, and selective memory. Now, with two sets of eyes watching very closely, that argument wasn't convincing. This backgammon game was completely unequivocal. I didn't know if it would ever happen again, but now I knew for certain that scientists who denied the existence of paranormal events literally did not know what they were talking about. I understood how they came to their conclusions, but doubted even the staunchest critic could have gone through that backgammon game with his skepticism intact.

After spending five months in Vermont, we moved back to New York City. We stayed at an apartment owned by Kitty's family while we looked for a new place. About a month later, we settled in nearby Weehawken, New Jersey. Just before the move, a couple of odd things happened:

September 24, 1989, New York City
I sat at the table in our apartment as I worked on some ideas for promotional mailers. My art supplies were laid out in front of me, but the phone on the far end of the table occupied my attention. I hadn't even made the mailer yet, but thought I'd better give art director Sara Eisenman, from Houghton/Mifflin books, a call to give her my new address.

I dialed the number.

"Sara Eisenman, Hello."

"Hello Sara, this is Andrew Paquette. I'm just calling to give you my new phone number and address."

"Bonk, clunk, clunk." I heard the sound of the phone falling on the floor.

"Oh my God."

"Sara?"

"I'm so sorry, it's just that, who is this?"

"Andrew Paquette."

"It's just, this is amazing. I was just on the phone with another art director, she called from New York, she wanted your current phone number, but I told her I didn't have it. Then I said that if you happened to call and tell me, I'd let her know. I was still holding the phone when you called! I had literally just put it in the cradle to hang up, but still had my hand on it when it rang again and it was you!"

I had not spoken with Sara since I last worked with her, almost two years earlier on the cover for *Oil Notes*, the same illustration I was working on when Kitty burst in with news of Sumi's death.

The idea to call Sara came to me as a suggestion, "Why don't you call Sara Eisenman?" My reaction was, "I might as well, but why now?" I didn't really want to call her at that moment. First, I wasn't ready to contact anyone for work yet, and secondly, I wanted to re-establish contact with clients in New York first. Sara was in Boston, and I figured I could get to her later. Instead, this idea that popped into my head put her at the front of the line. It made no sense to me, yet there was no great cost attached to it either. So I thought, "...why now?" and then got hit with, "Why not now?" and that did the trick. I picked up the phone and called her.

At the time, I didn't think too much about these details. I accepted it as a plain example of telepathy. Sara was thinking of me, was actually talking about me with someone else at that exact moment, and I happened to pick up on it. Except, that isn't the way the information came to me. I felt a question pop into my mind, "Why don't you call Sara Eisenman?" as if from someone else. Another thing about the message is that it wasn't in words. The entire idea described by those words was contained in a non-

27

verbal package that hit me in a subtle, non-aggressive way, even her name, just two words, was not presented as words, but as *her*.

The message was presented as an attractive option I might take, without explanation why. When I did question it, I was rebuffed, but coyly, "Why not now?" In retrospect, it felt very much as if the suggestion to call Sara did not come from Sara directly or from me casually picking up on her interest in me, but from a third party.

September 20, 1989

Just a couple hours after going to bed, I woke up suddenly and heard myself shouting, "There's just been a plane crash at LaGuardia!"

It was as if I'd just seen it. I didn't remember a dream at all, just my shout when I woke. I went straight to the TV and turned it on, sure that there would be a story about the crash. It had just happened. US Air flight 5050 had aborted their takeoff at LaGuardia, hit a light stanchion, and crashed into the water. Two died and forty were injured. Kitty had woken up with my shout and then watched the news report with me.

Earlier that week, I had started recording my dreams in a journal.

## Chapter Three

# A brief pause for some details

The first entry in the dream journal was made on the morning of September 15, 1989. It covered one and a half pages, and described one scene. At the time of this writing, March 21, 2010, it is a little more than twenty years later. There are now 24 journals that contain over 2,900 records, and the number increases every week. Most records contain multiple scenes, sometimes numbering in the dozens per record. Digitally transcribed summaries of the journals total over 420,000 words. Many records include detailed drawings to augment the written descriptions. In total, there are hundreds of drawings contained within the journals. Early dreams that went unrecorded prior to starting the journal were recorded after the fact in a section of the second journal. The total amount of material contained in all these records is not insignificant.

I have relied on my journals as primary source material for many sections of this book, but they are not the only sources. They are, however, the best source I have for contemporaneous accounts of my dreams. The quality of the records varies depending on numerous factors. As I noticed which decisions, habits, and events had an adverse affect on the readability or reliability of the records, I took steps to mitigate the problems and in many cases was able to eliminate them altogether. For this reason, the quality of the records improves over time.

There is a difference between my dreams and the journal records of them. One is a memory fragment of the thing itself, the other is an attempted verbal distillation of it. The process of translating a dream into words, just as with any other translation, can be inexact. I have made every effort to record my dreams accurately, but have found that there is no way to record everything I remember or to completely describe certain things for which no translation can ever be adequate. Despite this, the records are very detailed and paint a fairly accurate portrait of what I remember.

I have been able to remember my dreams for as long as I have imaged memories. My earliest memory of any kind is of a dream that I had when I was about four years old. I have remembered some dreams from childhood with the same amount of vivid detail, while others fade almost as soon as I wake. The general rule is that if I don't tell anyone about a dream or write it down, I am more likely to forget it than if I do describe it in words to someone else. Describing dreams to others is a way to bring the dream into the waking world, and that act alone makes them easier to remember. It is possible, though I have no easy way to check this, that the only dreams I remember from before 1989 are dreams that I described at least once to someone else.

The amount of detail I recall, as is evident when reading the journals, varies widely. Sometimes I recall only a simple idea, like one morning when I remembered dreaming of an oil tanker spill (one happened that morning in New York). That is all that I remembered, and all I wrote down, "an oil tanker spill." I didn't remember anything but those words. No images, no context, nothing. Other dreams took hours to write down and could fill as many as twenty notebook pages without fully describing what I remembered.

Some dreams are "solved" or "verified," meaning that I have some non-dream information that correlates with a dream. This could be, for instance, the TV broadcast of the Ramstein disaster in combination with the dream. One thing I discovered with the journal is that I usually remember multiple scenes from different dreams every night. To keep this distinction clear, everything I describe for an evening is called a "record," and individual scenes are described as "scenes." A "dream" can be a single scene or multiple related scenes.

Most records have multiple scenes, as many as twenty on a given night, but more often around four. For records that contain a large number of scenes, several scenes are usually found to be related. If instead there are a small number of scenes, they are ordinarily not related. If a record is considered either solved or verified, it is because at least one scene in the record has been checked and correlated with something else, not because all of the scenes have been checked and verified.

Depending on the amount of detail recorded in a scene, confirmation may be of as many as a dozen (or more) elements, or just one. Here is a quick reference chart to illustrate how I evaluate the strength of a scene:

1 **(highest quality)**: Multiple connected scenes, vivid, coherent.

2 **(good quality)**: A single scene, vivid and coherent.

3 **(average quality)**: One or more related scenes, not vivid, with some confusion.

4 **(junk)**: Any quantity of detail, from none to extreme. If no detail, it may be coherent but it won't matter because of the low level of detail. If a high level of detail, it is incoherent.

Looked at this way, I have about one hundred high quality dreams in the journals, most of which I recall very well, another three hundred of good quality, and then just under a thousand of average quality. Of the dreams so far described in this book, only the Amsterdam dream qualifies as an "high quality" dream. The others fit in among the thousand or so more ordinary dreams. If it had been a dream, the descending doubles incident would have landed in the "good" category rather than "highest" because the scope of the event was small, though it was completely accurate and rather startling. There are about half a dozen "big dreams," whose scope is completely off the charts.

The remaining dreams I classify as "junk." These dreams, whatever they might be of, are more the product of imagination than any kind of verifiable reality. I have been surprised on occasion by the discovery that a junk dream really was of the future, but this is rare. An example of this is one dream I had in about 1998, while I worked for the video game company SquareUSA.

In the dream, I hired a man I knew to do something for a Scooby-Doo project. At the time of the dream, this man and I weren't speaking to each other. He was angry with me for not agreeing to do him a favor, and had told me to never speak to him again. In addition to that, I was a senior animator at Square, not a hiring manager. I couldn't imagine being in a position to hire someone, let alone this guy, who had more experience than I did. On top of all that, I couldn't imagine Square, creators of the successful *Final Fantasy* series of games, making a Scooby-Doo themed game. A couple years later I was working for a different company on a Scooby-Doo project as an art director/hiring manager. I needed to hire someone to do some texture work fast, and I wound up calling the man from the dream. To my surprise, he accepted.

This is not a common outcome for a junk dream. Those dreams are usually so hopelessly jumbled up that it would be too complicated to figure out which part related to which event. My impression is that they are the result of my thoughts creating dream images from scratch, or the same, but overlaid on something real. It is this mixing of the two that gives me the clue that a dream is junk, because I can often tell when my thoughts are guiding a dream. In the Scooby-Doo example, I mistakenly identified an improbable event as impossible. If I'd looked more carefully, I would have noticed that it lacked the traits of a true junk dream.

Here is a record that contains many of the most common

features of a junk dream:

January 4, 1990
> Kitty and I fly around the country on a little invisible two-seater battery-powered anti-gravity unit. I have to get a new battery for it. Kitty and I have a tiff while we fly around on the thing. I get so annoyed that I reach out and snuff a burning cigarette as it dangles from an old woman's lips as we pass her with this flying gadget.

A Chinese man whose face is easily recognizable to strangers, thanks to being reproduced on bags from McDonald's, is in a swamp. He demonstrates some psychic abilities for a group of people. We are on a raft with two girls as we watch him.

Dali paintings in a book that isn't about Art. They are used to illustrate something else. One is a painting of Cher and her daughter Chastity, but if you turn it around, it becomes a picture of a wanton woman...

This record immediately presents a problem: the anti-gravity machine. No such thing exists, so it would either have to be invented, or I'd have to be very clever about explaining how something else came to be remembered this way in the dream. Another problem is presented by the cigarette snuffing incident. I get irritated with Kitty, see the woman smoking, reach out, and snuff her cigarette. In a dream situation, this is akin to an audience member reaching into a movie screen and shaking hands with one of the actors. The only problem is that in a dream, it is always my imagination that causes a scene like that, and they have never proven to be verifiable. I might dream of an old woman I will meet later and she might be smoking, but I will not snuff the cigarette. So right there, I know there is an error.

This is not an insignificant error, because it means that I cannot tell the difference between the dream and reality from within the dream. Whenever I try to interact with a scene, and I do it often, it is for this reason. The clearer a dream is, the less likely I am to think of interacting with it, let alone act on the desire. This doesn't mean that the dream is hopelessly polluted, but it is a warning flag that I have to pay attention to.

The Chinese man segment sounds like the kind of thing that cannot ever be verified. His face is on a bag, does that mean he is missing? He is doing psychic tricks, does that mean, like me, he is dreaming also? If so, I won't be able to verify it. The raft is interesting. Like the anti-gravity unit, it allows Kitty and me to travel through the dream inconspicuously. I frequently dreamed of this sort of device in my earlier dreams, but later have replaced them with variations on floating, flying, and "swimming" through the air. All of these, I think, are a way for my mind to make sense of something that otherwise would be impossible; how I travel great distances through the air with my physical body alone. This then, is a construct that makes me more comfortable while traveling in dreams, so the mode of transportation doesn't distract me from the dream itself. This is another item that indicates a poor quality dream. If I can't handle the notion of travel within a dream without a mental crutch of some kind, then the rest of the dream will be affected also.

The "Dali" painting sounds like a mental picture of my impression of the singer Cher, which, judging from this dream, wasn't that good. The realism of the image might have made me think of Dali's more realistic paintings, even though Dali may have no connection at all to the image. Maybe I ran across a disparaging reference to Cher elsewhere in the dream and this is how it was expressed, but there is no way to know. Another possibility is that in the dream I saw a particularly provocative photograph of Cher and drew the wrong conclusion from it. What is important is that the image of Cher changed as I looked at it to conform with what I was thinking. This is a very bad sign in a dream, because it means that my thoughts are affecting the dream. Therefore, the dream cannot be trusted.

Overall, I can imagine that a few things from this dream might relate to true events, but cannot realistically check them. Other parts of the dream make it perfectly clear that I am too involved in the dream to be objective. That is a key factor in identifying junk dreams. When this happens, the plasticity of the dream becomes too easily manipulated by my thoughts and it is no longer something I am witnessing, but something I am making. The disjointed action is another clue to this dream's junk status. I cannot take this dream as seriously as one where several scenes are thematically linked and have clear, logical action described within them. A man comes to me and says "Follow me, I have something to show you" and then he brings me somewhere and shows me something (the Ramstein crash), that is a coherent sequence. Here, it is like I am on a boat in Disney's Pirates of the Caribbean attraction, and I'm trying to interact with the animatronic puppets, not realizing they are puppets. Worse, it's as if I black out between every other change in the route, am totally disoriented, and every time I look up, I'm in a different part of the park.

This is the kind of dream that I will record, but not think of again unless I have a good reason to. About the only reason that would justify revisiting it would be if I thought something from the dream had just happened. For example, on November 29, 1989, I had a dream that had a very strong image in it of two enormous Statue of Liberty replicas, painted black. Another part of the dream indicated a slaughter of South Africans. This is what I call a "marker" in a dream, a strong image that I will see at the same time as some other event from the dream.

With this one, the image of the statues was so vivid that I told Kitty on numerous occasions that when I saw those statues, on that day there would be mass bloodshed in South Africa. Several months later, on February 3, 1990, we were driving up Sixth Avenue when I saw the sculptures. I didn't know where they came from, who the artist was, or any other details, just that there were a couple of multi-story black statue of liberty sculptures outside a skyscraper on Sixth Avenue. I told Kitty "this is the day," and sure enough, when we got home there was news on TV about a riot that left twenty people dead in South Africa.

What I did next is go to my dream book to look up this one specific dream and to make notes in the margin. I might have glanced at a few others while I searched for this one, but I knew exactly which dream I wanted, and as soon as I found it, was able to write in some corroborating information. This is how it usually works. I do not periodically read through my journals, randomly looking for something that matches. There's too much material to do that, and most of it is written in a dry, dull, sleep-inducing style.

When I do recognize an event and go looking for the dream, I frequently find that the one dream that comes to mind, once found, contains additional detail that also relates to the same event that sent me to the journal in the first place. On rare occasions, I have confused two dreams and have had to look for a second one if disappointed by the first. Again, reading the first will remind me of the second and will inspire me to search for a specific dream.

My ability to recall dreams varies based on a number of factors. I usually remember at least a portion of a dream on about five out of every seven nights, but if I have to get up early to go to work, I am much less likely to take the time to remember more. When I have more time, I may meditate on my dreams for about twenty minutes, to reveal more dreams and more detail. I remember more the more I write. If I try to remember everything before I start writing, I usually forget something before I get a chance to write it down. This is why I like to write a block of fast notes as soon as I wake up, and refer to them as I write out more detailed descriptions.

The strongest factor in remembering dreams has to do with my waking activities. If I am intently focused on my work during the day, then my dream recall tends to be much weaker. If instead I have been spending my days more contemplatively, doing Yoga exercises or painting landscapes, my dream recall can be excellent. One thing that has a strong negative effect on my ability to remember dreams, is playing video games. Somehow, this activity disturbs my ability to concentrate and relax more than anything else.

One thing that has always annoyed me about the way I remember dreams is that they are normally remembered in reverse order. I wake up with the most recent dream or scene in my mind and then as I write it, I remember the scene that led to it, and so on. On the occasions I have tried to circumvent this effect by meditating on the dream before writing it down, I have occasionally forgotten the recent scenes while writing the earlier ones.

I have tried to figure out a way to predict when I have the best dreams, but am at a loss how to do this apart from the already noted factors that have an influence on dream recall. I have had amazing dreams during very short naps, when exhausted from lack of sleep, when sick, and when in perfect health. The same is true of junk dreams. They come to me when they want to, the only regular characteristic of their comings and goings being the number I can expect in any given one-year period. The rate in most years is about three extremely strong dreams, twenty strong ones, the balance either ordinary or junk, so several hundred of each, and once every several years a chance of a big dream.

There are some long gaps in the journal, including a very long one between 1993-1998, during which I focused on my career to the exclusion of the dream journal. Other breaks occur for shorter periods of time, but for similar reasons. The two most fruitful periods are between 1989-1990 and 2003-2006, when most of my time was spent making paintings.

In 2005, I decided to preserve a digital version of the journals, and transcribed them by hand. This took the better part of a year to accomplish, and then about another month every year after that to catch up with new dreams. At first, I wrote one-line summaries of each scene, but later wrote out complete word-for-word accounts. Transcribing the journals was so tedious that on occasion I was tempted to throw away pages of uninteresting dreams, just to save the trouble of transcribing them. I did do this a few times, but then thought of a better solution: I stopped recording new dreams until I had caught up to existing records. After I renewed my record-keeping responsibilities, I was more careful about which dreams I included, to reduce the overall quantity of paperwork and transcription. Dreams of the future became so common that I stopped recording all but the most interesting ones. Scary dreams were sometimes left out or were only briefly summarized because I didn't like reliving them in my notes. Luckily, I've never had many.

The first difficulty of writing my dreams every morning is that I don't always feel like doing it. It took some time to discipline myself to do this, and a few tricks as well, like making a deal with myself that if I didn't remember anything, I would write, "I remember nothing tonight," or if I was in a rush, I would write that too. These devices had the effect of shaming me into making either a better effort to remember dreams or to spend some extra time writing them in greater detail.

I had no idea what was going to happen with the journal, so the way it was recorded and what was recorded changed a great deal over time. At first, I tried to record everything I could remember, but after awhile, I realized that it resulted in excessive detail that interfered with the clarity of the records. For instance, initially I would record the thoughts I had during a dream. These were often misleading, so, after discovering this tendency, I either left them out of the record or would take the time to describe the discrepancies between what I thought and what I saw so readers wouldn't get confused.

For a brief period, I got in the habit of writing in the time I went to sleep, the time when I woke up, and other external details surrounding my sleep habits, like whether I had a headache, a cold, was not in a good mood, or if neighbors were making a racket with their stereo at three in the morning. I was too impatient to keep this up for long, and stopped within a month or two. The reason I did it in the first place was to see if there any correlation between these factors and the dreams, but I never saw anything to indicate there was.

At first, I made no effort to design the recording process for optimal results. I just bought the first notebook I saw at a local newsstand, and started writing. That simple choice caused some problems. Because the notebook was spiral bound at the top, and because I didn't want to waste any paper, I had to keep turning it upside-down to write on the reverse side of each page. This made the first journal very difficult to read. In the second journal, I switched to a three-ring binder so that I could turn pages without having to flip the book upside down every time.

Writing in the dark wasn't easy, and doing it without waking Kitty was even harder. Sometimes I was so sleepy and the room so dark that my writing had to be literally decoded in the morning. There are at least five or so early entries where I sat there with a separate piece of paper, trying and crossing out all the possibilities for various letter-like shapes in the journal until I could puzzle out what the entry actually said. Some, I never completely decoded. This led to the purchase of a small lamp, then a flashlight, to help with my writing. I also made a resolution to be more careful with my handwriting, and for a while I block printed everything.

It took several years to realize that by not separating entries, they became very difficult to find later because the dreams blended together into a huge mass of words. The goal was to save money on paper, but later when I was earning more money, I relaxed and always started new dreams on a new sheet, even if this meant the entire back side of the previous page was left blank. This was probably my favorite of the "technical" improvements in the journal, because it made finding specific entries so much easier.

It has taken twenty years to accumulate the material needed to write this book. The dreams in the journal form clusters, or groups, that taken together describe different aspects of the same event or of the dream experience in general but the chronological order of the dreams does not match the order of the events they depict. When presented chronologically, a reader loses all sense of how these dreams fit together, as if they are all pieces of twenty different jigsaw puzzles mixed together. To solve that problem, I have first gone to the trouble of sorting out the puzzle pieces to present each puzzle separately. Within each puzzle, the pieces are presented chronologically. Some pieces, or scenes, belong to more than one puzzle. In those cases, I have tried to keep the scene in question grouped with other events that are most similar to it. Sometimes, separate scenes from one record are split up into different sections. The first puzzle is made up of scattered scenes from the future, seen literally.

## Chapter Four

# The ordinary future

The first future dream in the journal, at least, the first one I knew about, was pretty simple. About two weeks after the journal begins, I dreamed of my Aunt Terry calling me on the phone. Later that day, she did call. The next incident was more interesting, but no less mundane, I dreamed of a talking egg in a sock that gets smashed into a wall. The next night, October 21, 1989, I saw Saturday Night Live on TV. They had a skit called "Eggman" about a talking egg in a sock that gets thrown into a wall. Many of the dreams I found myself recording were like this; unremarkable domestic moments. Some had unusual details, like the "Eggman," some didn't.

The reason the dreams went abruptly from airline disasters to TV shows and telephone calls is that normally, these dreams wouldn't have been interesting enough to write down, and were forgotten. The rare dreams of clearly newsworthy subjects, were so powerful they couldn't be forgotten. The journal captured things that would otherwise have been lost.

Until these ordinary dreams were recorded, a skeptic could suggest that "selective memory" caused me to remember only dreams that were superficially or coincidentally similar to a later event. What the journal demonstrated is that the dreams I had been forgetting were also of the future.

It is here that the mundane dreams become very interesting. Tragedy may be exciting for ratcheting up the drama of the narrative component of a dream, but mundane dreams are just as good for the purpose of comparing to later events. Most offer details that, while not as newsworthy, are so ridiculous that when they do correlate with something else, they can be even more remarkable than a public disaster.

Ordinary dreams are valuable for another reason: they are more numerous than other dreams. This makes it possible to test observations made in the dream and the way they are recorded. Like anything else, the more data points there are in a sample, the more accurate you can expect your conclusions to be. Therefore, the large number of ordinary dreams in my journals gave me an excellent opportunity to check the quality of my records and observations. This is like the cliché that you can have a dozen witnesses to the same crime and each will describe the scene differently. The same problem existed in the journal. Sometimes I would see an event accurately in a dream but would report it incorrectly.

In a dream from January 21, 1990, I recorded "...news snatches that indicate massive food shortages had caused riots and the overthrow of a Latin American country. I see a crowd of 30,000 outside a McDonald's in this country." Later that night, the evening news had the same *images* I remembered from the dream, but the stories were different. One of the stories was about the opening of the first McDonald's in Moscow. Outside, a crowd of 30,000 patrons waited to get in. The next story was about the recent invasion of Panama, a Latin American country. Footage of the looted city from the day after the invasion was played.

If I had written what I had seen, instead of drawing inferences from it, then my dream journal record would have matched what I later saw on TV, including the fact that the McDonald's was in Moscow. I saw that in the dream, but because I couldn't reconcile Moscow with the strong images of a Latin American city, I combined the two. The "food riots" comment was added as a logical explanation for the crowd outside of the McDonald's.

"Dream correction" errors are common in the early portions of the journal. Thanks to the McDonald's dream, and others like it, I learned to report exactly what I saw, without interpretation. It wasn't always easy to do, but the quality of the records noticeably improved with practice. The key to doing it right, was to avoid identifying anything within a dream without some kind of objective reference for it. Outside the event, I had an absolute reference: the event itself, and this helped a lot.

When I teach 3D modeling, my students make replicas of existing objects. If the student makes an error, I can say, "This vertex doesn't match your reference, fix it or your grade goes down." and then point to the reference. This is the absolute standard against which their work is measured. In the same way, real events that correlate with my dreams provide an absolute standard. By comparing them with my record of the dream, I taught myself where I was most likely to make mistakes and to avoid them. The key to this was recognizing the probability that my dreams might describe something real.

On the same night as the McDonald's dream, I also dreamed that Lisa Powers, an art director I knew, gave me an illustration assignment and that I saw president George H.W. Bush smoking a hookah. Later that day, Lisa did hire me, and I did see "Bush" smoking a hookah, but it was a comedian on TV doing irreverent impressions, not the president.

The reporting is flawed, but these last two elements combine neatly with the McDonald's scene to create a "combination lock." A combination lock dream is actually a group of thematically unrelated scenes from the same night that correlate with other events that occur on the same day, regardless of when that day is. Combination locks of the mundane variety described here, happen on the same day as the dream or very soon after. They are fairly common in the journal, so common that I very soon learned to expect that if any one scene from a dream happens on a certain day, then I can expect other scenes to happen also.

An "identification error" is when I cannot identify someone in a dream. In one typical dream of this type, I couldn't tell if it was about Marcus McLaurin of Marvel Comics, or Mark Evanier, a writer who worked with Marcus, who mentioned some original art being returned to me. Later that day, I received the art from Marcus, and the identification error was resolved.

I had a tendency to confuse certain people with each other, but with no one else. As examples accumulated, identification errors became increasingly rare. I made these mistakes because I had a tendency to forget names in dreams, while other characteristics, like personality, came through more clearly. If two people had a similar personality, or a similar relationship to me or to each other, I could get them mixed up, like dyslexia, but with people.

Identifying strangers is more difficult, but not impossible.

DB6/68, 3/9/00 (nap)
I walk through some big glass doors into 3DO's Redwood City offices. Two men are with me, one of whom worked at Industrial Light and Magic (ILM) for some time.

Just fifteen minutes after this dream, I was inside the 3DO building for my job interview with Bill Hindorf. Instead, a stranger came out to get me. When he turned his back to pass through a glass door, I saw a "Skywalker Sound" logo on his jacket. Skywalker Sound is a part of ILM, so I inquired if he had worked there. He said he had worked at ILM for fifteen years.

In my memory of the dream, I didn't remember why I thought the man worked at ILM, but knew that he had. I discovered it only because the dream made me curious about the one clue that presented itself: his jacket. With all of my dream identifications, it comes down to objective clues like this, combined with logic and later events, to confirm them. If I hadn't had the confidence to ask, though, I wouldn't have ever had his confirmation. How often does that happen?

Just as I can mistake one person for another, I can mistake my motive for doing something. This is a "motive error." It happens frequently in dreams, but also while I'm awake. It first happened in 1989, when I had a date to meet Kitty at a movie theatre. After I'd left the apartment, I had a strong urge to go back to get something I'd forgotten. It was against my nature to return, but I did anyway.

I scanned the small apartment from the dining table, searching for whatever it was, but there was nothing. Then I looked down and sitting right in front of where I was standing, was Kitty's spare pair of glasses. I knew she had the good set with her and didn't need these, but I grabbed them anyway and stuffed them into my pocket. When I got to the theatre, before even saying Hello, I handed her the glasses.

"You heard me!" she said.

It turned out that she forgot her other pair of glasses at the office. When she got to the theatre, she realized this, but didn't have the time to go back and get them. Because of her knowledge of my dreams, she tried shouting at me in her head, "Andy! Bring me my glasses!" I didn't hear anything, I didn't even know why I turned around or why I brought the glasses, I just did it. Kitty had slipped her message in under my radar and that was good enough. I didn't need to identify her or the message to act on it.

The incident with Kitty's glasses appears to be direct communication from her to me, or telepathy. What of dreams of phone calls that I receive later in the day? Almost any time I dream of a phone call, such as one surprise call from my father, telling me he was shipping out to Puerto Rico with the Navy, the call itself takes place later in the day. Skeptics like to suggest this is telepathy, not a glimpse of the future, but it is a poor explanation.

The same information can be conveyed by telepathy, but a dream of a phone call is not a telepathic communication any more than you can "hear" an image. When I have received telepathic impressions, they do not include a visualization of the message or the future form of its delivery. When I went back upstairs to figure out what I forgot to bring to the theatre, I did not have a flash of Kitty phoning or writing me with a message. In a phone call dream, I see exactly how the message is delivered.

The following dream is an excellent example:

DB12/38, 12/12/02

Envelopes from United Media and Jay Kennedy of King Features. Jay's envelope is big. One contains a check, an offer letter, and a bunch of paperwork. The other envelope is similar, but no check.

Five days later, Kitty received a large envelope from Jay Kennedy, postmarked 12/11/02, containing a large fold-out poster and a card. She also received a $1,000 check, but not from Jay. Kitty was expecting the check, but I didn't know about it.

I confused King Features and United Media in the dream, but of greater interest is the postmark. Jay's envelope was postmarked the day before my dream, but it didn't arrive until almost a week later. Jay wouldn't have known about the check, sent by someone else, and the only reason for me to see it is the connection to the day Jay's envelope would arrive. Therefore, although a slender argument can be made that Jay or the sender of the check could have sent a telepathic message that would result in a dream, neither could have known their envelopes would arrive on the same day.

Ordinary dreams tend to be realized quickly, often later on the same day, but there are exceptions. On May 14, 2003, I dreamed of Saddam Hussein being captured, photographed, and inoculated by a doctor. Seven months later, shortly after his capture, I saw this happen on a news bulletin. Despite this example, experience shows that the more ordinary a dream is, the more likely it is to happen that day.

My dreams often contain memorable images that I draw rough sketches of in the journal. One dream from June 14, 1990, was confirmed later the same day, largely because of the sketch I made in the journal and how well it resembled a postcard received that afternoon.

Here is the way I described it in the journal, "It is a political subject, like an editorial illustration. I don't like it very much, it seemed crude. Dark colors; red, black, dark blue..."

The name I tried hard to remember, and wrote down as "Ted Garret" for the artist, resembled the real artist's name in only the slightest way, such as the consonant/vowel pattern of the names "Ted Garret" and "Kay Miller," but this was less important than the correct relationships between the parties. The card is from my friend Ron Robertson, who is the primary subject of the dream, and it involves an artist's agent (the gallery) as stated elsewhere in the dream. Both images have the same colors, both are the same aspect ratio (more than twice as wide as they are tall), the Miller subject does appear to be political, and my sketch shows a helicopter-like shape right where there is a helicopter in the Miller painting. The similarities are enough to convince me that the dream and the postcard are related. After that, the differences become a higher priority. Where are they different, and how can those differences be accounted for?

The rough "helicopter" from my sketch is a decent approximation, given that I had no idea what the shape was supposed to represent. In Miller's painting, the whirling blades of the vehicle are blurred in exactly the spots where my drawing loses detail. The lack of detail in those two spots then, is understandable. There is a semblance of a landscape in the sketch, from a perspective that is appropriate for a view of a helicopter in flight, but there is no background in Miller's painting, unlike my journal sketch. This looks like an attempt to complete an image that doesn't make sense without a background, but it could also be an attempt to combine the landscape in Ron's piece with the Miller piece. The rough marks on the left of my journal sketch indicate another foreground object in about the same spot a giant dragonfly occupies in the Miller painting, but without enough detail to recognize it, unlike the helicopter.

The sketch from this dream scene is an example of how something real gets distorted in a dream, and how it happens. For fun, Kitty, my daughter Nina, and I performed an experiment related to this. Kitty and I are both professional artists, and Nina is well on her way to becoming one also. I wanted to see how well we could reproduce images we'd seen while awake. We decided to use our recent Paris vacation for the images, because we'd seen a number of famous paintings there, including the *Mona Lisa*. With every painting we tried, we made the same kind of errors found in my dream journals. If anything, some of the compositions drawn in my journal were better approximations of the real thing than the sketches we'd made of paintings we'd just seen while awake.

I've dreamed of movies, videos, and television broadcasts prior to seeing them. With videos, some are of movies I had seen before. These can be connected to the specific day I see the video. Therefore, even though I'd seen the movie before, the dreams aren't manufactured from memory. An indication is that, while they depict movies I am familiar with, I usually don't recognize them until the day I see the video.

When dreaming of the literal future, I am stripped of my normal knowledge of everyday things, just as a baby sees everything on a street he is looking at, but understands nothing of what he sees. In literal dreams, it is difficult to identify what something is, despite remembering what it looked like well enough to make a drawing in my journal.

On June 9, 1990, I had dreamed of a decapitated head that talks, a man with what looked like many spears stuck in his body, and shots of a large and dangerous insect. I interpreted the images as being part of primitive Cambodian rituals, and wrote them down that way, along with detailed drawings. Later that night, I watched the movie *Alien* on video and immediately recognized the images from my dream. The talking head was Ash, the decapitated science officer robot, the dangerous insect was the first, small, form of the alien creature when it bursts out of a crewmembers stomach, and the man with spears related to a shot of the John Hurt character just after his abdomen bursts open. Blood trails around his body resemble the spear-like shapes I remember from the dream.

The difficulty of recognizing scenes from this famous movie reminds me of an incident when I was about twelve years old. My family stopped at a Bob's Big Boy restaurant for some dinner late at night. I was very tired, but when I saw some comic books at the register, I went right for them. One was *Spider-man*, which I took out immediately and started leafing through it. Very quickly, I had a disconcerting revelation. I couldn't read. I looked at the word balloons, and had no idea what anything said. I had forgotten how to read English. This truly terrified me for all of about two minutes, when I suddenly realized that the comic was written in Spanish.

With the Spanish Spider-man (*Hombre Araña*) and the decapitated Ash, my assumption about what I was seeing was so powerful that it overwhelmed what I was really seeing. People do this all the time. They mistake garden hoses for snakes, trash near a garbage can for a sleeping homeless person (or vice versa), and smoke for fog. In 1966, a fisherman off the coast of Spain watched as a hydrogen bomb fell into the ocean, attached to a parachute. He thought it was a man. Immediately afterwards, a second chute trailing ribbons fell into the ocean, and he thought it was a man also, but torn in half, with his intestines hanging loose. If this can happen when you are wide awake, think of the possibilities when you are asleep and the environment has a tendency to bend to your imagination, like wax in a flame. In the *Alien* video, I did my best to understand what I was seeing, but could only go so far without understanding the context. For the comic, I had to know it was Spanish before it became clear. With the video, because I was missing that key, whatever it was, I may as well have been an aborigine looking at a photograph for the first time, thinking it was just a bunch of multi-colored ink smears. This is just one of the reasons why I consider literal dreams of the future to be of lower quality than non-literal varieties.

One characteristic about movies that penetrates into my dreams is that they are made of powerful, memorable images.

### DB11/5, 3/29/02

I see a young girl being held by a criminal. I hope this isn't Nina, but she has a "daughter" feel to her. I watch helplessly as the criminal injects the girl with a drug. I can't see him, but I know there is another criminal in the room. The girl accepts the drug the bad guy gives her. I worry about his intentions.

Later the same evening, on the first day of its release, I went to see the movie *Panic Room*. The dream is straight out of the movie. Jody Foster is trapped outside a panic room, her diabetic daughter is inside the room with two murderous robbers. Foster talks one of the crooks into giving the girl an insulin shot as Foster frets outside the room. The daughter accepts the shot with relief. This time, as in most movie dreams, everything I saw was described very well, apart from the obvious identification error. In movie dreams, remembering scenes accurately is not much of a problem, but differentiating them from reality is.

I think the reason movie dreams have such powerful imagery is that, unlike real life, they are a concentration of drama, both in time and space. Everything takes place directly in front of the audience, all time-wasting moments are cut out, the film plays in a darkened room, and the filmmakers use every other trick they can think of to enhance the dramatic qualities of the film. This exaggerates the power of the images well beyond the ordinary, making them memorable.

I confirmed the Ramstein disaster from a TV broadcast, but the dream was not of a TV broadcast, it was the thing itself. The same is true of the Sioux City crash and the Amsterdam dream. All of those dreams were much more vivid than a movie dream, but the movie dreams came close enough to be weak imposters. What conclusively distinguished between them is that movie dreams had an additional quality; they carried with them a passive stupor, not unlike the mental state one might relax into to watch a film. Once I recognized this, I could predict which dreams would prove to be of movies with reasonable accuracy.

Movies aren't the only thing that can be confusing, memorable, or realistic in a dream. Here is an example of how our perception is different when we sleep:

DB2/17, 2/16/90

Two girls smashed flat by panes of glass, but in such a way that while they are now paper thin they are still fully rounded figures. They appear unmarred by the accident and the red-haired girl is very beautiful. I spend some time examining her face which even has a half-smile on it despite her current circumstances.

Later the same day, the mystery was solved. The "two girls smashed flat" are two of several young ladies I saw represented in a painting at the Philadelphia Art Museum. The dream was of the painting *Le Grande Baigneuses* by Pierre Renoir. The figures of the girls in this painting are fully-rounded and completely flat at the same time. I did not comprehend how this could be so in the dream, and made up my own explanation.

I saw a flat representation of three dimensional objects, but because I didn't understand the context, could not make sense of the image. To reconcile my expectation with what I saw, I imagined that the girls in the painting had been smashed flat.

The explanation doesn't make sense, but it does retain the integrity of the image.

I could have recorded the image as a series of brightly colored paint strokes, but I knew they represented three-dimensional figures and that those figures were a group of young ladies. Why was I unable to distinguish them from real people? In movie dreams, I am often unable to distinguish between real people and images of actors on a screen, but in a film, the images are more realistic thanks to photography, motion, and audio.

What it felt like, is that I was re-experiencing something that had happened in the future. When I went to the museum later, I examined the painting closely for two reasons: I liked it, and because I recognized it from the dream. This is why I examined it closely in the dream also. Then there is another layer of thought superimposed on the image. It is what my dream self is thinking, and that is not the same as what I see from my future. I look at the painting without any idea why, leaving me free to come up with my own ideas, as if I am two people. One is the character in the dream, the other is the dream observer, but both are me. The painting itself doesn't make sense for the reasons already given, so I puzzle that over in a fashion typical of literal dreams.

Why is it sometimes difficult to identify dream objects? Here, it gives rise to a theory that borrows from the Sumi experience and a bit more from Kitty's glasses. In both incidents, I reacted to invisibly provided information without consciously acknowledging it. What if, when we recognize and identify people, it isn't purely a visual recognition? It may feel that way because we pay such close attention to what we see, but what if there is a kind of psychic identifier also, a kind of mental handshake that helps us identify each other? Could it be that without such a device, the people in our environment would be as difficult to sort from their surroundings as the characters in this Renoir? Is this why it was so hard for me in the dream? Because I was relying only on what I saw?

So far I'd been thinking of my dreams as either one-way communications, like warnings and opportunities, or tourism, where I explore a small portion of my immediate future, as if it were a place, rather than a distant time. This next dream pair expanded my horizons just a bit more.

DB3/1 & DB3/27, 5/1/90-5/23/90
5/23/90
I wake up with a strong urge to call my mom. It is probably connected to a dream I can't remember, and that is why I didn't want to do it. I called anyway, and got her answering machine. Feeling silly, I left a fast and somewhat embarrassed message, "Mom, I had a feeling this morning that I was supposed to call. Never mind, and good morning."

In the kitchen, I found a pile of books Kitty checked out of the library the previous day. I grabbed one, a book about the commercial photographer Al Satterwhite, and brought it into the living room to read. While reading, my mom called. Not wanting to lose my page, I left the book open on the couch and answered the phone.

She had a dream that morning also, where she was told to call me and give me a certain message. She wasn't going to because it seemed ridiculous to her, but my message changed her mind. When she told me the message, I had my doubts. It was, "Tell Andy to go to the first entry in his dream journal and go very slowly." Here is the relevant section:

DB3/1, 5/1/90
A painting or photo of a rock. > A book or set of books with photos of palaces around the world. > A camera with sand in it slows the auto focus lens. The sand is put inside on purpose [see illus.] > A photo or painting of a blurred oval blip of light surrounded by medium dark browns and yellows. A very grainy enlargement of a tiny portion of the photo. I consider painting it.

The entry was loaded with references to photography and books. Then I got to the "blurred oval of light" and recognized a very similar image on one of the open pages of the Satterwhite book on the couch. There were other correspondences, but that was the most striking.

If any event is going to be recognized as related to an earlier dream, many complex dependencies must be satisfied. Usually, these dependencies are purely physical. Sometimes, like the Amsterdam and lottery dreams, a response to the dream itself is also required. Here, it is a response to two dreams by two different people. Without that, this dream cannot be realized. The dreams had to be coordinated.

I probably called my mom because I'd had an urgent message to do so in a dream. Like the LaGuardia crash, I didn't remember the appeal itself, but I did remember the message. If it really was a "message," then it implies a sender. My mother also had a dream "message." If we can accept this, then both of us received a synchronized message from an independent source that relates to an earlier dream of mine.

We didn't want to act on the messages, and for the same reason: we thought it was thin. My call then, becomes essential to carrying out the realization of the first dream, just as her initial reluctance may have also been necessary, to time the call to the moment when I was on the right page of the Satterwhite book.

The dream referred to in my mother's message is "the first dream" in the journal. That is an easy to remember location. Because it was the "first dream," the message she was supposed to communicate was easier for her to remember. Is this intentional? Is it a kind of message compression, like we saw with the descending doubles, where a message is reduced to its bare essentials? For that to be true, I had to have the right dream on the night that produced the first record in the journal. Was the dream manipulated to produce that result, or were later events adjusted to match whatever dream happened to be recorded on that day? Or were all of these things always a part of a future that had already happened?

My impression, is that the first dream was about a future that could only happen if certain other things transpired as they did. This means that a coordinated psychic element of some kind was essential. If my mother and I had not had the two dreams we received later in the month, this dream could not have been realized as it was. Kitty might have gotten the Satterwhite book anyway, and I may have looked at it, but stopping on that one page was a product of my call to my mother and hers to me, both of which had a psychic origin. This dream then, for the first time, gives a clue suggesting the existence of some kind of coordination between my waking reality, and the one experienced in dreams.

The dreams in this chapter are mundane, but not without interest, because of what they can tell us about the dreaming process. This is not a small thing, because seeing a thing is not always the same as understanding it.

## *Chapter Five*

# The distant future

I met my father for the first time when I was sixteen years old. Within a year, I was living in his house. While there, I had this dream:

DB0/11, 1982, Boyes Hot Springs, California
I wake up beside a woman I know is my wife. I look at her sleeping and reflect on the seven years we've been together, during the most recent years of which we've argued. Without waking her, I go to the door, where I am met by two men.

My impression is that they will take me to prison and that I am going there because of the arguments I've been having with my wife. I am not happy to go, but follow them out of the room regardless. It feels like we go up for a long ways, and then they leave me in a large open area, along with all the other inmates of this place.

It isn't like a prison at all. I have full freedom of movement, and seem to be able to do anything I like, except go back to my wife. I meet a couple here who become my friends, and we meet frequently to play board games or have dinner. I experience what feels like every day of a full year, and most of those days are normal in every way.

Then, on a day when I am expecting my friends, they bring a third person. I recognize him, but am surprised because he isn't expected. We start playing a game when suddenly there is a flood that covers the ground as far as I can see. Everything is swept up in it and I worry about drowning. Just then, I notice that the door I came through when I first arrived is unlocked, and has been the whole time I've been here. I swim over and open it, causing the flood waters to drain.

With the door open, I realize that I could have left at any time. I am overcome with remorse and loneliness and rush down the stairs, hoping that my wife will still be where I left her, and willing to take me back. Alongside me, I hear my friends talking about what they will do with their freedom. I tune them out and run all the faster.

When I get to her room, she is still there. Better yet, she will take me back. I am grateful for the opportunity and give her a long hug. I tell her I will be more sensitive in the future and less abrasive.

Now there is a gap of many years. In the next scene, I am outside painting a self-portrait from my reflection in a pond. I stand in my backyard, with my house about a hundred feet away. The landscape is lush and green, the house is white with a black roof. My wife comes to the sliding glass door with a towel around her head. She tells me it's time to come in for lunch. I put my paints down and go in.

Waking up as a seventeen year-old who had never dated was strange. In the dream, just minutes before, I was an adult. For the next few days after this dream, I still felt married, or the echoes of it. I didn't think the dream might relate to someone I would marry, but couldn't get over the creepy feeling left by seven years of memories from a life I hadn't lived. How could I experience so much in so little time? And why was it so realistic? I told my friend Ernst Halpern, a local art supply store owner, about the dream. He had once been a psychologist and answered from that perspective. The possibility that the dream might describe future events never occurred to him either.

In the next two years, I moved to Maine with my father and then back to California to live with my mother again, where I attended Art Center College of Design in Pasadena. One night I said to myself, "Tomorrow, I'm going to meet the girl I marry." It was the first and only time I'd ever had such a thought, and this night I repeated it several times.

The next day, I was in Mr. Robbins' drawing class when a young Asian woman walked in during a break. She wore a long black coat, the kind one never sees in California except on transplanted New Yorkers. Mr. Robbins and I discussed some drawings, but I had a hard time paying attention as she walked through the room. This was the first time anyone had made me think of that dream. After a few minutes, she stopped at my workbench and paged through a sketchbook I had sitting there. I paid attention, but couldn't break away from my conversation for another ten minutes or so. She remained at my bench, absorbed by my sketchbook.

I finished my conversation with Mr. Robbins and introduced myself. She said her name was Kitty, and she was from New York. We talked about my drawings at first, then about art in general. She wasn't in any of my classes, because she'd already earned her bachelor's degree at Barnard College in New York. She was in California to take supplementary classes and improve her skills in general. When she came into my room, it was out of simple curiosity. She paged through my notebook because she liked my art. We talked a lot, but I did not tell her much about my dream, only that she resembled someone I'd dreamed of once. We started dating within a month.

We lived together as an unmarried couple for the first three years we knew each other. We married when I was twenty-two and she was twenty-nine. Not quite four years later, a little less than seven years from the day we'd met, things were not going so well. In 1985, I moved to New York City to be with Kitty, in 1988 we moved to Vermont to be in the country, and then within a few months we moved back to the New York City area, but in New Jersey. I didn't like living in big cities, and only tolerated it for

Kitty's sake. I complained often about the city, and Kitty didn't like hearing the complaints almost every day. She didn't like the country, and her complaints while in Vermont were a significant factor in the decision to return to the New York City area.

After bickering about this for several years, we decided to separate. The idea was that I would try to learn how to draw comic books for a living from Portland, Maine, a location that was enough of a city for Kitty's tastes, and close enough to the country for mine. Kitty would stay in New York to pay the bills on a temporary basis. It was up to me to replace her income in a reasonable time frame from Portland.

On the morning of the move, I woke up early to answer the door. When I opened it, I was face to face with two men who looked familiar to me, like the men who brought me to "prison" in my first dream of Kitty. These men were the two movers we'd hired to pack our U-Haul truck for the move to Maine, they weren't jailers or prison guards at all, nor was I going to prison. I was going "up" in the sense that Portland was three hundred miles north of New Jersey, and I would be separated from Kitty for awhile, possibly permanently, just as in the dream.

With no one else to talk to, I re-acquainted myself with some friends I had met while attending school in Maine a few years earlier. I didn't recognize them from the dream when I first met them at school in 1983, because the context was different, but these friends were the people I played cards with in my first dream of Kitty, the one where I had to go "up" for a year and live in this other place.

One night almost exactly a year after moving to Maine, I waited in the apartment for a couple I had invited over to play some board games. After they rang the buzzer in the foyer below me, but before they arrived at my door, I realized that they were the couple from my dream. I also knew, thanks to the dream, that they would bring another classmate, Allan, with them, even though he hadn't been invited. When the elevator doors opened, he was with them. That day, I received my first real assignment as a comic book artist, from Marvel Comics. This was the day in the dream where I was let out to rejoin my wife. Curiously, Hurricane Bob had just lashed its way through Southern Maine a couple weeks earlier, leading to widespread flooding in nearby areas, including the president's home in Kennebunkport. It had its effect in Portland also. Because my apartment was along the wharf facing the ocean, I had to tape my windows and set up buckets and pans to catch all the rainwater that was pushed through various cracks in walls and around the windows. It wasn't exactly what I expected from that long ago dream, but the hurricane and its effects weren't that different from the "flood" that happened just before I went back to be with my wife.

I called up Kitty and, based on the money I expected from the job, arranged to have her move up to Maine. Right then, all but the last scene from the long ago dream had come true. As I write this in 2009, the last scene has not yet happened, but I do live in a location that has many houses resembling the one from the dream, including mine. I do not, however, have a backyard pond.

Unlike the other dreams described so far, in this one, the events unfolded over many years. This isn't a dream about a single incident, but of histories, decisions, and personal growth, all of which came to pass. I was seventeen when I dreamed this, and could not have known that after moving to Maine, I would marry a New Yorker I met in California, split up after seven years, go to Maine, get back together, and then quite possibly end up in Holland, a place I hadn't yet been to or considered visiting.

In 1982, my dad, my stepmother, Stella, and I lived on the outskirts of Sonoma, California, in a three-bedroom house surrounded by about ten acres of dried grass. It was about as far from New York, Los Angeles, or Maine as you could get. I thought about art, school, and my "new" father to the exclusion of all else. My only playmate was our cat, Porgy, who followed me into the fields while I painted landscapes. Marriage, separation, and whatever else went with it, were ideas as alien to me as a flying saucer from another planet.

When I saw Kitty for the first time, I didn't even need words, I just thought "!" it was *her*. But then my logic took over and just as quickly changed my mind. "No it isn't. Look at her, she's Asian. Did you remember her being Asian from the dream? Of course not. Let's not be silly here. She resembles her, but it's been a couple of years, don't be ridiculous..." After that, I tried to put the dream out of my mind, but, just like the call to Sarah Eisenman and the coy challenge, "Why not now?," it kept coming back. For the first couple of years I'd be looking at Kitty at odd moments, comparing, and thinking, "Nah..."

There were a lot of reasons to think we wouldn't get married, either by our own choice or the will of others. My family and Kitty's both had qualms about an interracial relationship, for a start, but there was also the fact that Kitty was a Christian and I was an atheist. I told her, in unnecessarily harsh terms, that there was no chance she could ever share or express her religious life with me. If she wanted to be with me, I didn't want to know about her religion and would never participate in it. The fact that I was vegan didn't sit well with her family, just as I didn't like being around non-vegan food when visiting. Our families were from totally different social spheres. She came from a well-known and sophisticated successful immigrant family in New York City, and I came from the wrong side of the tracks, raised by a wonderful, but single, mother.

Despite all these things, I did marry the first and only woman I ever dated, and twenty-four years after we met, we are still married. The key to all of it may have been that dream. The reason is that Kitty and I had an irreconcilable problem: she loved the city and I hated it. We couldn't figure out how to solve the problem and had all but given up on ever doing so. The dream gave me the hope I needed to persevere. Living in Maine while separated from Kitty was very difficult for both of us, but unlike her, I was not surrounded by supportive family members and friends. I was on my own in a cold and unknown place. My solace was that dream. I'd think of it, and it would give me the motivation I needed to stay up a few more hours at the drawing table to improve my skills a little bit more, to get closer and closer to the day when we could be back together again.

In the Satterwhite dreams, timing was very important. The three dreams all had to happen when they did, or they couldn't have been confirmed as they were. Other dreams, like the Amsterdam dream, also had to happen at approximately the right time, or their effects wouldn't have been the same either. Unlike Amsterdam, this dream did not affect any of my immediate options. Even if it had inspired me to move to a place like New York (where Kitty lived at the time) or Los Angeles, or anywhere else, I couldn't have done anything about it because of my age. I went where my dad went, and that's all there was to it.

The closest I can get to an answer is that, at around the time of the dream, Stella was trying to get me to start dating. Once, on the pretext of seeing some of her friends at a restaurant, Stella urged me to dance with one of her friends' daughters. Maybe the dream happened at just that time to remind me that I was spoken for? Maybe, just like when I accepted the premonition about Sumi, I unconsciously accepted what this dream told me. The result is that I could focus single-mindedly on my art studies so that, when I did finally happen to be in the drawing room on the day Kitty came in to audit the class, my skill would be evident to her already trained eye. This would attract her attention while simultaneously ensuring that I was unencumbered by pre-existing romantic attachments. Maybe that is why, on the night before, I was so confident I would meet my wife, because on some unconscious level I remembered it from the dream?

In some ways, this might be the first "big dream" I remember having. I haven't had many big dreams, less than a dozen, and each is different from the other in many respects. One trait they all share is their scope. Big dreams cover a lot of time. Some cover much more time than this dream of Kitty, some less, but it is always quite a lot, generally experienced in minute detail. Sometimes, like this one, they are literal, others are not. The subject matter of my big dreams are usually domestic, but not always. This dream of Kitty shares one other quality with the big dreams, and that is its importance to my life. It gave me inspiration, hope, and comfort just when I needed them.

Sometimes I have a dream that is so strong I am sure it will happen, but it doesn't. I wait weeks, then months, wondering why it hasn't happened. Years go by, and it still doesn't happen. There was one dream like this from 1990 about a certain person I would meet. I was so sure I would meet this person, that I mentioned her to Kitty several times, and showed her the drawing I made of the mystery woman in the journal more than once. By the time I did meet her nine years later, I had stopped recording dreams in my journal for almost four years. It was this dream that convinced me it would be worthwhile to start the journal back up again:

DB3/80, 7/8/90
I give a psychic reading to a woman from Long Island. The reading: She wants me to tell her where she is from. It is Long Island, but a certain part of Long Island. She is from forty to forty-five years old, dark haired, tall, large-boned, overweight (because of her height, it might not have been so bad as it seemed.)

Just before coming over to where I am sitting she has an urgent desire to bring a photograph of a man who, although he doesn't look like me, a verbal description of us would match fairly closely. Then we talk about a bunch of different things, and it is much easier than I expected because I thought she would be difficult. Long Island Sound? That sounds right to me.

At times I just gave her what seemed like good advice, but about half to three quarters of what I said was actually psychic. A quarter of what I said just served to point me in the right direction for the advice. She was married, and was experiencing a difficulty she wanted to have straightened out. I don't think I'd ever seen her before.

This is very much like a reading given to me, as opposed to the other way around, by a psychic named Carol Dreyer in 1999. She thought I looked like a friend of hers, a writer named Michael Talbot (author of The Holographic Universe), so she came rushing out with a photo of him and wouldn't stop talking about how similar we were. A friend of hers was there too and both kept remarking on this uncanny resemblance, yet I didn't see it at all. She was from Long Island, dark-haired, overweight (a lot, not a little) and had a chronic problem with her leg that she periodically complained of. The reading itself had a couple of interesting moments, but most of it seemed like she was just guessing, or maybe wandering blindly while waiting to bump into the occasional tree. When that happened, she could describe it reasonably well, but would then descend into the fog again. Overall, my impression of the reading was not extremely positive, but it did seem like there were a couple spots where she made some genuinely interesting statements.

When I met Carol in California, I recognized her immediately. Because of this, one of the first things I asked her was if she was from Long Island, long before she had a chance to say anything on the subject. I'd forgotten many of the details of the dream, so when I got home and looked it up, I was surprised to see the description of her making a big production of showing me the photograph and how I looked like this man, even though I didn't, among other things.

I am not in the habit of visiting "psychics." On this occasion I made an appointment with Carol because I was researching a screenplay (later published as *Peripheral Vision*). It didn't matter to me whether she was genuine or not; I just wanted to know what a $100 storefront "psychic reading" was like because I was considering including a scene of one in the screenplay and didn't want to just completely make it up.

I dream of moving house fairly often, probably because I find myself actually doing it often also. In a list of addresses I made recently in an effort to recall every house or apartment I've ever lived in, I came up with over 50 addresses. Most of these were from the period between 1968-1982, when my mother's intermittent employment forced us to move twice a year on average. since then, the average quickly dropped to once every two years. The next dream relates to one of the more unusual, least expected of all my moves.

DB1/3, 9/16/89, Manhattan, New York

I have just moved into a decrepit house on a hill near a body of water (an ocean or river) and am unpacking when the landlord, a nice man in his late forties and dressed like a cowboy, comes by to say Hello. There is an extremely dangerous steep cliff behind the house I am in with five mansion-like houses on it. A sign with arrows points up to the houses and reads, "If you can make it up the cliff to any of these houses, you may claim it and live there rent free." It looked impossible to me, but I tried anyway and got to the top. With that accomplished, I picked a house and moved in. It is a beautiful home. Later when Kitty and I are unpacking, two older women come in to look at the house but I tell them it is taken.

Fourteen years later, I saw the house in person. It was located in Arizona, on the steepest, most death-defying hill I'd ever seen, and it was one of three houses bought on spec by a writer/producer named Harry that I knew in Hollywood. There were two undeveloped lots on the hill, for a total of five lots. The problem was, Harry wasn't offering them to me rent-free. He wanted $4,000 a month. This was the identical rent I was trying to avoid paying by leaving Hollywood. I told him no deal.

Harry was surprised because he knew I made a good living as an art director, but then I told him how I'd lost my job at Sony. While working on a military contract for the Army, I discovered that about $2.3 million dollars had been misdirected by our business partners and that my boss had helped cover it up. I first tried to solve this with in-house counsel, but was blocked internally, then terminated after persisting with the issue. After that, I turned them in and was rewarded with an active and successful campaign by Sony to interfere with my job prospects. By the time I was thinking of moving to Arizona, it was because I knew that my Hollywood career was finished and I had to start all over.

After a considerable amount of talk, during which I repeatedly refused Harry's every effort to get me to move into the house, he finally made the offer I couldn't refuse: he wouldn't evict for non-payment of rent. By then he'd also reduced the rent to $3,200, only half of which was payable immediately. If I found myself unable to pay the rent, I would owe it. This wasn't exactly "rent-free," but it could be described that way if I ever lost the ability to pay rent, as I was sure I would, and ultimately did, after eight months. The man who let us into the house the first night was a friend of Harry's, who reminded me of the "cowboy" from the dream, and the two ladies were two estate agents that came to look over the place before they knew Harry had a tenant.

I had nine other dreams that appear to be related to this same move. The first of these came on the day after this one, as if it was a continuation of it. In it, Kitty and I moved to the house, and it described certain details that are consistent only with this one move. Later dreams describe us as living in Arizona, the appearance of the house, size of the basement, a drawing of the view from our living room, the fact that I spent my time filling the house with large format paintings, and a decent description of the art gallery in Scottsdale where I showed my work as well as its floor plan.

At the time of the first few dreams in this series, fourteen years before they would be re-enacted before my eyes, none of the houses on that hill in Arizona had been built. It was built in 2002, thirteen years after the first and second dream. I didn't meet Harry until 1997, or eight years after the dream. Harry didn't move to Hollywood until shortly before I did. At the time of the dream, I was working as an editorial illustrator, computer generated (CG) effects were not yet an industry of their own, and Sony Pictures had not been created yet. If someone had told me that artwork could be made on a computer, I would have been amazed. It would be three years before I discovered that the bizarre water tentacle effect in the film *The Abyss* was computer animation.

Despite all this, fourteen years later, not only did I come to live in that mansion on the hill, but the CG industry that brought me to Hollywood became an industry in its own right, Harry moved to Hollywood, the houses were built, Sony Pictures was in business, and, in the event that ultimately directed me towards Arizona, I became a whistle-blower on a video game-based infantry training simulation that I couldn't have conceived of in 1989.

One of the oddities about dreams of the future is that, the farther forward they project into time, the more they predict. If I dream of a colleague bursting into my office to announce the death of a colleague, and then it happens within hours, as happened when I worked at Rhythm & Hues on the *Daredevil* movie, that is about all that is predicted by the dream. But if I dream of meeting a psychic nine years later, or moving into a certain house fourteen years later, then all the other events necessary for their realization are by inference predicted also. In the case of Carol Dreyer as well as the house in Arizona, both dreams require the CG industry to come into being, as happened, that I become a CG artist, as I did, and that I move to Hollywood, as I also did. Both of them predict all of those things, but without explicitly showing any of them. My dream of Kitty from 1982 implicitly included a great many things, and if the last scene is indeed going to prove to be located in Holland, as I expect it will, then it will also have predicted the events that led to my first going to Arizona, and then to Holland, also without explicitly showing them.

Looked at this way, long range dreams, or even long range premonitions, like the one about Sumi's suicide, contain knowledge of unsaid things, things that are necessary for the realization of the primary prediction. All this means is that a remembered dream of future events is only part of a continuum of information, all of which exists in its entirety at any given time, and from which we may extract snippets on occasion, and all of which are inextricably linked together, like the colossal stones of the great pyramids in Egypt. For the capstone of a pyramid to remain in position, all the other stones must remain beneath it. For my dream of occupying a mansion on a hill to come to pass, many other things were required as well. That I only saw the topmost portion of this group does not mean that the other parts weren't there, just that I didn't bother to look, or my view was obstructed.

Whether a dream is poorly remembered, poorly recorded, or a garbled communication, it is based on something. If it is based on the future, it is coming from the same place and is part of the same thing. This is how I can have nine dreams about living in a house on a hill in the desert of Arizona, and other dreams about different subjects, all of which require the identical circumstances to occur. With dreams of the future, the effort to isolate individual dreams from each other can cause misunderstandings.

Learning how dreams fit together, on the other hand, can bring out new information that might not otherwise have been discovered.

## *Chapter Six*

# Visiting

"Andy, have you had any dreams about me recently?"

Lisa Moore asked this unusual question as if she knew the answer was yes. With it, the tone of our conversation changed dramatically, and became serious. I asked her why she thought I might have dreamed of her but she wouldn't say. She wanted an answer to her question first.

I thought about it for a moment, and was surprised to remember that I had written her name in the journal a couple weeks earlier. I asked Lisa if she'd like me to try and find it. She agreed to wait. By the time I got back to the phone, I'd found the dream. I didn't see any way for it to be meaningful to her. To me, it was a junk dream. She insisted I read it, so I did.

DB1/81, 11/28/89, Weehawken, New Jersey
A brightly lit room filled with hard reflective surfaces. On one end of the room is a pair of circular windows cut into a pair of thin steel doors. A man bursts in and I see that the doors swing both ways. The man wears a white apron and carries a stainless steel platter in his gloved hands. On the platter is an animal, but of what variety I am not certain. It may even be two animals, huddled very closely together, I can't tell because it looks like such a confusing bloody mess. It isn't a large animal, no more than a foot and a half long on the platter, and its hair sticks up in a bristly fashion like a pig.

The chef sets the platter on a steel-encased kitchen island directly in front of me. Behind him I see the faces of two girls looking in through each of the two windows. One is Lisa Moore, an old friend from high school. She cries silently and the other looks on in horror.

A woman carrying a knife walks up. Like the man, she wears an apron and gloves. She goes to the platter and separates the animals somehow. Then she holds the animal's body securely and places the edge of her knife on the neck of one of the creatures. She lowers it slowly, carefully cutting the animal's head free of its body. The head tilts forward, resting about an inch away from the neck. A pool of blood rapidly collects. The animal's eyes are still open.

I have an urge to comfort Lisa, then wake.

"Does this make any sense to you?" I asked.

"Yes."

Three nights *before* the dream, Lisa's cat Nikki was run over by a car. Nikki survived the accident, but was severely injured. One of the car's tires rolled over the cat's head, leaving it hanging loosely from her shoulders, partly decapitated. By the time Lisa arrived at the veterinarian's, Nikki's fur was thickly matted with blood and was sticking up in spiky formations. Nikki was brought into surgery, where the vet worked on her neck wound. The work was delicate and difficult. During the surgery, Nikki was accidentally decapitated and she died.

This dream shares many characteristics with my other dreams, but it is not the same. It had nothing to do with my future, or my life. It is about someone else, as if I'd gone for a visit at a particularly emotional moment. Until this dream, I hadn't considered the possibility that a dream of a friend might actually be of a part of that friend's life, not mine. If Lisa hadn't asked whether I'd had any dreams of her, this dream would not have been verified.

And why did she ask? The entire time we spoke on the phone, I wondered why she seemed so sure that I would have had a dream about her on this specific topic.

"The reason I expected you to mention a dream, the reason I knew you would know about Nikki, is that I saw you in my room that night."

Her answer floored me. I was already surprised that Lisa was able to verify the dream, but this explanation of hers was totally unexpected. According to Google Earth, we lived 2,876 miles apart. Lisa insisted that she saw me in her room and that she was awake when she saw me. On the night of Nikki's death, she thought of a dream I'd described to her previously and it gave her the idea that I might be of some consolation. She made an effort, just as Kitty did with her glasses, to get me to pay attention to her plight by calling out to me mentally. Afterward, she saw me in her room and that I said, "It will be alright, Nikki will be alright. This will be for the best, to take her pain away," and after that, I vanished. Three days later, I had my dream. Whether she really saw me or not, I cannot deny that my journal backed up what she said.

When I looked at my dream journal, I saw that as many as a third of all the dreams were like it: visits to friends, family, and strangers. Lisa's phone call became the Rosetta stone that unlocked a large group of dreams that had gone unsolved up to that point. The key to solving them, I now knew, was to correctly identify who a dream was about, call that person, read the dream, and then ask "Does any of this sound familiar?" I had no idea how successful this formula would prove to be.

DB1/123, 1/11/90

Richard works at a table in a laboratory. To his side, a box rests on the table. Richard is doing something to some little wafers, or tiles. They have letters written on them like Scrabble pieces, but they are a little bigger. Richard tosses them into the box when he is done with them. Physically he pays no attention to me, but mentally I hear him say, "I'm busy, but Hello."

-

I hadn't tried calling Richard since he moved to Japan, but on this occasion I thought it might be worth the effort. When I had him on the line, I told him about the dream. He seemed impressed that I went to the trouble of calling from so far away, and surprised at the reason. I described the dream in more detail than is written here, for the simple reason that I almost always remember more than I am comfortable writing. Here is an excerpt from the letter Richard sent in response:

"..As a Research Physicist supported by the National Laboratory for High Energy Physics in Tsukuba, Japan, and also by the University of California, Davis, I am paid to be skeptical...

"..this is the first time [that the main purpose of one of Andrew's phone calls] was to recount a dream. He simply told me that he had just had a dream with me in it, with at first no indication that he might suspect that I would recognize details in it of my life or work in Japan (which, by the way, he has not seen, nor at that time had he seen any photographs).

"He said he pictured me working at a large desk, perhaps metal and grey...He saw some sort of machine in front of me, and that I was doing something with the machine to square or rectangular blocks. He said the blocks had letters on them, sort of like Scrabble blocks. After this, I placed the blocks in what he described as a trash container strapped to the side of the table. (Note: since I am writing this from memory, I may have a tendency to remember most clearly the details that correlated most closely with what I had been doing. He may have told me other details which did not correlate and I have forgotten.)

"It so happens that I had spent several hours earlier on the day he called, and also on the previous day, sitting before a large, white table, slicing electronic pre-amplifier cards with a cutting machine...after this I got a piece of Teflon tape and wrote letters on the card to identify it (A,B, C, ...,AA, BB, CC, ..., AAA, BBB, BBB, etc) with a black magic marker. I then placed the cards in a cardboard box sitting on the table.

73

"I was astounded by the accuracy of his description of what he had seen in his dream in also describing what I had been doing earlier..."

Richard added the following,

"In and of itself, this correlation, while significant, would not support a hypothesis of pre-cognition over more mundane explanations."

Richard was a good sport in his responses to requests such as this one. He reported what he remembered objectively, and usually put in a disclaimer similar to the one here. "It's interesting, but not enough to prove anything," he seems to be saying. I was developing a different opinion, but then I had a better view of what was going on than Richard.

Unlike the dream of Lisa Moore and her cat Nikki, in this dream, nothing special is going on. It is easy to imagine Richard sitting at his workstation cutting these pre-amplifier cards all evening, and that it was a boring, repetitive task. The sheer boredom of it may have caused his thoughts to wander, maybe even to me. Is this what attracted my attention? Did his relaxed mental state make it easier for me to reach him? What of his comment to me in the dream, "I'm busy, but Hello"? Was he able to interact consciously with his work and simultaneously interact with me on a different level of consciousness?

From my point of view, this was an exciting dream because I knew that I was dreaming when I saw Richard. This was not one of those literal dreams of the future where I am so caught up in events that I don't realize I am dreaming. Not only that, but I knew I was visiting Richard in Japan. When I woke, I was all but sure that he'd be able to verify, in some way, what I managed to remember from the dream. That was why I was willing to spend ten dollars for the phone call.

In Manhattan, I earned money as an illustrator. I very much

wanted to work for *Time* magazine, and eventually did make thirteen illustrations for them, most of which were unpublished. By the time I was in Weehawken recording my dreams, I was no longer very active as an illustrator. Instead, I spent most of my time painting. In all of 1990, I might have had a total of five illustration assignments. I continued to hope that *Time* would hire me again, but no longer went to their offices as I once did, and hadn't seen any of my acquaintances there for several months.

DB2/5, 2/5/90
An instructor in a classroom wants to show my illustration portfolio to the class. He had been showing covers that had been paid for but not used by *Time* magazine.

This is an early record, from a time when I was starting to learn how to record my dreams accurately. A couple of perception errors are immediately evident: The "teacher" is an art director at *Time*, his "classroom" is one of their editorial offices, and although I certainly would have liked to show my illustrations to the "class" (probably editors or other art directors), I wasn't there.

The image itself was difficult to remember. My first attempt was at a landscape, but I knew that was wrong, because I saw a field of small objects, evenly spaced. Then I remembered it clearly and drew what I saw, it wasn't a landscape, but even rows of soldiers in camouflage uniforms and face paint.

I knew from the art directors at TIME that covers were decided during a Saturday meeting. This meeting, I believe, is what I witnessed in this dream, and that is why I put it in the "visiting" category instead of as a literal dream of the future. The cover image couldn't be verified until the following day when the issue was released, but the dream was of a past event, the meeting when the cover was chosen.

Overall, I am pleased with the correspondence of the two

images. As an artist, I am accustomed to making thumbnails, and wouldn't have drawn it much differently if I'd been trying to remember it a few hours after seeing it somewhere else. In comparison to the descending doubles incident, this impressed me much more because the number of variables for any given image are much greater than the six sides of a die, even if probabilities are easier to calculate for dice than pictures.

I used the "cover search" function on *Time*'s website, and checked every single cover for the year of the dream and the twenty-nine years preceding it, for a total of thirty years worth of covers, or 1,570 covers. Out of all those covers, the only one that matched my dream is the one that was delivered to my door the day after my dream.

This does not mean there is a 1:1,570 chance of a match, or that if I went through all of the covers for *Time*'s full history of approximately 4,472 covers that the chance would be 1:4,472. There is literally no way to calculate this because of the endless range of possibilities for any given image.

The problem with using probabilities or chance as an explanation for psychic events is that doing so requires a person to first assume that "chance" is a better explanation. Probability theory, by its very definition, can never prove anything. All it does is indicate "probability." When the outcome is different from expectation, it has a "probability value" that is "against chance." All this means is that the outcome was different from expectation by a certain amount. No matter what that value is, from small to incredibly large, probability theory can contain it because the theory also states that even the unlikeliest of events is likely to happen at least once. The beauty of this is that while it cannot be proven, it cannot be disproven either. For me, the problem is that I do not agree that true randomness, or "chance," exists at all, so it is very difficult to adopt it as an explanation for dreams that appear to be directly related to real things, such as this TIME cover.

DB2/55, 3/22/90

I am in a big parking lot, where a reddish sporty-looking car has been totaled and cannot be driven...

I am with a woman but she doesn't talk to me, so I assume she is angry. I keep thinking the car is my mom's Ford EXP, but it doesn't look right. It's a different car, but it's hers.

When I called to confirm this dream, my mom said she half-expected it. I wanted to know why.

"Because I saw you in my room last night."

Just like Lisa, she insisted that she saw me in her room. She said that she was sleeping when she heard me say, "Hi Mom." This woke her up, and when she looked at the ceiling, she saw me and Kitty sleeping in bed as if she was looking down on us from our ceiling. She said "Hi Andy" in response, and then I disappeared. I tried to suggest she was still asleep, but she disagreed, "No. It was very, very vivid. I could hear you, I could see you and Kitty, like from the ceiling looking down. When I answered back, I thought 'Goodness, we don't even need phones'."

As for the car, my mother was able to confirm that the EXP had been repossessed, so she had a new car, a "junker" as she called it, that matched my description perfectly.

My comment that "... she doesn't talk to me, so I assume she is angry" is something I later ran into often in my visit dreams. I would be with someone I know, would try to communicate with whoever it was, but wouldn't get a response. This made me think they were either angry or deliberately ignoring me. Sometimes I didn't mind, other times I did and would try to get their attention by yelling or attempting to break things. These efforts usually failed, which only bothered me more. The effort to make the other person acknowledge me would only stop if I woke up or gave up.

In the dream of Lisa's cat, the event it described was three days old when I dreamed of it. When my mother's car was totaled, my dream was roughly simultaneous with the event. In the dream of the Sioux City crash, a dream that was probably a "visiting" dream, even though the subject was a stranger, the event was in the future.

Sigmund Freud believed that all dreams are traceable to prior events in one's own life. When applied to the records in my journals, it is possible to conclude that this has not happened once. There are some where an argument could be made that a dream is related to a prior waking event, but in each case an argument may also be made that it is of a similar future event. Either way, Freud's conclusion is poorly supported by my journals. When examining them, an interesting fact about the timing of dreams as they relate to waking events becomes clear: dreams of visits often relate to an event in the recent past of someone else, whereas dreams of my own life may always reflect my future.

The way it works is this: Something happens to someone I know, or someone I know happens to think of me. If I am asleep, and the power of the message is strong enough, it may be incorporated into a dream immediately, or draw my attention to the scene and I will dream of it in more detail. If I am not asleep, then the information darts under the door of my unconscious, stored until later that night when I sleep, as a kind of message on an answering machine, waiting for me to get in to play it back. At that time it becomes a dream that appears to be off in time by a few hours or days, depending on when the message was sent and when I have the time or inclination to review it.

A variety of factors may interfere with an immediate response, and this may delay the timing of a visit dream, but when the dream occurs, it may very well be a real time viewing of a past event that is actually seen from the past, just as a dream of the future is seen from the future. Either that, or both views may be obtained from a neutral, or timeless, perspective. The point is, to always view the past and present as separate from the future is a mistake. They are all part of the same continuum of information, all of which is equally available together, like different points along the same three-dimensional surface. What this means is that I am not being "told" of the past any more than I am merely "seeing" the future. In both cases I experience them from the present, but localized to their time coordinates within the overall continuum, in exactly the same way we experience the present.

DB2/68, 4/4/90 2:38 AM

Richard and Tosh-ie, or a Japanese woman, get out of a little car or small car-sized object in an indoor garage or warehouse. There is a large lightweight object in the car. It is silvery colored and is "for" Tosh-ie. It is interesting how everyone seems to be Japanese, because Richard really sticks out as a foreigner. "Tosh-ie" may be wearing an unusual hat. They don't seem to notice me even though I try to help them.

Richard and "Tosh-ie" are at the lab. They will be in contact with other people soon, and there is some expectation related to showing off this object. It is about three and a half feet wide. It may be from America. It seems to be made mostly of aluminum colored vinyl, closely resembling an inflatable object. It had a great deal of visual detail, much more than indicated in my journal sketch. The drawing gives the impression there are no nooks or crannies - this is a false impression. It is like a miniaturized New York City skyline mounted on a heavy base.

Once they get it out of the car, Richard and "Tosh-ie" take it into a sterile looking hallway with low ceilings for an institutional building. We are on an upper floor, third or higher. There are some cleaning supplies on a cart with a lot of dust pans and other similar articles on it. I try to pick up a few and throw them. I'm not sure if this meets with any success, but I think so because a young man in the hall looks really shocked by something.

I remembered leaving my sleeping body to visit Richard, and

was highly aware of this fact throughout the visit. I had just had a similar experience but then turned right around and left again to see Richard. It required intense concentration on my part to stay with Richard and stay "conscious" within the visit for a prolonged period of time.

I put a lot of effort into describing things exactly as I saw them here. It was difficult to do, and resulted in sometimes tortured descriptions, ."..a little car or a small car-sized object...." It is amazing how difficult it can be to describe something when you don't know what it is. When I called Richard in Japan to check on this, I made a cleaned up set of drawings and sent them by fax. Richard said it didn't sound familiar, and I'd have to count it as a miss.

This was the first time I'd tried to verify a visit and failed. Then, about three weeks later, on April 25th, I received a letter from Richard. In it, he writes:

"Sorry I missed your visit here on 4 April. It would have been 3:30 in the afternoon in Japan. Your dream did not trigger any profound feelings of simultaneity, but a couple of details are worth noting. It was actually a student who works with me, Jeff, who noted that the floor plan that you drew has similarities to our offices. The room you put [me] in, second from the end, corresponds to my own office, also second from the last on the 4th floor (while you said 3rd). On the opposite side of the hall you draw too many doorways (there is only one) but you put a window where there is indeed a window, along with several others, that look out into a center space of the building to allow light. Some months ago, one of the secretaries (Japanese, of course) helped me carry an electronic keyboard into the central office that I had just bought and had delivered, so that I could show her what it sounded like. It did not look like the skyline of Manhattan, but it was 'black and white, mostly white and came out of a large box. You drew the office where this occurred in approximately the right place but with many more offices separating mine from the one that was shown...I would not want you to claim this as an unambiguous victory, but there are some interesting coincidences."

I'll add here that I disagree with his statement that a keyboard isn't reminiscent of the NY skyline. To me, the long black rectangles punctuated by white are very much like silhouetted skyscrapers against a flat sky, as seen in many graphics of the city. As soon as I read the mention of a keyboard, I mentally slapped my forehead and said, "of course!" It was the shape I tried so hard to describe, but just couldn't figure out what the thing was. Even the references to it having some kind of "inflatable" quality made sense now, because I'd always thought that plastic piano keys on keyboards looked inflatable.

To illustrate how difficult it is to record something like this, try to describe a common object to someone else. The catch is, you cannot say anything about the function of the object, what it does, or how it works. I tried this on Kitty and Nina, and in every version of the challenge, we had no idea what the other person was describing until the object was pointed out. Only then was it obvious what the target was, and at that point it was clear that the descriptions were quite good, despite being incomprehensible. It is easy to forget how much we know about things, or to remember what it was like before we knew.

For example, here is an object in my room: it is wide, about the span of my arms, gray and black, but mostly gray, and has some nicely engineered pieces that allow it to move in a grid-like pattern. Most of its parts are flat, and can move. One part of it can spin in a circle, with long flat fingers sticking out.

Keep in mind that I know what this object is when I described it, and could look at it as I wrote. In a dream, neither of these things is possible. If you guessed The object is a 72" Mutoh drafting arm, congratulations, you've done better than I did every time I tried this exercise at home with my family.

It may have been a reportage error, but at the end of the record for this scene, there is a description of what it felt like to visit Richard in this way. As part of that description, a visit and a dream are differentiated. As I remember it now, I think it was because I had a higher level of awareness during this visit than I am accustomed to in other dreams. As I was to discover later, this is an important distinction.

Early in 1990, I read a book about precognitive dreams, *Dreams that come true*, by Dr. David Ryback, PhD. A couple months later I visited him in Atlanta. One outcome was an experiment to test my dreams. I would copy my dream journal entries every morning and immediately send them to David by mail. I used a code to identify dreams in the journal, and made notations on the outside of the envelopes so that we would know what was inside in case anything interesting turned up. After a few months, I stopped sending envelopes, having decided he had enough.

DB3/12, 5/10/90
I try to find Dr. Ryback and finally locate him in Atlanta. There is a car with its roof smashed in by a tree branch after a wind storm. This is the second time this has happened to the car. After looking over the car, I go to a nearby building where I find David. He says I should be quick because he hasn't much time. He seems very closed, as if my presence is far from his consciousness. In fact, he is simultaneously engaged in conversation with someone else while I try to talk to him. He asks me "What happened to the letters? Why did you stop sending them?" I answer it is because he needed only so many to prove the point, and after that if someone didn't believe, they wouldn't be convinced by more of the same.

I called David about this dream later the same day. At first he said it didn't relate to him, but then he remembered a conversation from that morning with a colleague who works in the same building. The man told him how, early in the previous week, windstorms caused a tree branch to fall on the roof of his car, caving it in. Then, on the previous night, another windstorm knocked a branch onto the roof of his wife's car and caved it in also.

Just like Richard, when David said to me, "I'm busy, but Hello," he communicated with me while his attention is simultaneously occupied elsewhere. Do we regularly interact with others on this level without realizing it? Who suggested that I predict matching descending doubles? Where did that come from? When Kitty had me get her glasses, she had to turn her attention to me on a conscious level to do it, while I received it below the surface and acted on it, without knowing what the message was. Is this no different from my conversation with David in the dream? Are we bombarded with these communications all day long, like radio waves or wireless Internet communications, and how often do we act on them without realizing it?

DB3/50, 6/10/90
Aunt Terry and Uncle Tim discuss a painting made by Tim. It is a horizontal landscape divided into three bands; foreground, middle ground, and sky. The foreground is very open and a white or gray color. The middle ground is a bunch of stylized yellow and yellow green strokes resembling bamboo. The sky is blue or turquoise. It is about fifty inches wide.

I thought it was strange to be dreaming of my Uncle Tim painting landscapes when it is my Uncle Tom who is a professional artist. I called Terry to see if this dream made any sense to her. She surprised me by saying that about a month earlier, thanks to a visit from Tom, Tim got the idea he'd like to try painting and had just finished a painting. Terry asked me to send a drawing of what I'd seen in the dream.

I cleaned up the drawing from my journal and sent the following fax (Fig. 5.4)

*Fig. 5.1, Fax of "Tim's painting" sent to Terry McGlynn on morning of dream.*

After she got the fax, Terry called me back. She told me that Tim had just finished a painting that resembled my drawing. That very morning she'd discussed it with Tim because he wanted to hang it in the kitchen, but she didn't like the idea. She said my little cartoons on the side were interesting because they mimicked their moods in the conversation.

"I put those in for scale," I explained.

"You got that right too."

About a week later, a letter arrived from Terry and Tim that contained a photo of the painting in question.

The correlation was as good as I could expect if I had tried to make a sketch of a painting I'd just seen in a museum. The things I put into my drawing are in his painting and the colors are right. I missed two rocks in the foreground, but when you look at my drawing, it is like I am reaching for those shapes but don't remember them well enough to put them in. The other error is that I put the bamboo where a rock wall is, but do so in the shape of the rock wall, as if reaching for that shape, but not quite sure what it is.

So far, my visits have mostly been of mundane events, here is an exception:

DB4/269, 4/3/91

Walter (a pseudonym) has a tiny baby boy that he throws out in such a way that I am certain the baby will die. I recover the baby, but Walter says he wants the baby out of his life (dead) (is this an abortion?)

Nine days later, my friends Kate and Dennis Dix are at my apartment. During the visit, Kate told me of a dream she'd had on April 3rd, the same night as my dream of Walter. In it, she also saw a baby left out to die, and then I showed up and told her to make sure and tell me of the dream after she wakes.

Kate and I both knew Walter, so it makes sense that we would dream of him, though neither of us knew if his girlfriend was pregnant or had recently had an abortion. I didn't have the stomach to ask, and Kate, for all I knew, didn't either. For me, the fact that we'd had dreams of the same subject on the same night was interesting enough. What I found even more interesting was my appearance in her dream. In essence, I gave her a post-it note reminder of something I already knew, to make sure I remembered it, as if I was aware of the difficulty of penetrating the sleep/waking barrier with information.

By 1995, I was focused on my new career as a video games artist working for Epic MegaGames (later called Epic Games). I didn't have time for the journal, and had written my last entry almost a year before. This didn't mean I stopped having dreams or that I didn't remember them, just that I no longer felt like writing them down.

At about 8:00 on the morning of May 1, 1995, I was working on my computer when I heard our landlord walking down the steps to go to work. I rushed out to catch him to set up a racquetball ball game later in the week.

Richard had introduced me to Stev (this is the correct spelling) about a year earlier, and that led to me renting the bottom half of his house. While talking with him, I realized that my memory of having been with Richard and his wife, Pat, earlier that morning had to have been a dream. After all, I lived in Maine, he lived in California, and I had just woken up. Even then, my memory was so realistic that it was hard to believe it had been a dream, though I knew it had to be. Here is the dream:

I'm with Pat as she gives birth to twins, and then I am in the room with her and Richard. Richard sits in a chair near the window.

For fun, I told Stev of my dream, then excused myself to write an email to Richard:

Date: 01 May 95 08:21:14 EDT
From: Andrew Paquette
To: "INTERNET:breedon
Subject: Congratulations!
Last night I dreamed you had your twins, so I'm guessing you are officially a "dad" now.
Andy

Here is Richard's response:

"DATE: 5/1/95 6:38 PM
Re RE: Congratulations!
Right you are! Born just hours before the time your message arrived here. How do you do it? I showed your message to two professors I work with. One said you had had to get it off the Internet (although I made absolutely no postings), the other simply said, "very good!"
...They are in the neonatal intensive care, but only because they are a little small. Tell Stev.
Thanks, Richard"

Richard was so surprised by this dream that he mentioned it to a correspondent of his, the well-known magician and psychic debunker The Amazing Randi:
"I received many other e-mail messages about the birth of our twins with the subject "Congratulations!," but this is the only one

I got BEFORE I sent out the birth announcement! Before this I had not communicated with Andy, who was on the east coast, for at least a week or two.

"He certainly knew my wife was pregnant with twins but could only guess when delivery might take place. It is a remarkable coincidence that he guessed correctly as delivery occurred 6 weeks before my wife's due date. As it was, we went in to the hospital for a routine exam, when my wife's water broke. We stayed there, and she delivered between midnight and 2 am. I slept in her room at the hospital. The only person I called in the morning was my mother. Andy's message arrived in my account at 5:24 am California time, even before I called my mother (in Ohio)...

"I should also point out that this was the only such message he sent me—it is not as if he was trying every day to make sure."

Randi was, as anyone who has ever heard of him might expect, skeptical.

"From your long account, I see a glaring problem: how do you know how many guesses this person made that were NOt [sic] correct? You don't know. How many times did he have a statement notarized, and then discard it, unpublicized, because it failed? When I was a kid, I successfully predicted the outcomes of hockey games by having some 30 different letters notarized, each different from the others, and merely produced the correct one after the game."

"Again, think for a moment. If this had NOT been correct, you would not be recounting it, would you? It would not enter into your "evidence" at all. And, if it had been off by a day or two, or a week, that would still be a "hit," wouldn't it? And, if he knew when your wife was expecting, he could have made a simple calculation, and hoped to get lucky.....?"

The way Randi saw psi, or as he would put it, "claimed psi," they are all mechanically explicable hoaxes of one sort or another. Because he sees it that way, he looks at any incident as a fraud. This is like assuming that all money is counterfeit because some money is. Randi's assumption that all psi is fake creates a very narrow funnel for his ideas on the subject. Genuine psi is so far outside the experience of a person like Randi that he cannot be expected to trust anyone on the subject until he experiences it himself. If he's anything like me, he won't accept it until after it has happened to him multiple times.

Although Randi makes several incorrect suggestions in his emails, he does get one item right: "I'm not a prophet, but basing my prediction on past experience — extensive experience — I would venture to guess that this man will (a) not be able to come to an agreement for a test, and/or will fail the preliminary test." What he is referring to here is his semi-famous "Million Dollar Challenge," a prize offered to any person who can prove almost any kind of psi effect to Randi's satisfaction. From my point of view, the contest is not legitimate because it is designed for the publicity gained by withholding the prize. Awarding it would destroy the actual, if not the ostensible, purpose of the contest. As I told Richard, who would like to see me try the challenge, I'm not interested for a number of reasons. Randi's fundamental misunderstandings about psi are one reason, but also because the "Contest," as Randi calls it, is in poor taste. Randi says he'll give a million dollars if anyone can prove any kind of psi. It is a boast.

Visiting dreams are easier to corroborate than any other kind of dream in my journal. It is rare to have one I cannot verify, which makes those odd dreams that can't be verified very strange. They look like all the others, their signal strength is about the same, and yet, their subjects cannot confirm them.

If it were possible to verify only ten or twenty percent of the visits, or even fifty or sixty percent of them, it wouldn't bother me as much. But with something in the neighborhood of seventy-five percent verified, the few left over stick out as real oddities. My gut feeling is that the corroboration rate alone indicates the likelihood that all of these dreams are proper visits, but that for some reason, my friends don't remember the event they describe. It is also quite possible that my descriptions are too difficult to understand for the subject to verify them. Without corroboration, it is very hard to know for sure.

I have had a number of dreams of certain people despite their having only minimal involvement in my waking life. My friends Richard, Ron, Carol, and Dino appear more often than anyone else after Nina, Kitty, and my mother. Another friend, Gokhan, an animator I first met when I was working on *Space Jam* at Cinesite, showed up quite often in my dreams for awhile even though I barely talked to him during the day. In one dream, he addressed me directly and said, "You know, we are very good friends." The statement, in the context of the small amount of daily contact we had, didn't make much sense, but on the other hand, if true on some other level, it would explain the number of dreams he appeared in.

It seemed to me there should be a relationship between the number of hours spent in common social activity with a person and the number of appearances they make in dreams, but there wasn't. I had much more contact with another employee at Cinesite named Juan. We lived in the same building, played racquetball almost every day, and had dinner together on occasion. Despite this, I never had a dream about him. Gokhan, whom I also saw socially, but probably less than ten percent as often as Juan, shows up more prominently in the journal than many other people.

What this indicates to me is that there may be another layer to our relationships that we aren't consciously aware of, perhaps linked to the kinds of communications I experienced with Dr. Ryback and Richard, but more extensive. if so, are these pre-existing relationships? Can a friendship be initiated before physical introductions are made?

Visits, it turns out, are much more than just proving you were "there." They imply many levels of social interaction between people and spirits, and that spirits aren't necessarily of the deceased.

## Chapter Seven

# Ghosts

In 1981, half a year before I moved in with my father and stepmother, they adopted two black Manx kittens. Stella named the male Porgy and the female Bess. One morning they were resting on top of the wheels of Stella's car when she came out to go to work. Just before she started up the car, Porgy jumped off the wheel. Bess didn't, and was killed when the car backed out of the driveway.

A few months later, I moved in with my dad and Stella, and became great friends with Porgy. He followed me out to the fields when I went painting, chased me into town when I would ride there on my bike, and liked to jump on my shoulder from our roof as I walked by. He was with me when I collapsed from acute appendicitis and when I stupidly covered a yellow jacket hive with my foot and then got stung a dozen times when I had to lift it. When we moved to Maine in 1983, Porgy went with us. A little later, I moved out. Porgy stayed with my dad.

Summer, 1984 (Portland, Maine)
Porgy is huge, like a werewolf. He accuses me of something, but I'm not quite sure what. He finds me and slashes ferociously with eight-inch long razor sharp talons. Deep gouges are carved in my arms and torso with every stroke. He growls something, but I can't make it out. It is speech, but what he said is lost in pain as he slashes again. I don't know what to do, there's no way out...

...And then I woke up, my heart pounding blood to my system so powerfully that I can see my blankets vibrate in time with my heartbeat. My arms are unmarked, as is my chest, despite fading phantom pains from the dream. Then I went back to sleep...

...Porgy is still there. This time he is small, scrawny, and clearly diseased. His claws are broken, his fur mangy. He attacks, but this time instead of huge talons, his diseased claws dig narrow festering trenches in my flesh. He speaks in a low rasping voice, accusing me "How could you let them kill me! How could you? How could you let them murder me?"

He accuses me again and again, but I have no idea why. What did I ever do to Porgy? He says I let him be killed, but he's wrong, what is he talking about?

And then I woke again. My heart pounded harder than before, and sleep was out of the question. The dream had to be a fantasy, but it was hard to think of it that way. The idea that I could have somehow harmed Porgy, my friend, kept coming back and I wondered if maybe I had without realizing it. It was silly to contemplate such things, but the dream forced me to think of Porgy.

Two weeks later, my dad called to say that my Grandpa Paquette was in town and they intended to come visit me. "Fine with me," I said, and then, because I thought it was interesting and the sort of thing my dad would think was funny, I told him, "I had a dream about Porgy a couple weeks ago."

"Oh yeah?"

"He slashed me to ribbons in the dream. At first he was a big werewolf, and then he was this scrawny little diseased thing shouting, 'How could you let them kill me!'"

"You don't say."

"Crazy huh?"

"Well you know son, Porgy is dead. We put him to sleep two weeks ago on the vet's advice. He was very sick with feline leukemia. The vet said he could live awhile, but it was very painful and he thought it best to euthanize him."

When I heard that, my reaction was pretty simple: "!" No words, just surprise, and then a creepy tingle that moved up my spine. I was eighteen when this happened. I didn't believe in spirits, ghosts, animal ghosts, or any other oddball supernatural idea. My dad, a former Navy man, didn't offer an opinion. "Your granddad an' I are gonna be there at 15:00. See ya then."

If I had been honest with myself, I would have acknowledged that it was a dream about a real ghost right away, because I knew that's what it was from the moment my dad told me what happened to Porgy. I didn't believe in such things, so I labeled it a coincidence and shoved it as far from my thoughts as I could.

Stella, my father, and the veterinarian, at a minimum, knew of Porgy's euthanization and could have telepathically contributed the information to me while I slept. What they likely would not do was counterfeit Porgy's reaction to it, or his appearance.

If I had picked up on Porgy's death from any of the witnesses to it, this dream would have been in one of the previous chapters. It would either be a dream of how the news was conveyed to me (my dad's phone call), or a dream of the actual scene of his death (a visit). Instead, Porgy came to me directly. This was Porgy's ghost.

I dream of ghosts often. They make up what is probably the third largest category of dreams in my journal. The dream of Porgy is unusual because it concerns someone I know. This is unusual for ghost dreams, most of which involve strangers and do not provide enough information to easily identify them. For this chapter and the next, both of which deal with ghosts, my criteria for selection is whether the dream has any interesting ideas to offer. Some of these are verified, but others are unsolvable because I have been unable to identify the ghost. This does not mean they are incorrect, but that they lack sufficient information to be verified.

Below is the first dream that I was willing to take seriously as a dream of a real ghost. It is the same dream that inspired Lisa to think of me when her cat died.

DB1/25, 9/26/89

A young woman stands on a riverbank. She tells me that her father died of drowning here fifteen years ago. I enter the water and am surprised to discover her father is still here. He seems alive and well, but is unaware that fifteen years have passed since first entering the water. He is confused to find himself 'breathing' the water and so is constantly alternating between choking and not choking. He periodically sinks to the bottom and then rises up to the top again. He accomplishes this with feeble paddling motions.

I go to the surface and point out his daughter to him. He doesn't understand why she can't see him even though he is right here in plain view. After a few unsuccessful attempts to attract her notice, he starts his "drowning" sequence again. An older couple swims by, momentarily distracting the drowning man from his plight. He swims after them in order to make contact but he is too slow because of his periodic slow "falls" to the bottom.

He doesn't understand why he is able to breathe underwater and why people don't notice him. He also seemed to forget everything every time he relives his drowning. This might be why he thinks it is happening now as opposed to fifteen years in the past.

This ghost had been trapped for fifteen years, re-enacting his death, over and over again. It may have been a kind of punishment, but it didn't look that way. He simply couldn't drag his attention from the drowning experience long enough to realize that he died long ago. He came close to escaping from the loop several times, but then he would falter and succumb yet again.

This ghost's problem is that something prevents him from making accurate observations about his environment. He is seeing more of what he expects than what is actually there, and reacts more to his own thoughts than anything else. Because of this, when he shed his body so many years in the past, it becomes just another confusing fact to be set aside while he deals with his more immediate problem, survival. This is exactly like those dreams where I visit someone and try to interact as if I am physically present. This man has just emerged from his body into the equivalent of a permanent dreaming state and doesn't realize it.

When I "died" in the Amsterdam dream, I didn't expect to survive the experience, but when I did, I didn't hang around my body. I thought of Kitty, went to her, and knew that I had died. I didn't know what I was supposed to do, but didn't ignore my new environment or condition either. The ghost in this dream was so obsessed with his fear of death that the experience cannot end until he is somehow snapped out of it.

I tried everything I could think of to help, but nothing worked and I eventually gave up. How many other ghosts like this are there? What does it take to ignore something like this *for fifteen years*? In previous dreams, it is always when my own interests or ideas are superimposed on my surroundings that this kind of confusion results. It is the desire for self-centered activity that drowns out the reality around me. For this man, his fear created that self-centered reality and trapped him within it. As soon as I saw him, I wanted to help, and did so to the best of my ability. Unfortunately, I couldn't get past step one; getting him to accept that he had died. If I had succeeded, what would have been next?

The next "ghost" dream to catch my attention turned out to be a false alarm. In it, one of Kitty's friends from work, Joe Fazecas, had just died and was at the hospital. When I told Kitty about the dream, she was so worried that she called the office and found out that Joe *was* in the hospital, but he hadn't died. He had had a heart attack followed by triple-bypass surgery.

It was tricky for me to identify ghost dreams at first, because they came in so many forms. With Joe, I think there may have been moments when he was clinically dead, or so close to it that there was no meaningful difference. I picked up on that and thought he was really dead. Maybe there is a way for one spirit (my dream self) to identify whether another spirit is still tethered to a living body, and his tether was so weak that I assumed incorrectly that he was dead. In dreams, not just this example with Joe, I have found that I can be every bit as confused as the drowning man when I am looking at another spirit.

In one dream I saw the body of a woman *and her spirit also* lying in the middle of the street after a hit and run accident. She said something to me about the accident, but I reassured her, "No, no, you look fine." I could see her dead body, but her spirit radiated health. Her body was irrelevant.

"Vibrant health" is a fairly consistent feature of ghost dreams. When my grandfather died of complications related to an ulcer in 1998, I started dreaming of him regularly. I had not dreamed of him when he was alive, and had only seen him in person a few times in life, so I did not know him well. He was pleasant, but that's all I could say of him. After he died, he became a frequent visitor in my dreams, and he always looked terrific.

I think the reason most ghosts look pretty good after they are released from their physical bodies is that they are able to project whatever appearance they want, and most of them tend to either remember themselves as healthy, or that's what they want to look like. Either way, when I've seen ghosts of people I know who've passed on, they tend to look better than they ever did in life. There are some exceptions, like Porgy, who used the plastic responsiveness of his spirit form to express his anger towards me when he came to me immediately after his death. Other ghosts have done the same thing.

In one dream, a ghost demanded that I look at him as he decapitated himself, rolled his head into a fireplace, and then waited while it rolled back to where it belonged on his shoulders. Another spirit did the same thing, then wanted to try it on me, to demonstrate the plastic nature of our spirit bodies. This is what they did to amuse themselves as ghosts. It may be more interesting than repeatedly drowning for fifteen years, and it does shed some light on how a dreamer can manipulate his dreams with his thoughts, but it is not a productive way to spend one's time.

I don't enjoy this type of dream and usually ignore the "prankster" type of ghost when I encounter them. What many of these ghosts have in common, at least those that know they have died, is a desire to interact physically with other people. They cannot easily do it, but they try anyway. Sometimes, if they try hard enough, they can produce poltergeist effects.

In one dream where I saw this happen, in classic haunted house style, an extraordinarily angry (and frightening) woman named Susan caused so many poltergeist effects in her former home, such as plucking and igniting hairs from the arm of a woman who lived there, that the owners put the house up for sale. Two other ghosts in the same house were peaceable. Without Susan, the owners of that house would never have noticed it was haunted. The difference is that the Susan ghost was trying to be noticed, but the others weren't.

My ghost dreams fit into a small number of distinctive categories. Each of the different categories represents a different level of awareness on the part of the ghost subject of the dream. The lowest level are my dreams of death. In these, I see someone, or sometimes several people, at the moment of death. Usually there is a very short preamble to establish a context, but in most, it's like an editor snipped out the death scene from a person's life, cropping it as tightly as possible from the exact moment the death is initiated and the exact moment when life is terminated.

Death dreams contain only the death scene. They do not reveal any ghosts. In them, I have watched a young convict stabbed to death with a makeshift knife in a prison cell, a mother and daughter tied to chairs and buried alive, car accidents, drowning, shootings (war and crime), and many other scenarios. Ordinarily, I am not too affected by the deaths if they are accidents, natural, or the result of war, but the crimes are horrifying. In those, I try to interfere, but as a spirit myself, it is not possible.

In one dream, I saw an American aid worker in Kashmir. There was some political strife there, and militant factions on both sides. I saw her riding a bicycle, then she noticed she had a bloody sock and screamed as she dismounted her bike. She'd been shot in the foot. As she examined the wound, she was shot again in the neck. She jerked involuntarily and then tried to crawl away from the direction of the shot (and mistakenly crawled towards it) but died in less than a minute.

Another death dream, but a massive scale death dream, was of a World War II naval battle where sailors from both sides were plunged into a dark ocean and had to fight the water, their wounds, their gear, and enemy soldiers. In the next scene I saw coffins laid out in a service for American soldiers recovered from the battle. The family of one soldier in particular caught my attention, a man who drowned while trying to fend off another soldier.

The reason I put death dreams in the same category as ghost dreams, even though no ghosts are present, is that in the *next* class of dreams I do see ghosts and the thing they most want to show me is how they died. My conclusion is that death dreams are a truncated form of a dream where a ghost shows his or her death scene. Most likely, I simply fail to remember the connection to the ghost from the dream, so I count death dreams as a reportage error connected to this next class of dreams, the "how

I died" dreams.

With these, I have a very hard time recognizing a ghost as a ghost. Instead, I find myself talking with someone who describes how someone died. While describing it, I can see the entire event as if I am there. After I wake, I just about kick myself as I realize that the person who showed me the death was the person who had died. Therefore, it was a ghost.

It isn't as if there aren't any clues. In one, my daughter and I are dreaming together and I show her the skeletonized remains of a woman in a partly submerged car. At the same time, we see the ghost of the woman herself. She tells us a tragic story of a husband and wife who die in an accident when their car runs off the road. I thought the story was interesting, but failed to connect it to the ghost or the skeleton. When I woke I figured it out right away, but in the dream, I was too busy paying attention to the story to bother thinking about it in any detail.

I've had many dreams like this. A list of them would be long and boring, but suffice it to say that the variety of ways these people died is large, and within that variety there is one near constant factor: almost all of them died unexpectedly. I have dreamed of people who die peacefully, but they don't ordinarily get categorized with these low-level ghost dreams. What makes them "low-level" is that the ghosts are earthbound. They hang around either their bodies or places that were meaningful to them in life. All by itself, this is a bad idea because it cannot help but frustrate the ghost, if it is aware that it is a ghost.

My grandfather and grandmother were practicing Catholics. They had some expectation of an afterlife, and maybe this is why my dreams of my grandfather are so different from these maudlin ghosts who cannot let go of their previous existence. After he died, my grandfather fairly sparkled with energy in my dreams. His clear blue eyes, which always seemed to project some measure of childish delight even when he was alive, now gleamed with health and pleasure.

Over the next few years, he told me that my grandmother was quite sick (we found out a little later that she had Alzheimer's disease) and that he was waiting for her to die. After that, I wouldn't see him anymore. Until then, he would wait. It was difficult to communicate with my grandmother, he said, because she was in such a confused state of mind. He tried, but it didn't always work out. Then one night, I saw her in a dream:

DB14/58 July 3, 2003
My grandmother is here. She is literally shining, like sunlight through diamonds. She is very beautiful, radiant. Has she died?

I was peripherally aware that my aunts and uncles were looking out for my grandmother, but this dream is what told me she had died. Later that day I received confirmation from my Uncle Tom. She was so beautiful in this dream that it is hard to describe. Maybe this is what one gets from raising eleven children and devoting your life to good works. Shortly afterwards, I dreamed of my grandfather and grandmother, together again. He said goodbye to me and left with her, both happy.

It was a completely different story for Kitty's grandparents, who died the same week as my grandmother. Unlike my grandfather, who stuck around out of love for my grandmother, Kitty's grandfather, C.C. Wang, had a less happy reason to stick around. Just before his death, he discovered that he had been robbed by his youngest daughter, her husband, and their son, his grandson. The majority of his cash had been transferred out of his accounts, and his world famous art collection was almost entirely missing.

C.C. tried to have his daughter and her husband arrested, but had a severe stroke before the DA's office sent anyone to talk to him. When Joel Vengrin, an assistant DA, did show up at the hospital, C.C. was too sedated to talk. He had managed to cut his daughter out of his will and to file formal statements with his lawyers, but this would not be enough. C.C. and his wife died shortly after, within days of each other, making a prosecution of his daughter impossible.

Within a week of his death, C.C. showed up in one of my dreams. He was with the ghost of a friend who died before him as he watched his (living) great-grandson play, a boy he had always taken an interest in and who has always had a noticeably pleasant disposition. In the dream, he was confused, worn out, and didn't seem to know what to do. Over the next few years, I dreamed of him often. With each dream, he became more aware of his condition. At the same time, he tried to figure out a way to right the situation created by his youngest daughter.

Before long, just like my grandfather, Kitty's grandfather looked like a robust and handsome man in his early forties, full of health and determination to fix things for his remaining family. Later, his enthusiasm waned. Like other ghosts who find that it is not easy to deal with the physical world, he gave up. After that, he didn't appear in my dreams anymore. At this time (2009), the statute of limitations has run out on all crimes committed against C.C. and issues related to his estate are still unresolved. His world-famous art collection remains missing.

Anyone who has seen the clairvoyant John Edward on television cannot help but get the impression that the space around us is constantly astir with multitudes of spirits. As if I needed any proof, I had the following experience:

In 1989, when we still lived in Vermont, I dreamed there was a ghost in the house with us, and had been since before we moved in. Kitty woke me up, asking if I wanted to go for a walk. I didn't, and went back to sleep, still dreaming of the house ghost, a middle-aged, balding man. When I got up later, Kitty was gone. After just getting out of the shower a little later, our doorbell rang. Outside, I was confronted by several policemen who wanted to know who I was, and then they searched the house for an intruder.

It turned out that in the middle of the night, Kitty had woken to find a middle-aged man staring at us from the foot of our bed. He stayed where he was for a long time, as Kitty, terrified, wondered what to do. At one point, he seemed to shift to a different part of the room. She woke me up then, and tried to get me to leave the house with her. When I didn't budge, she went to our window, on the second floor of the house, and jumped out. She ran to the neighbors and called the police.

The police couldn't find any footprints around the house, despite mud that completely surrounded it, nor any other sign of an intruder. Kitty's description of him was interesting though, because it matched the ghost in my dream. Had she seen a ghost? Who was he, and what did he want?

As long as these ghosts remain anonymous I cannot be of any help, but help is clearly something they all either need or want. Looked at this way, the dreams become easier to understand. Porgy was angry with me because he thought I should have prevented his death. The drowning man needed to know he was dead and that he should move on. Others showed me the location of their bodies, and a woman who died at the hands of a club-wielding murderer may have wanted, like Porgy, some kind of action taken against her killer.

With Porgy alone, even if he is "just" a cat, survival of consciousness after bodily death is certainly indicated. Others make it clear that this is what we can expect, whether we believe it or not. More important is the nature of this survival.

Most of the ghosts described in this chapter may as well be inmates of an enormous hospital, wandering the halls, trying to find a doctor. Unfortunately for most of them, the intensity of their focus on their former lives completely blinds them to their actual surroundings. This doesn't mean that there aren't any doctors, just that the patients keep walking away from them or refuse to take their medicine. What they need to do, as my grandfather seems to have done, is "wake up" to their condition. Until they have done this, they remain in what must seem to be a very strange and callous place indeed.

## Chapter Eight

# Disconnected

Ghosts sometimes have specific reasons to contact certain people after they've died. Because of the sudden disconnection caused by their death, they desire to tie off loose ends, as Kitty's grandfather did, before moving on.

When my family moved out of the San Jose area in 1977, I lost track of my best friend, Dayton Ewing. A ghost would help us get back in touch. Twenty-two years after I'd last spoken to Dayton, his name appeared in my journal for the first time. Within two weeks, it happened again. Four months later, I had a dream about his parents. At first, I thought Dayton had died. This led me to make a fruitless search for him on the Internet. By 2001, a little over a year after this unusual trio of dreams, I took another look. This time I was more objective and noticed a few key details: 1) Dayton was present in only one of the three dreams, 2) his mother was present in two of them, 3) the only person who spoke directly to me was his mother. What this meant to me was that the dreams were of his mother's death, not his.

To confirm it, I did an Internet search on her name, Sarah Ewing, and the word "obituary." I immediately found it, dated January 20, 2000, or right in the middle of the three dreams from the previous year. Using information contained in the obituary, I managed to contact Dayton again. I had been confused because Sarah spoke of Dayton and death, her own, but I focused on Dayton instead of her, and delayed resolving Sarah's request by over a year.

Some ghosts aren't expert at sending messages, and many people aren't practiced at receiving them. I don't know exactly where I would fit on that scale, but have the impression that there are others who are much better receivers than I am. This is because there are clairvoyants who can hear or see ghosts while they are awake, but when I get these messages in a dream, it can take some effort for me to figure them out, as with Sarah Ewing in the example just given. A clairvoyant who can receive a message while conscious has already brought the message into our waking world. Receiving the very same message in sleep adds at least one extra barrier to understanding because the message must pass through from the dream and into waking memory.

Several years after Kitty's father died, he appeared in a dream with a message for Kitty. Instead of listening, I kept talking with him about other things. He tried to get a word in edgewise, but I didn't give him a chance and he finally left. He may have been able to express his message if I had understood the context of our meeting better, but I didn't. In dreams, I forget there is a time limit. When I wake, they're over.

Two years later, I dreamed of Kitty's father again, this time along with Kitty's mother. In it, I ask them why they are there, and they answer, "You called us." This reminded me to go get Kitty, and I do. When I told Kitty about the dream, she told me that on the same night she dreamed of her father for the first time, and reconciled with him.

Just like Sarah Ewing, it took some time for this message to finally get through. As a result, Kitty's father may now feel released from his earthly burdens and is able to continue on. her grandfather stuck around for several years, as did mine, but both of our grandmothers seemed to have vanished instantly, unencumbered by whatever held their partners to the earth. Perhaps they had already tied up their loose ends. Ghosts are spirits who have some kind of business to transact, whether a final message of love, fixing a problem, or simply acknowledging that they have died.

DB0/20, 7/20/95; Portland, ME

Sumi appears to me, saying she has a message for Richard. It's pretty simple, she just wants him to know that she loves him and that she is sorry.

The content of this dream is so ordinary that I wouldn't bother mentioning it except for an interesting synchronicity connected to the day I had it on. After waking, I went to my computer in the other room to check CompuServe for messages and news. Right there was a big story about George Carragonne, someone I knew from my days in New York. He had just committed suicide by leaping from the 45th floor atrium balcony at the Marriott Marquis hotel in New York City.

George and Sumi are the only two people I have known personally who committed suicide, and they did it in the same way. To dream of one within hours of the other one committing suicide is, at the least, synchronistic. The way I think it worked is that first I dreamed of George's suicide, this in turn reminded me of Sumi, and thinking of her gave her an opportunity to pop in with a message for Richard.     The following dream should help make these connections clearer:

DB3/47, 6/8/90; Weehawken, NJ

I attempt to communicate with some school kids in a parking lot. Then I feel a pull from Richard, as if he is asking me to visit him. When I arrive, it is like a large classroom full of people and they have somehow called my spirit to them while I am sleeping just by thinking of me. I am very aware that my body is sleeping and that this is my "other" body (astral body,) I have no doubts about this during the dream.

At first I am unnoticed, but then a woman seems to know I am there and before long they are all talking about me as if I am really there, but invisible. Two people stand out most strongly; Richard, and a girl.

I go into another room and sit down. One man in particular is focusing hard on me, but I stop at an older woman instead because I have the impression I can do more for her than the man. I see that she has an infection in her urinary tract that needs to be looked at. There is something else weighing heavily on her mind, possibly a death or serious illness in her family. I think it is her husband.

I put my hands on her head to accomplish a few things; to let her know I am here, to heal her, and to comfort her. She is aware of me on a telepathic level, but not consciously. She is very dense this way, very "closed." I don't have the energy to go to the man, so I don't, even though I would like to because he wants me to come to him.

Then I look at the end of the room and to the right where I sense Richard's presence, but I don't know where he is. He wants to know what would be some good stock tips as he looks over his investments. I get the idea that "Helman's" and "Chevron" will be good, Chevron less so than Helman's.

He looks at a financial listing in the paper, but I don't see either of the two recommended names printed on it. He definitely has money on his mind, and I try to help him. When the name "Helman's" comes up, I think of the mayonnaise brand and Lillian Hellman, the writer. The Lillian Hellman impression is stronger than the food product, so that is probably what is meant. Later, I am alone with Richard in a room and I ask him if one of the female class members has a dying or recently deceased husband. As soon as I ask him, the image of the woman I put my hands on comes to me. She is lying down in bed and reminds me a bit of Kitty's grandmother. She worries about her husband.

After waking, I called Richard and got confirmation from him that he was going over his investments that night, though he was looking at bonds, not stocks. He agreed that Chevron would be a perfectly good investment because it was a blue chip stock, but that it was so stable that the return wouldn't be that great. What neither of us knew then was that two months later, Saddam Hussein would invade Kuwait, causing a huge dive in stock prices for almost every company except for oil companies.

Even though I didn't write it down, there was something about the dream that made me think of Lisa Moore. Because of this, I gave her a call to read the dream and see if it made any sense to her. She said that on about the night of the dream, she decided to try and get me to diagnose a health problem that was upsetting her mother. She did this by making a conscious effort to attract my attention by thinking of me. During the call, she also informed me that her father was in fact deceased, a recent suicide. In a later call, she confirmed that her mother did have a urinary tract infection, in addition to some back pain that was alleviated after the night of the dream. She says that her mom loves Hellman's books and had one by her bedside the night of the dream.

In this dream, it worked like this: Richard was thinking of his investments while in a relaxed frame of mind, and I was inclined to visit him. Before I could do so, Lisa's insistent, and more urgent, request got in the way and I went to her instead. I dealt with her mother, but as I did so, the ghost of her father tried to get my attention, and succeeded, but not strongly enough to prevent my original desire to see Richard from taking over, and I then went to see Richard. Lisa was still thinking about me, and her mother was still thinking of her husband, so after finishing with Richard, I go back for another look at them before waking up in bed.

What this complicated series of travels indicates to me is that, even if we don't remember why we go to see a certain person in a dream, there is a reason, and it will make sense if you remember enough of the dream. This is a repeatable pattern, just as archaeologists know that paper is typically found in rectangular sheets. This allows them to identify paper scraps as fragments, instead of imagining that every article of paper they find is complete. If anything, my dreams have shown me that although I do sometimes remember whole sheets, more often they are scraps. If I am somewhat aware of the kind of shape they naturally fit into, it is easier to make sense of them. It is this theory that allows me to extrapolate from the dream of Sumi a connection to George Carragonne's suicide, as well as the expectation that there is a reason why I go to see the people I do, or see the people who come to me, even if that reason isn't immediately evident.

## DB3/67, 6/26/90

I am at a baked goods shop in India. Standing beside me is a forty or forty-five year old woman who comes from a large family. She is thin and has long black hair. She is not beautiful, not even plain, and she is haggard. Her aura is average to slightly below average.

She asks to look at a box of food because she is in love with the man behind the counter. She hints to him that she loves the man, but is very coy about it. I'm not interested in watching this scene, and leave.

When I come back, the woman's family is before me, the woman herself, and a woman who is psychic. No one can see me and I have the impression that I am somehow aiding the psychic. All of the people assembled are homely. One of them, a tall and skinny man sticks out to me. He has a big black moustache.

The psychic says, "I see a nose, there is something about his nose. It isn't the way it looks, but something else. It smells something, tells him something he suspects, it smells out his feelings which are hidden to him. He is in love with a woman, with your mother, but he has never told her this." The man she refers to is the same man I saw earlier in the bakeshop.

The psychic goes on to say, "She is in love with him. They would like to be together, but, I do not see her [in the future.] I only see him. She is not there. I am sorry, why is this?" Several persons in the gathering cried when asked this question as if the subject, their mother, was dead without paying any attention to the fact that she is sitting right there. But, like when I was at the bake shop, no one could see her. Apparently she is an earthbound spirit, at least for the time being.

One of her children, her eldest son I think, says something about how the family had chipped in to buy a used car for their mother. I had the impression this was what killed her somehow, and then I wake up here.

As far as the psychic in the scene is concerned, I am as much a "ghost" as the Indian woman who died, but that is the wrong term because I am still connected to my living body. More appropriately, I could be described simply as a "spirit," or the "astral body" of someone living. Both words have problems because they do not distinguish between a spirit that is connected to a living body and spirits that are associated with a dead one.

In English there is no single term to properly distinguish between a ghost and the spirit of a living person. This distinction is important because, just as "ice" and "water" are made of the same thing, they aren't the same. If both were called "water," and one were to try to describe ice *and* water, how could it be done?

The failure to acknowledge the difference between spirits of the living and the dead has undoubtedly caused meaningful misunderstandings, where, for lack of any other terms, all spirits are labeled "ghosts." While writing this book, I have already been tripped up several times because of the inadequacy of available terms, so I have invented a few new ones to solve the problem. Starting with the fact that many terms in Psychology are German, and that "poltergeist," a word for a certain kind of ghost, is a well-known German word that has been borrowed into English, I used German roots for the new words, designed to distinguish between spirits more exactly.

The new words are:

"Lebengeist" (lay-ben-guyst), or a "life ghost." This is a ghost or spirit with a living body.

"Todgeist" (toat-guyst), or "death ghost." This is a ghost or spirit that does not have a living body, but remains attached to at least some portion of its former life. Most "ghosts," including poltergeists, are also todgeists.

A "freigeist," is a spirit without a living body that is not attached to earthly things.

Using these definitions, in the dream of the Indian woman, I am a lebengeist and she is a todgeist. In the dreams of my grandfather, he is a todgeist until he leaves with my grandmother, at which point they are both freigeists. The Susan from the previous chapter is a poltergeist, or a "noisy ghost." Significantly, a poltergeist can be a lebengeist or a todgeist. For instance, if I had actually succeeded in making a noise in Japan as I thought I did when I saw Richard and his keyboard, then I would have been a poltergeist at the same time as being a lebengeist.

I am not always able to help when asked, and this can be quite sad. Sometimes, it stops at the attempt to communicate a simple message to me, as happened with the ghost of a woman who died in the 1970's. The dress her nearly mummified body was buried in was so interesting to look at, that all I could think about was drawing all the various patterns it contained. While I was occupied with those thoughts, the woman tried to get me to help her in some way, but I never fully received the message.

On a different occasion, the night of March 23, 2006, the todgeist of a young man in his late teens contacted me. It was a very tragic scene that he showed me. He had been abducted, sodomized, and killed. He showed me the entire appalling crime, then carefully gave me the full address of the suburban ranch house the crime took place within. He pointed out the small

111

amount of blood on the bedding in one room, a room I can still see in my mind perfectly clearly. He showed me the man who did it, and gave me his full name, carefully spelling it out for me. He was angry at the disgusting pervert who had done this to him, and wanted my help. He knew he was a ghost and could do nothing to aid in the capture of the man, who remained free and unsuspected of the crime. He gave me all the information that would be needed to have him arrested. And then I forgot.

By the time I wrote my journal entry, all I could remember were the scenes of what had happened. The specific words and numbers connected to it, the man's name and address, and the name of the victim, I could not remember. Next to the premonition of Sumi, this dream probably weighs more heavily on me than any other. I know he gave me the information that was needed, but because I was sleepy that morning and didn't feel like writing it down right away, the information I remembered when I first woke had been forgotten by an hour later when I finally wrote it down. This is not uncommon for me, especially in the later journals, but I wish it hadn't happened here.

The problem is related to this "information-under-the-transom" feeling, where everything in the dream seems normal, and therefore unremarkable. In this dream, even though the murder victim was urgent in his plea and commanded my attention completely, what he told me was so clear that when I woke it never occurred to me that I might forget. Feeling sleepy, I lolled in bed for some time before getting up and writing the entry into the journal, by which time my memory had faded and I only remembered the broad strokes. Luckily, it isn't always this way.

DB14/83, 8/12/03, Phoenix, AZ
At an art supply store. I am told that one of the employees of this place may be about to die. I think it is James from Arizona Art Supply. Someone in his family was very sick or had died, so he

started taking drugs, drinking, and had stopped taking care of himself. He will die because of this, or may have already.

I am very worried about him here. There is a pervasive feeling that he doesn't have to die, that it is unnecessary. He does not have to die at this time, but he will if he doesn't shape up.

Because of Sumi, I decided to pass this warning on to James, although I was very uncomfortable doing it. I knew who he was from maybe half a dozen trips to the store where he worked, but did not know him well enough to easily have a conversation like the one suggested by this dream. While writing this chapter, I ran across an old clip of Barbara Walters from her TV show *The View*, where she comments on the psychic James van Praagh. The previous week he had stopped her in a hall to give her some health-related advice that he'd picked up psychically. She was naturally worried, and went to her doctor, who said she was fine. Her response to her viewers was this, "I think it is a dangerous thing to do, looking at someone and saying 'oh there's an aura, you have an elevated white blood count' and then worrying someone about something that might not even be correct." I happen to agree with her. This is why I was uncomfortable with this dream.

Nevertheless, I was sufficiently concerned that I drove out to the shop, thirty miles away. During the entire drive, as I watched cars and saguaro cactus approach and then vanish behind me, I wondered how I was going to introduce this warning into a conversation with James. When I got there, the conversation went something like this:

"You know James, it's a bit odd to say this, but I had a dream with you in it last night."

"Really? Good I hope."

"Actually, no. The reason I'm here today is because that dream got me worried. Can you tell me if someone close to you, a family member, has recently died?"

He looked startled then, maybe even a bit ashen. He clearly did not expect that question.

"It was my sister-in-law, she was killed a couple weeks ago in a high speed police chase. A cop slammed into her car while she waited at a traffic light."

"Okay. I hope you don't mind my asking this next question, but, have you been depressed about this?"

"Yes, a lot. I was always over at my brother's, doing things with them. She was a great person. I really miss her."

"Well James, I think I dreamed of your sister-in-law, and what she told me is that you've been drinking a lot and you haven't been treating yourself very well lately because of this..."

"It's true."

"She wants you to know it is very important that you stop that kind of activity right now. It is very important that you do this, do you understand?"

"Yes."

"I'm not kidding here. You need to get on with your life and let go of this tragedy."

"I know. I dreamed of her a few times, and she said the same things."

I didn't mention the drugs because I didn't want to freak him out by talking about something illegal, nor did I mention that he would die if he didn't stop his self-destructive behavior, because I didn't want to give him any not-so-bright ideas. It was not an easy conversation. About a week later, I came by to pick up some art supplies. James wasn't in, so I asked after him. He had quit earlier in the week. I have no idea what happened after that. I never knew his last name, though I did know his sister-in-law's name, because it was in the paper. Unfortunately, I never wrote it down and now I've forgotten it. I'd like to check to see if he is okay, but haven't been able to.

What is obvious from James' statements is that his sister-in-law was using me to pass on a message in exactly the same way I passed a message back to myself through Kate Dix. That is even though she gave the message to James directly, James' sister-in-law *also* sent the information to James through another channel, just as my lebengeist did by asking Kate to get it to me as well. With James, reinforcing the message like this is useful, as a way to verify that his dreams aren't just his imagination. The mere fact that a todgeist would know this and take steps to counteract it demonstrates a kind of ingenuity that ghosts aren't traditionally given credit for having.

DB22/23, 9/22/08

A woman the same age as me, but young in appearance, attracts my attention by speaking to me directly. The exact words are gone, but the content of what she says is this, "Andrew, I wanted to say goodbye. It has been many years, decades, since we last saw each other. Since then I got married to A_____ (Avner? - a Jewish man) and we had children." As she says this, I see her husband sitting at a desk working at a computer. Nearby are two sons. One is 8-10 years old, the other is a lanky teenager, maybe 15-16 years old. The woman continues to tell me of the major events of her life, and again states, "I wanted to say goodbye." This doesn't completely make sense to me, so I ask, "Don't you mean 'Hello?'" She replies, "I wanted to say goodbye." and then I wake up.

My impression is that I knew her in school as a girl, but I don't know who she was. Even though I didn't understand it at first, the message she had for me, to sum up her life and then say goodbye, is not uncommon for todgeists who are about to be freigeists. After "death" dreams, these "goodbye" dreams may be the most numerous among dreams where ghosts appear. To me, this predictability adds at least a little credibility to dreams of ghosts, because it seems to me that if they were pure imagination, the results would be more varied. Instead, they are quite consistent. Todgeists like to show how they died, announce that they have died, pass messages to the living through our lebengeists, explore their newly malleable environment, and say goodbye.

DB2/46, 3/13/90, Savannah, GA (en route to Miami)
... Later I am flying over the city again and am drawn to a certain spot where I make a landing. My uncle Tom is there. I tell him that I have spoken with Rita, his recently deceased sister. I feel that she is "with" me somehow and I do remember talking with her. She asked if she could live with me. After I say yes, she asks me to tell Tom that she won't appear to him in his dreams anymore.

The next day, I was in Miami at Tom's studio. After I told him the dream, he told me that he had dreamed of Rita the same night. In it, she said goodbye. After a few years of wandering alone, somehow she'd come to grips with her new state and was willing to let go. I think with most todgeists, or even all of them, this should be expected even if it takes more time for some than others.

On a YouTube video, clairvoyant John Edward is asked by an interviewer, "What do you think happens to a person's spirit when they die?" This is not the right question. It should be, "What happens to you when your body dies?" To look at the phenomena of one's life from a body-centric point of view intro-duces error whenever matters of the spirit are evaluated. Your spirit does not die, but your body will, and it will decompose, but you remain. What you do from there is up to you.

## Chapter Nine

# To forget

It is unthinkable that certain things could ever be forgotten, and yet they are. "Forgetting" happens all the time. There are many types of amnesia, from the familiar blow-to-the-head variety to amnesia induced by drugs for traumatic surgery. If one takes a purely mechanical view of it, memory is something that can literally be lost or destroyed, because it is possible to damage or destroy parts of the brain that are associated with memory.

If you don't look at memory as being purely physical, other possibilities present themselves. It may be that certain parts of the brain are used to process memories, so if they are damaged, then it would appear as if the memory itself were lost. Ghosts appear to retain their memories, particularly of what could be considered the most traumatic experience of their former life: their death. Once the body is completely destroyed, brain included, a ghost's memory becomes difficult to explain as a faculty of the brain, or any other part of the body. If a ghost has a memory at all, and it does seem to be the case, then memory cannot reside exclusively within the brain. "Forgetting" is not a matter of destroying something forever, it is more like losing access to something that still exists.

Normally, when you want to know something, the answer comes to you almost immediately. If it is "difficult to remember," you might have to cast your attention inwards for some seconds or minutes, calming your mind, relaxing, and concentrating on the subject of your inquiry until it comes to you. If it doesn't, you may say you've forgotten, but that you might remember by the next day, and probably will. The difference between forgetting and remembering is the amount of time it takes to recall the desired information. If it is short, you "remember," if it is very long, you've "forgotten." If it comes back to you, you've remembered it, even if you'd forgotten it before.

DB1/128, 1/16/90

I am brought to the estate of the owner of a department store. He sits on a large lawn with a manservant, his younger son James, and his elder son, me. James is a teenager, and I am nearly twenty. I experience a tremendous longing when I see my father again, because I know it has been many years since I last saw him, and that I had totally forgotten him during that time. Seeing him again reminds me of those years, and the many fond memories I have of being his son.

The year is about 1928 and we live in a large manor on a lake near Chicago. I can see a green Duisenberg auto parked in the driveway, and a tennis court to the side. My 'father' has a dark olive-skinned complexion and thick eyebrows, as does his man, making me think we are Jewish or Arab. They are both in their sixties at the time and in good humor. I do not have any awareness of having a mother. James is spoiled to the point of being unpleasant. I am studious and responsible.

After our lunch, I returned to the house. The walls of my room are lined with bookcases that extend all the way to the twenty-foot high ceiling. Stacks of books litter the floor. I experienced vividly the next several weeks as the son of the owner of this department store. I work for him in a clerical capacity and spend most of my off hours in academic pursuits. Employees from the store recognize me and treat me well. We have an art collection housed in its own small building adjacent to our house.

I experience every activity you might expect over a couple week period, even repetitive things, like combing my hair, getting dressed, and eating meals. At first it feels like I am exploring the new environment, but pretty quickly I distinctly feel like I belong there and am involved with the family business.

About one month after I had this dream, I spoke with my father on the phone. We were talking about something else when I mentioned that I didn't remember much from before I was eight years old. His reply was totally unexpected. He said, "I can remember from before I could talk, and even before that."

"Pardon me?"

"I remember being someone else before I was me. A past life. I've always remembered this, even when I was a baby and couldn't talk about it."

At the time of this conversation, my father hadn't heard of this dream, my other recent dreams, or even my interest in the subject. I had only lived with him for about two years when I was younger, and hadn't started tracking my dreams until much later. We didn't talk much, and when we did, I was guarded. On his end, he was a former Navy man (newly re-enlisted) whose entire life was based on nuts-and-bolts practicality. He had never struck me as the kind of person to have an interest in anything paranormal, yet here he was talking about a past life.

He remarked that he hadn't ever had 'dreams' about another life, but that ever since before he could talk, he had strong imaged memories of one. One of those memories was particularly strong:

His name was 'James'; he lived in a large Art Deco mansion with a huge library beside a lake near Chicago. The family owned a Duisenberg (not sure of color), an art collection, and a boat. He had an older brother that was aloof. He was disconsolate and had been ever since his mother's premature death. He wasted most of his time playing tennis. The time period was evocative of the twenties and thirties of the twentieth century.

We had never discussed the subject of reincarnation, but his "past life memories" match up with my own "memories" from a recent dream. The time period and location is the same, description of the house is consistent, as is the car. He remembered a few things that weren't in my dream, all of which are consistent with the dream. If my dream and his memories are accurate, then he was my younger brother in the lives we remembered.

The principal objection to the idea of past lives from a skeptic's point of view is that there is no physical way to transfer memories or personality from a corpse to the body of a living child. As discussed earlier, if memory is not connected to the body, then this argument is overcome.

We understand spirits primarily in the context of a spirit that is either attached to, or recently detached from, a body. When a spirit becomes attached to a body, it is called an "incarnation." How is incarnation different from reincarnation? It is the same thing, done a second time. Is there any reason why incarnating two or more times should be impossible, when incarnating once is not? It is not the same as eating an apple and then eating it again. It is easy to see that a body rots and is destroyed completely after death, so this will never be restored, but the spirit is independent. What would prevent it from incarnating in another body?

Consider the status of a todgeist or freigeist prior to being associated with a body. It is identical to the state it will be in after that body dies. What of the material it is incarnated into? There will always be more babies, and each baby will require a spirit to animate it. Some Christian denominations believe that reincarnation is a "false teaching." This is based on their interpretation of ancient documents, but these documents are unclear and inconsistent on the subject. These same denominations accept that we have a soul that exists independently of our body, that it is brought into our bodies shortly after conception and leaves upon death. Mechanically, this is all that is required for reincarnation to occur. From their point of view then, it isn't that reincarnation is mechanically impossible; their doctrine accepts all of the necessary elements for reincarnation to take place. For them, the issue is a matter of permission. We are not permitted to have more than one life. If this dream of mine and my father's past life memories are anything to go by, this doctrine is wrong.

I had several others dreams related to this life in Chicago, all of which served to flesh out my personality and the memories a bit, but not so much that it is worth presenting them here in any detail. Suffice it to say that I was conscious of my social status and insufferable because of it. I dabbled in watercolor painting, but was not very good. Most interesting is that some habits from the previous personality have carried over into this life. When I was a child, I very much wanted to run a shop of almost any kind, and had a precocious success as a young merchant, buying and selling comic books and antiques to neighborhood shops. When I was about nineteen, I lost interest in that to pursue painting, which was an avocation in the Chicago life. In Chicago I was, and now am, a voracious reader.

Recently I had a kind of postscript added to the dozen or so dreams that refer to this life:

DB21/30, 11/30/07
Kitty and me in Riverside, California, in the year 1941. We go to the hospital where my father is born. Somehow, we see several variations of my parents' early married life. Someone showed us several "what would have happened if..." scenarios, all of which involved some kind of modification to how my parents met. The only scenario that results in pleasant co-existence for them is one where they don't have children. That causes a problem for someone else though.

The funny thing is, it seems someone wants me to be born when I am and through these parents, so it is considered the best of all possible alternatives for them, despite making impossible the one variation where they remain happy together.

The "Chicago life" isn't the only past life that has shown up in dreams. In total, I've had dreams that refer to no less than eight previous lives, with no indication that there aren't more waiting to be discovered.

DB3/76, 7/4/90

A woman sits in the front passenger seat of our car, but Kitty pays no attention to her. The woman faces me from her seat so that we can talk. She has reddish or strawberry blond hair, is in her early twenties, and has a strong Southern accent. She says that I am the one with an accent.

I have the feeling I'd met her or known her a long time ago. In fact I was certain I knew her from a past life, but I cannot remember anything about her beyond recognizing that we'd known each other before. This emptiness in my memory about her is so strong it is almost painful, like a part of me is missing. I wondered where everything had gone, because I was sure I knew her and that there were things to remember, but now there was nothing.

I wanted to remember her name more than anything else, but it was beyond my ability, so I asked her, "I just can't remember your name, please tell me." She says something like "Marcia" but when I repeat it back to her she says "not exactly, but close. It is also similar to but not the same as a department store. My last name is exactly the same as a department store." And then I woke up.

This dream was so strong that I was sure I would meet this young woman during the day. I wrote it down in my dream book and then told Kitty about it, extending myself so far as to predict we would meet her that afternoon at the Fourth of July picnic in Central Park that we planned to attend with friends, Barry and Nancy Fishman. When we picked up Barry and Nancy, I told them about the dream also, predicting we would meet this girl at the park. I thought it likely we would meet her at the picnic because it was the only opportunity I knew of to run into a stranger on that day.

Some hours later, I was resting in the park with my eyes closed while Kitty talked with Barry and Nancy. A new voice unexpectedly entered the conversation to ask about the cast on Barry's arm. I recognized the voice and accent from the girl in my dream! I sat up and opened my eyes and there she was, the spitting image of the person from the dream. I whispered to Kitty that she was 'the one', and then asked her name. "Macie Sears" was the response. Not only is it an unusual name, it matched the description from my dream perfectly. The spelling of "Macie" is similar to both "Marcia" and the store "Macy's," and "Sears," of course, is identical to the name of one of the world's largest department stores. She does have a Southern accent because she is from Florida, but her accent isn't strong. I told her about the dream and talked about it a bit, then exchanged numbers before she left to rejoin some friends.

Later that night, I dreamed about Native Americans. I thought it was a junk dream at first, but then something happened that made me wonder. On about July 20th, or two weeks after I met Macie, I called to ask her if she would be willing to write a statement for me about our meeting in the park. She surprised me by telling me that on July 5th, the night I dreamed about Native Americans, she had a dream with me in it. In her dream, I told her that we had known each other in a past life where we were both Native Americans. I then told her that it was very important to remember the dream and to call me with the details when she woke. She didn't intend to tell me because it seemed silly to her, but with me on the line, she decided she may as well tell me about it, and did.

That night, I dreamed of being a Native American, and how I died:

DB4/13, 7/20/90

Now I am in the past. There are three Native American Indians on a grassy slope. Two are male, and I am one of the two. The third, an old woman, sits under a tree on a hill not far from us. She is there to patch up the wounds of the victor, if any. The body of the loser will remain to be scavenged.

The reason we are fighting has to do with a loss of face of some kind. I had done or said something that made this other man lose face, or so he thought. At the time, I didn't intend for this to happen, and felt badly about it, but he was furious. I consider this man to be a good friend and do not want to fight him, but he insists. In his eyes, we may have been friends once, but now I am his enemy and he intends to win this battle.

We each have a knife and begin wrestling in the grass. We are both strong enough to prevent the other from moving, so while we're exerting all of our strength, we're barely moving at all. We do this for quite a while, using up tremendous reserves of energy but with no apparent result. As we are locked in this struggle, I know my heart isn't in it and that I may lose. While thinking this, I see that one of the laces of my sandal has been sliced. Before long, my foot will slide out of the sandal and I will lose my footing. I try to tighten the lace, but cannot reach it. This distraction is all my opponent needs. Almost as soon as I shift a part of my attention to the sandal, he suddenly shifts his weight and stabs me in the back. I think it is a fatal blow because he backs away as soon as he inflicts it and stops fighting.

As I die, I tell him it doesn't matter who dies on this day. "Yes it does," he says, and I die. Then I seem to float into another time, leaving those three Indians far behind on the grassy slope.

In the dream, I had the strongest feeling that Macie had been the man who killed me in this dream memory. During the dream, I remembered "my" life as this Native American. Though I don't remember the details, I do remember that I had no concept of a "white man," suggesting the possibility that the tribe I belonged to hadn't yet met European settlers. This would date the life to a period not much later than the early 1800's but could have been much older, depending on the tribe.

I only dreamed of Macie once more, two months later:

DB4/59, 9/4/90
A woman standing beside a disabled car on the road waves her arms to get my attention. It is Macie Sears. A number of interesting psychic things happen next, all of which are meant to convey the same message: that we had arranged as spirits to meet in Central Park in order to fulfill an old obligation related to the past lives referred to in the previous dreams. Now that we had met and briefly discussed it, this obligation was satisfied and we would no longer have any reason to communicate, in this or any future life, because our lives and interests were moving in completely divergent directions.

Here, for the first time, is an explanation for a seemingly purposeless meeting. I wondered how many other meetings had been arranged like this. Richard, for instance. Just before I met him, I had a dream that someone came to me and told me he was an old friend and that we'd be seeing each other soon. I was about to go to an ashram for a few weeks, so I assumed that if there was anything to the dream, I'd meet this "friend" there. On the last day, I met Richard, and we've been friends ever since. Did I know him in a past life? I don't have any indication apart from that one dream, but it isn't inconceivable.

In 2002, I had a dream that mentioned Macie, though she doesn't appear in it. In the dream, I am shown a kind of family tree, except it includes past lives. According to this document, at one time I belonged to the Seneca tribe. As soon as I notice this, someone tells me that someone I knew in New York (I assumed this was Macie) knew me at that time and was Seneca also.

I will skip over many of the past life dreams, primarily because they cannot be corroborated, but also because in many, the details are repetitive. For instance, I have had quite a few dreams about the life lived immediately prior to this one. In them, I was a soldier from Florida who died in the early days of the Vietnam war, when casualty figures were still very low. Most of the dreams are about how I was killed in an ambush on patrol. Some are about me running into the todgeists of other soldiers I knew then, and talking about our time there. In one from 2007, I am told that something from that life would soon have an effect in this one, but I didn't know what was meant. Irritatingly, I was given my full name from that life, but forgot it by the time I woke up.

I've had three dreams about a life as someone named "Mr. Geschen" that seems to have taken place in the nineteenth century. There is even less detail in these dreams than some of the others, but this name is always very clear in them.

There are several dreams of lives lived in very ancient times. I cannot imagine any way to corroborate them, but the ideas presented in some are interesting. In one, after going into some detail about the appearance of an ancient kingdom and its customs, it describes some aspects of my life there. I came to the kingdom with my sister, both of us strangers to the place. When we make our presence known to the authorities, one of the rulers decides that I am a strong psychic. This in itself isn't all that special, because at this time and in this kingdom, a psychic is about as common as a veterinarian.

The interesting part is this: at a certain point in the dream, I get into a conversation with some other psychics about "dreams." They sniff their noses when I use the word "dream," because they have different words to differentiate between what a psychic does when asleep, which, as they plainly state, is *not* "dreaming," and what happens when non-psychics sleep. It is only the latter category that is described as a "dream" in this culture. This meant that when I alluded to having "dreamed" of something, I may as well have said that I wasn't psychic.

They explained that when a psychic sleeps, instead of dreaming, he either travels with his "astral body," which is a kind of non-physical body, or he goes to "the Akashic records" for information. The term "Akashic records" comes from my readings of that time. It is a Sanskrit word used in Indian metaphysics to describe a kind of repository of all information that is available on a higher spiritual plane. I used this term when writing the journal entry because it was the only way I could translate what I was told in the dream.

In two other dreams, I was a slave in extremely ancient times. In one I remember being taken from my wife by my captors, never to see her or my family again. I spent my remaining years on an island doing what looked like roadwork, carving earth and rocks away to make a staircase and then a road leading from a dock at sea level to a flat elevation that was considerably higher. I knew I would die a slave, with nothing but work and punishment my daily fare, so I fantasized often about meeting my wife again in a later life.

DB19/60, 11/15/06

I am with a baby. She is the new incarnation of someone I knew before. She wants me to take her swimming, so I do. She swims off to a section of a wharf near a bridge onramp that goes to Manhattan or New Jersey.

When we get back to shore, the baby amazes me by writing some messages for Kitty's cousin Andrew on a menu. She wrote a few lines about how frustrating it is to not be able to communicate normally.

I point out that she's doing a beautiful job now, and that really sets her off. She then writes a lot in Chinese, describing all the things that are impossible to do purely because of her size, like going to university again (something she wants to do.) When she says this, I see an old-fashioned Chinese academy for boys only. It is the kind of place that would have existed before the Communists took over.

I think she just wanted me to say Hello to Andrew for her. But then I get her talking about other things (or writing, I should say). Next, the baby wants to go to a seafood restaurant she used to frequent when she was someone else. She makes it clear to me that the last time she was here she was an important man. A waitress tests the baby by asking a question that only this other person would know. She answers correctly.

There is only one person I can think of who fits the description of this baby, and that is Kitty's grandfather, C.C. I think the baby is indicating that she lives in either New Jersey or Manhattan now. I have had at least a dozen dreams like this, of babies that tell me of their past life, or tell me about mine. They are a bit like a todgeist who compulsively shows me how he died, but here they are showing me that they are alive again. My impression is that as babies, they don't exactly have a lot going on during their day, so this kind of communication may be easier to accomplish than when they are older and have to make a greater mental effort.

The "memories" in these dreams, corroborated or not, are every bit as vivid as they should be if they are real memories. If not for my father's unexpected corroboration of the Chicago series of dreams, and Macie's confirmation of the Native American group, I would be more skeptical than I am. This isn't because I am skeptical of reincarnation, but because I have no way of knowing whether there are any reportage errors in my records. I cannot easily compare these dreams to anything tangible, like a magazine cover or a letter in the mail. I like to be able to compare my dreams to something to weed out errors. Without any material to use for comparison, it's hard to know whether every detail of these dreams is recorded correctly, or if, like the Moscow

McDonald's dream, something is confused.

For instance, when I tried to verify the Vietnam dreams by looking up names of soldiers killed in Vietnam, at first I thought it would be fairly easy, but then ran into two potential problems: there were soldiers who were "from" Florida because they were born there, or because they'd enlisted there but were originally from somewhere else. If my life was from the latter category, he could have been from anywhere. Even the name gave me some problems as I quickly realized that some men aren't known by their first name. One man whose name was Jimmy, went by "Billy" because his middle name was William. Others might have had nicknames that had nothing to do with their real name.

My gut feeling is that the main thrust of the Vietnam dreams, and others, are correct, but that small errors exist within them that are probably significant enough to derail any attempt to positively identify a specific person. I am satisfied that the Chicago dreams are fairly accurate, thanks to my father's corroboration, and am prepared to accept the Native American dreams as-is. The others, at the very least, provide some insights into what these memories are like. Ironically, the existence of ghosts alone proves the mechanical feasibility of reincarnation, making memories of past lives irrelevant for the purpose of determining whether reincarnation is possible. They are useful for determining whether it happens, but where they can be most useful and at the same time most harmful, is the information they provide about why we behave the way we do.

In the Chicago life, I was guilt-ridden because I witnessed some boys attacking a woman but was too frightened to stop them. In this life, I have a very hard time not interfering when I see someone taking advantage of someone else. If I see a fire, I will immediately call the fire department. If I see a fight on the street, I will call the police. When an employer took advantage of employees, I helped them recover what was taken, and when a different employer, by fraud, put soldiers in harm's way, I informed the Army. Maybe the reason dates to the guilt in Chicago, maybe not. It's hard to know for sure. The reason is, I forget. Maybe it will come to me later...

## Chapter Ten

# Waking intrusions

One night in 1987, Richard and I discussed Uri Geller as we walked to his lab at Rockefeller University. Some years earlier, when Richard was an undergraduate student at Kent State University, his professor, Dr. Wilbur Franklin, organized a study of Geller and his claim that he could bend keys with the power of his mind. We were talking about this because I'd just come from a disappointing "metal bending workshop" where the cable TV personality Diana Gazes claimed to be able to reproduce Geller's effects.

Richard said that although they never caught Geller cheating, they never recorded any psychic phenomena either. He added that they had come up with a way that Geller *could* cheat, and assumed that he must have been. This struck me as wrong, and I said "Just because you figured out a way to imitate the result, doesn't mean it can't be done!"

I wasn't angry, just emphatic. At that moment, Richard had just taken his keys out of his pocket. A few seconds later, as he prepared to insert one into the door, he gasped audibly, uttered an imprecation, and dropped the keys on the ground.

The key he meant to use was bent at about a forty-five degree angle and could not possibly be fit into the lock. After some students let us in, we took an elevator up to a workshop Richard needed to fix the key. He was fascinated by what had just happened. He put the key in a table clamp and worked on it for maybe ten minutes.

Richard said he was about to put the key in the lock when he noticed it was bent. He was surprised by the coincidence of my statement followed by his discovery of the bent key. Two weeks later, he thought he had the answer. He said that he must have somehow levered the key against something while it was in his pocket, then moved his leg and bent the key. The way I looked at it, if that key was bent before it came out of his pocket, it would have snagged on something, or he would have noticed that it didn't feel right. I also didn't believe that he could have levered it in his pocket without noticing it or marking his trousers.

Neither one of us can say for sure what happened because we weren't paying attention at the time. I wasn't thinking of bending his key, nor did he expect it to happen. What we do know is that it was already bent when he looked at it just before he tried to put it in the lock, and that he hadn't seen it bent until that moment. Even if Richard had been carrying around a bent key that afternoon without realizing it, it would be an interesting coincidence to be discussing the unusual topic of Geller bending keys shortly before discovering his own bent key.

This is the first time I remember witnessing an "unintended paranormal effect." This is when a statement is made, and then something closely related to it immediately happens. The descending doubles incident and others from the same chapter do not qualify, because the results, though surprising, were predicted. In this case, I wasn't thinking about bending Richard's key, nor was I paying conscious attention to it. Indeed, it wasn't until Richard pointed out that his key was bent that I bothered to look at it.

An incident with my uncle Tom is less ambiguous. On October 18, 1989, he sat in our kitchen while Kitty made some dinner. When I walked in, I had the sudden feeling that If I asked Tom to name any character from popular fiction, he would name a certain character. I wrote the name on a piece of paper and handed it to Kitty. Then I turned to Tom and asked, "Name any character from popular fiction."

"Why?" he wanted to know. "Oh all right, Tarzan."

Kitty's jaw dropped wide open as she shrieked in surprise.

"What? What did I do?" Tom wanted to know. Kitty showed him the paper, and now it was his turn to be surprised, and he was. It read, "Tarzan."

When a skeptic hears of an incident like this and says "correlation does not imply causation," he means that my prediction and Tom's reaction are not an example of cause and effect. I agree, but it is irrelevant because there is a more fundamental issue: correlation does sometimes reflect a relationship regardless of whether it is causative. What that relationship may be can be unknown, but that doesn't mean it doesn't exist.

Unlike a television set, where the perspective of the image projected upon it does not change regardless of the viewer's position and angle of view, the exact perspective of a reflection in a mirror is determined by the viewer. This means that it is possible for two people to see different things in the same mirror at the same time. Depending on the shape of the environment reflected by the mirror and the contents of that environment, one viewer may be positioned in such a way that certain articles are visible to him, but hidden from someone else looking at the same mirror from a different angle. With Tom, it was as if I'd had a momentary glimpse of what he would answer if I asked this certain question, so I asked it, and the mirror didn't lie.

Rhoda Gubernick of *The Atlantic Monthly* magazine hired me in the first week of February, 1990 to make a double portrait of the musicians John Cale and Lou Reed. A week later, the art was done and I shipped it to her in Boston by Airborne Express. The next day, she called at about four-thirty in the afternoon with an emergency. "Andrew, we're just about to ship this out to Wisconsin to have it printed, but we noticed an error on your art." She said that because I used color overlays, she didn't notice at first that the color of the singers' skin in the portrait had the wrong percentage of black. "It's a hundred percent right now, it will block out all the line art underneath it."

It was a serious mistake and I wasn't proud to have made it. Without having the art to compare it to, I could only guess, so I said to change it to seventy percent, assuming it should be dark.

After hanging up, I worried that the problem hadn't been fixed. The darkness of a color doesn't matter as long as it contrasts with the line art. In this case, I made the line art lighter than usual. That meant that the new value I gave Rhoda might be just as bad as the first one. It took ten minutes to figure this out, leaving plenty of time to call Rhoda and give her another value. Doing so would require admitting that I'd made another mistake, but I didn't want to do that.

This mistake was embarrassing. I wanted to call, but at the same time I really wanted to fix the art some other way. A phone call on its own wouldn't be good enough. I had to see the art to fix the error. This was before computers were used to ship art, and I didn't have a copy of the illustration at home. While Kitty sat in the kitchen eating dinner, I paced in the living room.

"What I really want," I said, loud enough for her to hear, "is for the package to get waylaid on its way to the printers in Wisconsin and mysteriously arrive here without anyone knowing about it. I'll fix it and send it on its way and everything will be fine." The concept made no sense, but it was the only option I could think of.

I said this over and over again to Kitty as if it was a mantra. "Either I call, or it just appears, that's it. It can't happen any other way." I tried to think of other options, but the only idea that would work was the one that was impossible. "It has to show up here tomorrow." After two hours of pacing and repeating this, I went to bed.

The house phone woke me the next morning. There was a package waiting for me downstairs - I had no idea what it could be. The Airborne Express truck sat in neutral by the curb, punching clouds of vapor into the cold February air. The deliveryman handed me a box and a signature sheet. I was about to sign when I saw that the box didn't have an air bill. I turned it over to check the other side, but it wasn't there either. The Airborne employee was impatient, but I didn't want to accept a package if it didn't belong to me.

By now I was wide-awake and knew I wasn't expecting anything. This box had no address information on it at all. It didn't have a sender's address, a recipient's address, or even a single name to identify it in any way. It also looked like it had been opened and then artlessly resealed. To say it was suspicious was an understatement. "Where's the air bill?" I asked.

"Dunno."

"How do you know this is for me then?"

"My supervisor said to deliver it to this address."

"Where is it from?"

"Dunno."

"Do you mind if I look inside, just to make sure it's for me?"

"It's your box, man. Do whatever you like."

I borrowed a letter opener from the doorman and sliced open the box. Inside was every article, every original photo, every original slide, and every piece of original illustration art for the entire issue of The *Atlantic Monthly* to which I had contributed. Buried in the middle, I found my illustration.

I signed for the box and ran upstairs. "Kitty!" I yelled when I got inside. "You are not going to believe this!" I pulled out my illustration and brought it over to my worktable. I found the color I needed to fix quickly, because Rhoda had taped over the original value with a new piece of tape and a note in her handwriting. I didn't want any mix-ups, so I pulled her tape free of the art. Underneath, I found my original number. It wasn't written very clearly, but I was familiar enough with my own handwriting to see that it said "10%." Rhoda had read the percent sign as part of the number. I hadn't made a mistake at all, but if I hadn't caught the later error that Rhoda and I had made

135

jointly to "fix" the first, my first job for the *Atlantic Monthly* would have been a horrible misprint.

I called up Rhoda, "It's Andrew Paquette. You'll never believe what I've got."

"Pardon me?"

"The package you sent to the printers yesterday arrived at my apartment in New Jersey this morning."

"Oh my God."

"Just tell me where it needs to go. I'll send it on its way."

I asked Rhoda if she knew of any past occasion when all the raw materials of an issue had been lost. "Never," she replied, "Not in eighty years of publishing."

When I contacted Rhoda about this recently, her primary concern was that she thought this account made her look somehow responsible for this potentially ghastly error. It hadn't occurred to me that anyone might look at it that way, and I had to think about it for awhile before I figured out what she meant. On her end, she might have been thinking that she forgot to put the airbill on the box, a possibility that I hadn't considered until a few days after receiving her email.

I called DHL, the new owners of Airborne Express, about this. I was told that packages are shipped without airbills every day, but the procedure is to return them to the shipper when it happens. I wondered how that could be done without an airbill. "Easy, we just check the pick-up location and return it there." For me to get the package, it almost certainly was shipped with an airbill, but lost it after it entered the system. After this, someone opened the box in the hope of finding an address to send it to. My art did have my name, address, and phone number on it, but then so did all the other material in the box, numbering about a hundred items.

Oddly, if there had been anything inside the box to indicate who the shipper was, the box would have been turned back to

*The Atlantic*. This means that either there was no reference to the magazine in the box, or the Airborne supervisor wasn't able to distinguish it from all the other material.

Richard thought my email about his twins was amazing. For me, this was more amazing. This was something that *I wanted to happen, and it did*. When I paced the night before, repeating over and over again my wish, I was talking half to myself, half to Kitty. There was no one else to hear me. I did not know where the package was or who I would have to contact about it. I didn't even try. Even if I had known, I wouldn't have been able to achieve this result by normal means because I wasn't the shipper or the intended recipient. Airborne wouldn't have paid any attention to me, and everyone at *The Atlantic* would have already left the office. Instead, I focused on the end result I needed, having the package in my hands, and I got it.

I did not expect the package to actually show up on the following day. It was a total surprise when it did. I was not repeating a mantra with the goal of causing this outcome, I was worrying aloud. I paced because I wanted to solve the problem. I clearly communicated to Kitty the fact that I didn't see any other way to accomplish my goal, and that this was the only solution, as bizarre as it was. This is very much like the incident with Richard's key. I didn't intend to see his key bent, but I said something I felt strongly about, and there was a response.

One scenario I can imagine is that either my lebengeist or some other spirit influenced a person in the delivery chain telepathically, perhaps by distracting his attention, to treat the package carelessly. This caused the airbill to be lost. After this, simple telepathic communication, directing a supervisor to select my address, would accomplish the rest.

However it was done, my powerful desire caused someone or something with access to the package to accidentally destroy or lose the airbill and then fish my artwork out of the package for an address. That is a direct chain of causation, and that is not coincidence or synchronicity. It is an example of an "affinitas nebulosus," or an "obscured connection."

"Coincidence" is an acausal correlation, and "synchronicity" is a meaningful acausal correlation. What both of these terms imply is that causation is meaningful to the correlation, but it often isn't. I don't know what caused me to suggest my question to Tom or why he answered the way I predicted, but I don't have to know to detect a relationship between the two. If pressed, I would not argue that I *caused* him to say "Tarzan," nor would I have suggested anything similar with many of the other correlations in this book. Some of them do appear to be causally connected, like the *Atlantic Monthly* incident or Richard's key, but in both cases, the specific cause is unknown and that makes the subject of causation irrelevant. More germane, is the indication of a relationship between two things and an unknown third factor. This type of grouping, an affinitas nebulosus, can be a paranormal relationship.

Men who sleep in their clothes may tend to have liver disease, but not because one causes the other. The factor that links them is drunkenness. Drunks who have liver disease tend to pass out in their clothes. This is not a paranormal relationship, but that doesn't mean that all unexplained correlations are the same.

Sometimes I think the only reason there are people who don't understand this is because they have trained themselves to overlook examples of paranormal connections. This reminds me of the work of Dr. Richard Wiseman, author of *The Luck Factor*. In it, he describes how his associates placed a £5 note directly in the path of a self-described "unlucky" study participant, who proceeded to step right over the bill without a glance. A "lucky" participant, on the other hand, spotted the note right away and picked it up.

On the morning of March 28, 1990, I was meditating when I "saw" the cover of the new *Time* magazine. This was confirmed within hours, when our copy arrived by mail. It is the first time I know of that I had a waking premonition of an image like this. I wondered if I might be able to do better, by sitting down and concentrating on future cover images. I opened my sketchbook, and made thumbnails for ten covers, each with corresponding cover dates. About halfway through, I started feeling fatigued, and resorted to what felt like random guesses.

The following week, we received our copy of the April 9, 1990 cover dated issue. It was a near match for the thumbnail labeled "6·11·90." It was close enough that I decided to have the thumbnails notarized, in case any of the others came out right. This is the first time I ever notarized something like this.

A week later, I had another cover to compare to my group of sketches, and again it wasn't perfect, but it was intriguing. The week after that, the result was even better, matching for date and composition. The following week was again good, but after that, the results fell off. After four in a row that had some correlation, none of the rest could be described that way. Statistically, two of the covers are excellent matches, two are partial, and the rest don't match. Depending on how you look at it, this means I was successful from 20% to 40% of the time.

What this taught me is that these things cannot be forced. On all previous occasions, paranormal incidents were spontaneous or unintentional. There is something about the act of trying to cause a paranormal result that fights against success.

There are specific physical sensations that accompany each of the incidents described in this book. Broadly speaking, the most accurate observations, or "successful" incidents, are characterized by the same feeling I get when I am looking directly in front of me but am aware of something happening just outside the range of my peripheral vision. If I relax, but continue to look straight forward, a picture forms in my mind of whatever is just beyond the range of my vision. In this way, I can "see" one thing while allowing my mental focus to drift towards another. As soon as I move my eyes to get a better look, the mental image vanishes.

When I made the attempt to draw ten future *TIME* covers, I was making an effort to passively find the covers, but the effort was more fatiguing than I expected, and after the first few drawings, I was bored and wanted to get it over with. By then, the images were disrupted and I may as well have been guessing. Dreams put me in a more passive frame of mind, making it much easier to pay attention to what is in front of me without becoming mentally exhausted.

It's like something that happens when I'm painting outdoors: when I walk through an environment looking for a place to sit and paint, the wildlife runs from me. After I'm seated and have been painting for some hours, the wildlife will creep back, often getting quite close to me. As long as I continue painting, the lizards, chipmunks, rabbits, deer, and whatever other animals might be near me, are content to stay. If I look at any of them directly, they immediately scatter.

In 1989, Kitty and I went to the back room of New York's O.K. Harris art gallery to look at a painting. Directly in front us, a large wooden storage rack was bolted to the wall. This armature had enough slots to store about a hundred paintings in two rows, one stacked atop the other. At waist height above the floor, a wide wooden viewing shelf provided a place to view paintings. To use it, a painting is placed on the shelf so that its bottom edge is pressed into a thick wooden lip at the front edge of the shelf, and the top of the painting leans backwards about six inches to rest against the rack itself. Ethan Karp, the gallery director, pulled out a watercolor by Stephen Fox that he wanted to show us, and positioned it securely on the shelf. In its frame, the painting was about twenty by thirty inches.

To give us some privacy, Ethan discreetly stepped away, but not so far that he couldn't answer questions. Kitty stood about three feet in front of the painting. I stood four feet away and to the left. Ethan was the furthest from the painting, and stood about eight feet away, on Kitty's right. I asked Kitty if she liked the painting. "I do," she said.

"Then I think you should have it."

I saw a blur to my right as Kitty gasped and then was suddenly holding the painting in her arms. Ethan also gasped, possibly louder than Kitty. His first words were, "It looked like a ghost picked it up and dropped it on her!" Kitty said, "It just jumped on me! If I hadn't caught it, it would have fallen on the floor!"

*What happened here?* In other incidents, it was just Kitty and me quietly enjoying an evening at home. This time we were in the middle of a big city, surrounded by people, it was broad daylight, and this thing had just happened in front of the gallery director of one of Manhattan's finer art galleries. This was exactly like the incident with Richard's key, except this time, there were three sets of eyeballs trained on the painting when I said "I think you should have it." There is no ambiguity here, and no room for conversations about probabilities or chance. No matter what the actual physical cause was of that painting lurching onto Kitty, it did it at the *exact* moment I finished my sentence. My comment may not have caused the painting to move, but I think it is fair to say that both my statement and the motion of the painting are related.

Physically, there was very little to suggest what might have happened. As Kitty and Ethan both explained, the painting went *up* and *forward* before landing on Kitty. It did not simply rotate forward on its bottom axis. If it had, it would have fallen short of Kitty and she wouldn't have been able to catch it. When it moved, *it moved alone*. There was no earthquake, or even the kind of earthquake-like jolt that sometimes shakes the ground when a heavy truck hits a pothole outside. The painting was securely resting against the painting rack, and had been for some minutes before it jumped onto Kitty. There was no sound that might give a clue to how this happened. It was, and remains, completely inexplicable.

Ironically, we did not buy the painting. With that in mind, this incident acquires another dimension. I said "I think you should have it," and then, as if in immediate response, Kitty "had" it, but she did not own it. It is the kind of response one might expect from a child.

One thing this incident has in common with others described in this chapter, is the implied presence of a listener who reacts to what I say, in an attempt to satisfy an expressed desire. Whoever or whatever this is, it deserves a name to distinguish it from a neutral force of nature. I was trying to come up with a word for it that would mean something along the lines of an "unknown listener" when I ran across the Latin words "servo spiritus," meaning "the watching spirit." This expression also has the meaning "protective spirit," making it sound very close to the familiar English term "guardian angel." For reasons I will explain later in the book, the word "angel" may be a misnomer in this context, so I am happier with the less specific "servo spiritus" and will use it instead.

A year after the incident in the gallery, I wanted to sell a very expensive Photorealist painting that we had bought in New York. I called Ethan to see if he was interested. He wasn't, but he did want to know if any other odd incidents, like the jumping Fox painting, had happened to me. We talked about that for at least a half hour before I got off the line. Sixteen years later, when I was living in Arizona, I called to tell him that I was considering including an account of this incident in a book. He no longer remembered it clearly, but admitted that it "sounded familiar." Even so, he gave his blessing to publish it. Kitty was more adamant. "You have to publish it! That thing *jumped* on me! I saw it!"

Once, after seeing the performer The Amazing Kreskin on television, Kitty and I drove down to Atlantic City to see one of his "concerts." I was curious to see if he would be as convincing in person as he was on TV.

During the show, Kreskin asked for a volunteer from the audience. He asked the man to think of his birthday. Immediately after saying this, a birthdate popped into my head. Then Kreskin read off the date I was thinking of and the man in the audience, dumbfounded, agreed that he had given his birthdate correctly.

I've heard the theory that performers like Kreskin have collaborators in the audience, but I don't see how a plant in the audience could have given me a mental image of a birth date, just before Kreskin read it off, without some kind of paranormal process being involved. Even if they *were* collaborating and the birth date was invented, it still wouldn't explain how I picked it up independently.

On May 17, 1990, I had a paper jam in my home copier. It sat on the floor of our apartment, forcing me to get on my hands and knees to clear it. I reached into the copier with my right hand, seeking out the jammed paper by feel. My first try only resulted in tearing the paper in half, so I had to put my hand in even farther, and be very sure of my grip on the remaining scrap. When I did this, I experienced a weird sensation like I had plunged my hand into a bucket of cold ice cream. It was pleasant at first, so I allowed my hand to remain in this position as I struggled to pull free the jammed paper. After some seconds more had passed, I realized that I hadn't made contact with a cool surface on the interior of the copier at all, but a super-heated one.

I yanked my hand out as fast as possible (along with the paper) and observed in horror as my hand, which had just been pressed hard against the extremely hot fuser roller of the copier, began to blister. As I watched, the blister extended from the second knuckle of my right thumb to its base at the wrist. It was like watching a balloon inflate, but not quite as extreme. Even so, within minutes I had a patch of skin about three inches long and an inch wide that had bubbled outwards and changed color to a bright pink. Meanwhile, the pleasant sensation I felt at first had given way to pain. I yelled out to Kitty that I'd just burned my hand in the copier, asking for ice.

"We don't have any ice!" she yelled back. "Use the blueberries!" There were some frozen blueberries in the freezer, but as I watched, even with the blueberry package pressed against my hand, the swelling became worse. Next I tried cold water from the faucet, but this didn't seem to help much either. It had been maybe five minutes from the time I first made my interesting discovery in the copier, and the swelling hadn't abated at all.

I looked directly at my hand and, thinking of all my recent psychic experiences, I said aloud, "If there is anything to this psychic healing business, then heal this wound now." Within twenty or thirty seconds, as I watched, the blister reduced in size until it was completely gone. It was like watching a movie in reverse. Once the blister was gone, the skin smoothed out and went back to its normal color. There was no way to know that it had ever been burned from its appearance.

I found out later that a fuser roller is heated to about 180 degrees Celsius, or 356 degrees Fahrenheit. It had to have cooled a little bit in the seconds since I started the copy and when I shoved my hand into the machine, but it couldn't have cooled that much. In the few seconds of contact, it was enough to give me what I later discovered was a second-degree burn.

A sunburn can take a week to heal, and second-degree burns take about three weeks. As part of the healing process, blistered skin sloughs off or is cut off. With me, I had blistered skin, and retained all of it. Not only that, but the healing process, to say the least, was rapidly accelerated. According to the online sources I consulted, putting ice on the burn is a bad thing to do, but running cool tap water is a good thing to do. The tap water doesn't heal blisters, however, instead it cools the skin and stops the burn from getting worse. A blister, quite simply, is dead skin. No amount of water could have brought it back.

Incidents like these continue to happen in my waking life. All follow the same pattern: 1) an intentional or unintentional "request," 2) the request is honored in an immediate and inexplicable manner. This sounds like answered prayer, and in a way they are, but I was not praying in a traditional sense on any of these occasions. In the earliest ones, I didn't even believe in God. By the time my hand was burned, I acknowledged that God probably existed, but was a long way from accepting formal prayer. To me, calling these examples of "answered prayer," at least in a purely religious sense, is the same as reflexively identifying a servo spiritus as an "angel," or suggesting that liver disease is caused by falling asleep with your shoes on. Maybe it's true, but maybe there's something more going on.

## Chapter Eleven

# Indivisible bonds

The word "correlation" does not mean the same thing as "connection," as skeptics like to so often remind us. A correlation can indicate a connection, and sometimes there really is one. I move a computer mouse on my desktop and see a cursor move on my monitor at the same time. This is a correlation indicative of a connection, and there is a connection, as anyone can tell, by following the cord at the back of the mouse to the computer, then from the monitor cable connected to the computer all the way to the monitor. What is disturbing about paranormal events is that, like a wireless mouse, the means of connection are not visible. Worse, unlike a wireless mouse, they aren't understood.

What should be understood by now is that there are connections. Not only that, but these connections are so much an indivisible part of our physical universe, that they are not severable from it. It may be argued that some of the odd events described here are the equivalent of paranormal pranks, but what is more difficult to argue is that these same events would be possible without a firm connection between the physical environment we see and whatever non-visible forces act on it to cause these odd situations.

Poltergeists have the apparent ability to affect physical objects, not necessarily with their mind, but *somehow*. People have the apparent ability to witness events that will not occur until after they've first seen them in a dream. It is not necessary to know the process that allows this to accept that it happens. The fact that future events may be foreseen indicates that time either isn't linear or sequential, as we are taught it is, or there is a way to jump forward and backward in the sequence to observe, at the very least, future or past events. We are able, as my many "visit" dreams indicate, to see other people in other places, remotely. Sometimes the distant locale, or things witnessed within it, are remembered with enough clarity to convincingly identify those details when awake. All of these things require what is often described as a supernatural, or paranormal, component.

The word "paranormal" refers to something that is not scientifically explainable. It is the pared-down, secular version of "supernatural," a more robust term. "Supernatural" is a more religious word, in the sense that it can refer to the works of God or the devil, or to either of these beings along with a host of others, from angels to lowly ghosts. The primary meaning of "supernatural" is less exalted; it simply describes things that appear to transcend nature or that are attributable to an unseen agent. This latter definition appeals to me because it says more about the things I am trying to describe than "paranormal," but because of its religious associations, I have avoided it so far. It is, however, more correct.

While writing this book I have encountered some serious difficulties because of the paucity of words available to describe the various things I want to describe, and that most of the words available don't describe these things very well. I've already invented a few words and terms for this book, and will do so a few more times before the book is done, because the vocabulary for this kind of experience is weak. With "paranormal" and "supernatural," the problems aren't so insurmountable that I feel a need to change them, but they do hint at something un-looked at, an object in a mirror that can only be seen from a certain angle, and this does deserve some attention.

According to Merriam-Webster online, "supernatural" things may be attributable to an invisible agent, such as a ghost. This is exactly what we have seen over and over again in many of the experiences recounted here, but it is not clear to me who, or what, this agent is. There are other experiences that indicate the existence of ghosts: lebengeists, todgeists, and freigeists, but nowhere is there any indication that any of these are definitely responsible for certain of these events. My principal objection to "supernatural" is that it tends to identify the invisible agent, usually as a ghost, angel, God, or a devil. What I don't like about "paranormal" is that it leaves so much out, and at the same time sloppily characterizes so many things together without discrimination.

The best way I've come up with to classify these things is to first figure out where they come *from*, as a locale. In Part One of this book, I have described events that are concerned with, not just earth, as the title implies, but all things in the physical universe, as we know it. It is important to understand perspective in this context, because just like a mirror, my dreams have shown that point-of-view radically alters an experience. If I am "awake" now, but then dream of being "awake" while my body sleeps, who is to say in which I am awake and which I am not?

The word "earthbound" refers to the physical universe, as it is understood by those who occupy it *while awake* within that universe. A literal dream of a future event that takes place within that universe is therefore "earthbound" because it is a waking earthbound event. In the same way, a todgeist who is intimately associated with the death of its body, a lebengeist who visits friends and family while its body sleeps, or the mysterious invisible force that causes poltergeist effects, whatever it is, are all earthbound as well. All of these events require an element that is not earthbound to function, but the event itself is earthbound, because that is where the focus is, or where the activity is carried out.

To try and understand *supernatural* events purely from an earthbound perspective is not easy. For one, it presupposes that it is possible to do it. I'm not convinced that is true. If one is to try and detect something that is undetectable by a certain class of instruments, and only those instruments are used to detect it, then failure is unavoidable. Part of the key to this is that if our physical universe keeps us earthbound, then there is something else, either beyond it or within it, something undefined, but that is not earthbound. At a minimum, an understanding of this other locale is crucial to understanding the *paranormal* events witnessed so often in our earthbound environment.

When I dreamed of Porgy, where was he? When I "spoke" with Richard while he was working in Japan, was I "in" Japan? or was I somewhere else? When my grandparents said goodbye, where did they go? Where was my grandfather's todgeist before he said goodbye but after he died? One place they weren't, is earthbound.

The previous paragraph contains another of these language-oriented problems I was complaining about earlier. It says, "...after he died," when I am not referring to the death of my grandfather. Clearly, he did not die. His body died and was destroyed, but my grandfather lived on, and he did so *somewhere else*.

I visualize it this way: everything that can be encompassed by the word "earthbound" is like a stage. The stage is populated with props, backdrops, actors, lighting, and sound equipment. This is all most people ever know during their lives, which are lived entirely on this stage. Until their bodies die, they will not know any other locale, and even after their bodies are gone, some will continue to wander this enormous stage, unsure of what comes next. What most of them don't realize is that many of the things they interact with daily have hidden controls.

Backstage, an environment that almost none of the stage-dwellers have any concept of, are hordes of technicians, store rooms, and piles of equipment. There is the elevator under the stage, and the technician who operates it. In tandem, the effect on the stage itself is quite inexplicable, so long as the backstage environment remains hidden. There are many types of people that hang around backstage, and not all of them are useful. Some haven't been invited and don't belong, but they remain regardless, interfering with those on the stage for their own amusement. Others help the people on the stage, in many different ways. It is a symbiotic existence, with the backstage environment providing certain necessary elements of the on-stage experience, even as the on-stage experience provides a purpose for the backstage support staff.

When I see a painting invisibly picked up from a shelf and dropped on Kitty, or a burn blister healed almost instantaneously, or a dream of a future *TIME* cover, I don't ask myself, "was this precognition, an out-of-body experience [OOBE], telepathy or psychokinesis?" This is because I know that I've just had another helping hand from the backstage crew, whoever they may be. If I need to know who I will marry, they tell me. If I happen to be wandering around backstage while I am not needed on stage (while sleeping), I may take a peek at the script all by myself and discover the answer. The point is that it is the difference between these locales that both separates them experientially and that allows for supernatural incidents.

In books I have read on supernatural subjects, the focus is on the person who experiences or reports a supernatural event. These people are often designated as "psychic" or "clairvoyant." Regardless of whether these descriptions are accurate, to study a person as if that person is directly responsible for a supernatural event, is a mistake. The supernatural/natural connection is a permanent condition from the earthbound perspective. This means that the presence or absence of any number of psychics is irrelevant to the connection itself and the existence of the "backstage" locale. Cooperation clearly takes place between the stage and backstage locales, and this is where supernatural events are most likely to be found, but to assume that the causative force originates in one place rather than the other, and to identify it with a person rather than an overall characteristic of the environment itself, unnecessarily constricts the field of view.

When I paint on this stage and the animals come near, behind them, I have caught glimpses of yet more, quietly working and going about their business, sometimes helping me, but always busy. The earthbound experience, as fascinating as it sometimes is, is just the beginning.

*Part Two*

# Backstage

# Mundus Alo

*Chapter Twelve*

# An Entire Life

DB2/82, 4/17/90

I am wide-awake while my body sleeps in bed. It lies peacefully in its bedroom on earth, surrounded by the entire physical universe. Planets, stars, and galaxies are far below me and yet they are very near. I can pinpoint the location of my body with ease, even though I am outside the physical universe and my body is within it.

The space around me is vast. If the entire physical universe could be described as the inside of a mansion, then I occupy a tiny spot in all the space outside of that mansion. When I look at it, it is like peeking out from behind a black gauze curtain at a well-lit stage. The place I am in is above the stage in the sense that I can look down upon it from here, but at the same time it exists beyond spatial limitations.

Now that I am free of my body, I am also freed from physical desires and interests. Those things prevent me from seeing things clearly when awake, but now I have a totally clear view of everything. My "waking" state is like being completely unconscious compared to the way I feel now. Instead of simply seeing and hearing things within a certain range, all of my normal physical senses are immeasurably magnified in sensitivity. More importantly, I have knowledge of things that are hidden from me when my body is awake.

Part of that knowledge is that I remember that the word "I" does not refer to my body. "I" am the soul that drives my body, but "I" exist apart from it also. The body will die someday, but I won't. When I look at it lying in bed, it is like an overcoat or a pair of boots, useful, but no more than a covering, a shell.

My body is unconscious, but I am awake, and I am not dreaming. I know this with a clarity that I have never experienced while my body is conscious. I know I will have to return to my body but relish this time away from it. When I rejoin my body, I will surrender to the spiritual equivalent of a drugged state, where I will conduct myself with a reduced level of awareness. My responsibilities are not unbearable or impossible, but are more difficult than if unfettered by a body.

When my body sleeps, my spirit wakes and is freed like steam into the night air. When my body communicates a need to wake, then my spirit immediately returns to it, like water being poured into dough. In this sense, my body is like a heavy suit of armor that not only weighs me down, but that impairs all of my senses. We have eyes to see with, but seeing with physical eyes is like peering through tiny slots in an iron helmet. Touching things with my body is like the sensation of using a long cane to break through some spider-webs. There is a negligible amount of resistance, and that is all I feel compared to what I can feel as a spirit.

My life on earth is important to my work in this other place; though I spend no time contemplating what that might be, because I have a task that requires my immediate attention.

I turn my gaze from earth and focus on my surroundings. They are indistinct, but not in the way a fog can obscure a landscape. Here, there is no landscape to obscure. It is plain, clear, open space. There is only one thing to look at nearby, a line of spirits that I am supposed to join.

Near the queue, there is a building with a turnstile in front, operated by hostess-like spirits. They ask each spirit in turn some questions before granting entry, to ensure the spirit goes to the right place. The spirits are a mix of todgeists and lebengeists.

When it is my turn, I become aware that despite my elevated level of consciousness, there are spirits here who know a great deal more than me. For instance, I know that I am subordinate to both of the hostess spirits now facing me in the same way that a patient is subordinate to a nurse while in her care.

Although time as such does not exist here, I ask the year, in reference to earth.

"1924," says one spirit.

"Don't you mean 1973?" I ask, thinking that 1973 is preferable somehow.

"No, it is 1924," she repeats clearly.

Then I remember that I am selecting a year. 1924 is a year I have already been to, but liked it, so I say, "Fine. I'll get out here," meaning in 1924. I can't do it though because I've already been there, or it is closed off to me for some other reason. Either way, the girl has a suggestion for me.

"It's 1965 now, why don't you go now or you'll have to go much later."

Her statement is reasonable, so I agree to be born in the year 1965. I pass through the turnstile, and as I do, everything changes to become 1965. I see cars, haircuts, clothes, furniture, and architecture from the period all around me. A freigeist in the form of a distinguished looking man meets me on the other side of the turnstile. He behaves like a kind of usher, so that is how I will refer to him. He says that he is here because of my insistent call for some information. He asks if I am sure I want to see it. I am, and say so. With that taken care of, he escorts me through a barrier to a place where the entirety of my life will be shown. Passing through the barrier is accompanied by a peculiar sensation, like a yearning to break through to the surface after being underwater too long.

Inside, it is like a vast theatre with many thousands of screens. It isn't really a theatre any more than there are screens, but it is the nearest metaphor. It is an enormous space set aside for the purpose of viewing the entire content of my life in one sitting. The "screens" are the events themselves, played out in full three dimensions. At the end of the viewing, I can decide whether to accept this life.

The audience is made up of the spirits of every person I will ever have any contact with, meaningful or otherwise, and every person who will be affected by my life. The usher remains at my side as I watch an ongoing presentation of many things at once. He seems sad that I want to see these things. He doesn't think my life will be any more difficult than anyone else's, but that most spirits have to incarnate in difficult lives to overcome short-comings that would otherwise persist. His sympathy for errant spirits in general is what makes him look sad.

On a main screen, my life is shown from my perspective. Everything I see, hear, touch, taste, and smell is displayed. My emotions, motives, and thoughts are also played out. When a person or an event intrudes on my life, more screens pop up to show how that thing came to be. If in one scene I count the number of wooden matches in a matchbook, I then see how the matches came to be in the house.

In the same way, whenever I do something that affects anyone else, more screens pop up to show the event from their perspective, and then yet more screens for anyone else who is affected. In this way, a simple fistfight in a school playground spawns dozens of screens that simultaneously show the cause of the fight, the fight itself, and all of the ripple effects it had on every person who was in some way affected by it.

It is exactly as if I am reliving my entire life, from my birth in 1965 to my death at some future date. Nothing is missing, not even the smallest time-wasting moments like day dreaming while staring at clouds in the sky, or fiddling around with a puzzle on a long drive. Everything unfolds at exactly the same pace I remember living it, and then proceeds into the future at the same speed.

Because I experience the life from multiple perspectives simultaneously, I am able to evaluate all of my life choices. When I do something that causes harm to someone else, I not only see myself commit the act and the person's reaction on the screen, but I also see his spirit in the audience react as well.

Seeing each event from this variety of perspectives is crucial to my decision about the life. The ripples my actions will cause to those around me will define the success or failure of my life more than any other measure. The life has a serious purpose, and is not designed for entertainment.

My sister Debbie is here as a spirit. This is because she will be making a decision regarding the same family in the year 1967, the year of her birth, but also because she plays a large role in my youth. I walked in on a display of her life, but once I arrive, we are watching two different "movies," each displaying the images of our individual lives and their overlaps on the same screen simultaneously. She is as bound up in the playback of her life as if she is living it right now instead of being a member of a very large audience.

I sympathize with Debbie because she doesn't seem to be getting as much as I will out of life. She also takes a number of hard knocks throughout her life. Even as this thought occurs to me, the usher informs me that she will agree to this life partly as a favor to me, so that she can protect me from certain adverse influences while allowing me to take advantage of what would otherwise be a substantially more dangerous childhood environment. In addition, I am informed that her trials are something she can handle because she has a strength I lack.

There are far too many scenes to recount or remember and some are not from the present incarnation. There were memories of other lives that came to mind while watching as this one played itself out. My father in this life had been significant in at least one other life with me.

In a scene from an earlier life, my father [who is not my father, but a friend] had too much to drink and went out to a boat tied nearby to retrieve more liquor. He loses his balance in the boat and falls into the water. He dies of drowning amid fragmenting ice floes on a river. His spirit is pulled out then so that he can rejoin me in a new family. He has to leave before I do to be born in time to be my father. I travel with him and experience his early married life with my mother just before re-experiencing events from my childhood.

The thrust of our lives leaves Debbie in a blue-collar position as an adult, while I am in a rather good position. When I see the entirety of my life, all of the hardships of my childhood make sense in the context of what's required and what I want to be. I don't want to be poor (when young) but it doesn't seem so bad here because I can see the results.

In the end I seem to possess some personal influence and status. I wasn't 'just' an artist- there is something else to it. After watching the entire life I am pleased with the choice. I could have taken something else but chose this life and in the end it is pretty good in a number of ways. I discuss it with Debbie's spirit and she agrees. We see that the lives chosen in the same family are appropriate and beneficial *overall* despite isolated unpleasant events.

The criteria used to evaluate the quality of the life is very different from what some might expect. Money, prestige, fame, success in a given profession, fun, and satisfaction of desires are all things that have been used to rate one's success on earth. In this place, and in the context of selecting a life, those factors are of no importance at all. The only things that matter are the moral quality of our decisions and the net effect our life has on those around us. If by living our lives there are beneficial effects on those around us, then we have been successful. If, on the other hand, we have harmed those around us, then the life is a failure, regardless of every other factor.

When I focused on the early years, my dad doesn't come across very well. He drinks to excess, causing many problems for my mother. I'm surprised because it's unexpected but at the same time he chose that life just as we chose ours. I feel sympathy for him because he *had to* do those things and will pay the consequences for his actions.

When I woke up from this dream, though I hadn't had much sleep that night, I was wide awake. I dashed downstairs to our living room and wrote as fast as I could. The details were already fading and I didn't want to lose any more than necessary. I remembered the fact that I experienced every minute detail of my life, and at the time I woke, I still remembered what some of these details were. I knew I didn't have time to write everything, so I had to choose what would be recorded first. I decided to start with the outline of the dream, to make sure it was preserved. By the time I finished that, the small details were gone.

This is my first "big dream." In an earlier chapter I described the dream of being married to Kitty as being like a big dream in some respects, but this dream is the first that has all of the properties I have come to expect from them. The dreams of Porgy and the Amsterdam mugging were both vivid, but not this vivid. In other dreams I was aware that I was sleeping, but not like this. No previous dream had the scale of this dream or the level of awareness that this one had. On top of all that, there is the amount of time covered, an entire lifetime, and then some. It is all these things in combination that makes this a big dream.

There are two spirits in this dream identified as "hostesses" and one as an "usher." All of them belong to a class of spirits that I classify as "servo spiritus," a "protective spirit that watches over." These are spirits who help both lebengeists and todgeists. I suspect that the ranks of servo spiritii are filled by freigeists and lebengeists. They can easily be mistaken for "angels," and probably are, because of their helpful attitude and ability to render inexplicable assistance. If the Ramstein dream had happened a few years later, I would have described the man who brought me to the crash as a servo spiritus. In the dream where I helped Lisa's mother, I behaved like a servo spiritus also, and may actually have been functioning as one. It is because of this example and others like it that I am unwilling to assume that all servo spiritii are freigeists. I am fairly sure that a good number of them are lebengeists as well.

This dream is the source of my stage/backstage metaphor from the previous chapter. The backstage environment is described with some clarity, but the term "backstage" really doesn't do it justice. I prefer the Latin *mundus alo*, or "world/universe of comfort, aid, and support." This is exactly the feeling I get from the servo spiritii I find here, and why I like this term. For the "onstage" environment, or "the physical universe," I like *mundus limus*, or "world/universe of mud." To me, this is the defining characteristic of this locale, the stuff that everything is made of. Compared to the mundus alo, everything in the mundus limus is heavy and ponderous.

Servo spiritii are not mentioned in previous chapters because they are not earthbound, even if they assist those who are. Servo spiritii occupy the mundus alo locale relative to our waking physical universe, the mundus limus.

The major subject of this dream, depending on how you look at it, was either incarnation or reincarnation. Curiously, neither term was ever used within the dream itself. More to the point, although I have had many dreams on the subject of past lives or reincarnation, in none of them is the subject a matter of interest or controversy. Reincarnation is accepted, or taken for granted. It is something that everyone, including me, *knows*, just as I knew that Sumi would commit suicide. The information is there, it is true, and there is no need to question it. To question reincarnation, or even incarnation, which is the same thing, would display an impossible degree of ignorance.

There is one other subject of interest embedded in this dream: predestination and free will. The conflict between these two ideas has kept philosophers busy for thousands of years. Precognition implies predestination, yet everything we do feels as if it is done by our free will. Which is it? If I dream of a future event that requires a number of other, seemingly unrelated, events to also come to pass, some of them trivial in nature, then how can I imagine that I have free will? If I am meant to open a certain book of no real importance, and leave it open on a certain page at the moment I receive a call from my mother, how can I think that those actions were not designed prior to my going through the motions?

The dream presents an intriguing answer to this. I am shown the life and asked if I agree to experience it by living it. I agree, and become me. I exercised free will when I chose the life, but like a roller coaster, once it starts, I can't get off until the ride is over. Also like a roller coaster, there are a limited number of things that can be done within the car you have strapped yourself into. In this way you have free will when making the initial decision, and then again to a limited extent during the ride. This isn't a complete answer, as I discovered later, but it is the first time I'd seen anything to answer the paradox of simultaneously experiencing free will *and* predestination.

## Chapter Thirteen

# Sleepers

A "sleeper" is the lebengeist of a sleeping or unconscious person, operating independently of its sleeping body. The designation is used in situations where sleepers congregate with each other, as opposed to "visit" encounters with people who are awake.

DB22/66, 2/12/09
I jog towards a nearby highway. Street signs along the way bear the names of different towns in Texas, but where? I make my way to a rundown shop with a payphone, intending to call someone and find out.

A line of men wait to use the phone while others loiter inside. In total, there are about twenty men here. I ask one, "Do you know where we are?"

"Yes," he answers, though his manner is sarcastic.

"Then where?"

"I don't know."

I ask others, but they don't know either.

Startled, it dawns on me that none of these men know where they are or how they got here. Others enter, but they don't know either. The line of people at the phone and the men on the phone all had the same idea as me. We discuss our predicament and discover we have something in common. All of us had been sleeping, but woke up inside this place. We don't know where it is, how we got here, or how to get out. Then I wake up.

In the successful online video game, *World of Warcraft*, players connect from their home terminal to a group of servers. The servers maintain a constantly updated "image" of the WOW universe, which is visible to all players simultaneously. Using this system, a player may run into friends, enemies, or strangers within the game, but only while they are online. At other times, their characters are dormant, just as we are when we sleep. This design is analogous to what I saw in the dream.

I have run into "sleepers" in dreams before, like when I communicate with my mother in a dream while she is also sleeping. In this dream, I have run into a crowd of lebengeists who are strangers to me and that I have no interest in speaking with. We have nevertheless all arrived at the same location and in approximately the same cloud of confusion. Prior to the group of "sleeper" dreams, I hadn't thought about whether or not one sleeper could meet another in a dream. I had a vague idea that each dream environment was totally unique to each dreamer, and that this alone would make congress between parties impossible. Thanks to this dream and others like it, I have developed the opinion that there is a stable common environment that lebengeists may visit as a group, and that it isn't just an accidental meeting place.

DB21/38, 12/28/07

A woman is talking to me. Her manner is so urgent that I noticed it before I notice her appearance. When I do look at her, I see that she is slender, with tight skin, about thirty, and African. Her clothes are bright yellow and green.

At first, I wasn't listening, but she said it was important I pay attention because either she or I would be waking soon and would have to attend to our bodily needs. Surprised, I asked, "When is your body going to wake up? How long do you have?" She ignored me and repeated her message.

She first establishes that she has the authority and the ability to communicate the message. Then she said that I was similarly situated with her. That is we both receive information while we sleep. She showed me a list of other people who have earned the same privilege. There are only about 60-100 names.

I didn't understand the next part of the message, so she points to a statement carved into a wall. There are three parts to it. The first part is a stylized English king's crown. Second is a name, either "Winston" or "William" or possibly both superimposed on one another. Third, something that is true of, or happened to, the first of these two kings, would be true of or happen to the next.

The name Winston makes me think of World War II, but Churchill was prime minister, not king. There was a King William, however, and it is possible the current Prince William will be made king.

Just before I wake, I hear beautiful choral music. Then, after I wake, I can still hear it for a few bars before it goes away, so loudly that I think it is coming from one of our neighbors. I went downstairs to ask Kitty and Nina if they heard anything, but they hadn't.

To hold my attention, this woman reminds me that both of our bodies were sleeping at the time, and that either one of us might have to go at any moment. This acknowledgement by a lebengeist in a dream that she is indeed a lebengeist was amazing to me.

There is a strong suggestion made that one's bodily needs have a priority override that will instantly cutoff any activity as a lebengeist. If the body must wake, the lebengeist must return immediately. Because of this, I have had a number of dreams where I must get something done just before my body wakes, or as in this example, someone else's body wakes.

If linear time is an illusion, why would this matter? We could take forever, if need be, to discuss everything we wanted, and then could pop back into our respective bodies whenever we liked. Instead, we had to focus because either one of us might vanish at any moment, as if our time stream was coincident with the one we experience on waking. It felt like we'd left the main ocean of time-free information, to pursue our waking bodies by canoe up a small tributary that, the closer it came to a body at a certain time, the more linear time became. As our experience of time became progressively more linear as we approached the time our bodies would wake, the more subject to it we became.

The symbol message given to me in the dream may refer to any of several people: William the Conqueror, William of Orange, Winston Churchill, and/or the current Prince William. There are many things "true of" these men, so to isolate any one incident or quality doesn't make much sense, apart from one thing: The first two Williams were kings, and Prince William may be made king. At a minimum, I think the dream suggests that Prince William will be made king, though why it would be urgent or important to know, I have no idea.

If the lebengeist in this dream had not identified herself, I would have identified her as a servo spiritus because of her awareness of my sleeping state and the nature of her message. Even now, I am tempted to do the same thing, and in so doing to reveal that servo spiritii can definitely be lebengeists also.

DB5/432, 6/8/99

A series of earthly trials are laid out before me like a video game. At any point along the path, it is possible to step out and experience an earthly existence and its difficulties. While there, as with a video game, you may either go for a "high score" by finding all the nooks and crannies of the experience, or you may instead seek to gain direct passage to the game's ultimate goal [God]. The latter can be faster, but is much more difficult to accomplish.

At first I am curious about things I see on the way, but grow gradually less interested. It is at this point that I become aware of the nature of the course and can see that there are people who appear periodically and dash around all the obstacles in any given area. If these people, who are like gurus or spiritual teachers, are followed, the path can be navigated more quickly.

Until I saw this, I had only scattered knowledge of individual earthly trials, but now I saw how they fit together into a comprehensible experience that is much larger than any one life. As soon as I have this realization, a guru appears as if from out of hiding. He'd been there all along, waiting for someone to notice him. As soon as I spot him, he takes off through several trials. He moves many times faster than everyone else, but only because he moves straight from start to finish while others meander around all the curious inducements of the road.

I follow him through many earthly trials and incarnations, after many of which he stops in at a wayfarer's tent. It is erected just off the course and about midway between the beginning and the end. A sign on the door indicates that answers are to be found inside. My guru is not there, but has gone back to help others who are struggling with their trials. There are many sleepers like me in the tent.

A sign directs me to have some tea. After pouring some for myself and taking a sip, I become aware of an older woman who accepts payment for it. She says something about Chairman Mao misleading many people during his lifetime and as she says it, his name and portrait appear on the coin I give her.

She tells me that the tent and the metaphor of our earthly trials as a video game-like layout was the idea of the guru who led me to the tent. He is so far removed from the ways of the mundus limus that it is difficult for those who are below him in knowledge to understand his meaning. For this reason, he set up the wayfarer's tent and asked this woman, who is but one of many servo spiritii, to be here to explain the dream when I arrive. My impression is that she is a lebengeist I have met before.

After she tells me all this, I realize I am not in my body, but in the plane of the spirit, as a spirit, or in the mundus alo as a lebengeist. I see others around me that I assume to be recently deceased todgeists. An old woman looks at me and says "Isn't it wonderful!" I share her happiness and give her a big hug. Over near the tea table, there is a man and woman with a baby. I think they are all Scottish, and, like the old woman, recently deceased. Like me, they don't seem to know what's going on before talking with the guide, so they just follow the instructions on the signs. I wonder how he and his family died. As I wonder this, I think of things I've done in this life that need repenting or making up. As these thoughts press in upon me, I wake up.

The description is short, but this is a big dream. At the time, I worked long hours at my new job at THQ, and wasn't inclined to spend time writing notes in the journal.

The "earthly trials" referred to are entire lifetimes loaded with a variety of challenges. I saw them in great detail, with nothing missing. In my first big dream, the scenes appeared like popup ads in an Internet browser. Here, it was like looking at the flat outline of a great tree lying on the ground, where every leaf is a life, and every branch and twig a series of actions taken within and between lives that lead from one to another.

Like a real tree trunk, the "trunk" of this pattern led straight from root to tip of the "tree." If not for the powerful inducements of the lives available on either side of this path, it would be simple to reach the tip of the tree, which is the ultimate goal of the exercise. I didn't see anyone who was able to do it, not even the gurus.

Everyone is drawn away, in varying degrees, to become lost in the thicket of physical experience. This isn't necessarily a bad thing, because to find the tip of the tree through experience allows a spirit to arrive with knowledge it wouldn't otherwise have. There was some risk, however. By taking any of the innumerably branching paths that led to this multitude of experiences, a spirit risked never finding its way back to the primary path and to the ultimate goal. One could gain experience from the lives, but couldn't indulge too much without risking becoming forever lost.

This is where the gurus came in handy, because they could help bring a wayward spirit back to the main trunk of the tree, where they could continue on their way.

DB4/59, 9/4/90

I become fully conscious of the fact that I am sleeping. I think, "Oh, I'll remember this for sure, everything is so clear, much more so than when awake!"

Now I am brought to a place that is so beautiful that it is very difficult to describe. Its purpose is the spiritual replenishment of its guests, whether they are todgeists or lebengeists, like myself. The first thing I see are two enormous ornate entrances, each with a long ramp leading up to it. The structures are suffused with an inner radiance that I cannot see with my eyes, but fills everything with warmth and clarity. The brilliance of this light is beyond what would be comfortable to view without a visor or sunglasses, yet it is mild and soothing.

I enter with three others; an old man, a young man, and a woman. As I pass through the gate, music washes through me. It has such beauty, graciousness, strength, and love that tears spontaneously well up in my eyes and pour down my face. Nothing I have heard while awake compares to this music. It is powerful but gentle, harmonious and richly varied, all-pervasive but non-intrusive. It is like angels singing a song of limitless love and gentleness for those of us who are there and whom they pity and love.

After passing through the gate, I find myself in an anteroom. Signs in every conceivable language dot the walls, and the spirits in this room speak a wide variety of languages. We all understand each other, and I can read the signs, regardless of the language. Food is laid out for us to eat before going forward, like small crackers on spoons. A boy here has arms of unequal length.

I am overcome with sympathy and give him a hug, but he doesn't notice because he is busy examining the cabinetry upon which the crackers have been placed.

After we have had some food, a servo spiritus greets us. He takes us on a tour of the facilities. As we walk, I see many hundreds of cells containing lavish gardens. Signs hanging near these gardens say that they represent a comprehensive collection of gardens from every time period and of every category. One sign says that a "witch" has been put into the corner of one garden. I look in and see her. She is doing something to help the plants, like a gardener.

The guide takes us outside to see something specific. Once we leave the "building" we are above the earth and some distance away. Even so, I can see it very clearly, including any detail I direct my attention at. We stand on a promontory that overlooks a certain place on earth.

Everything on earth and the planet itself is very physical, or material, in a way that I hadn't noticed before. It is like everything is made out of the same material, regardless of whether we would identify it as being wood, stone, water, air, or something else. From here, it is plain that everything in the mundus limus, is made of the same substance.

We could see differences between objects, but the difference between water and stone was like a color difference between two different paint chips. They are both paint, but the color difference between them is enough to discriminate one from the other. Another thing about all this stuff is that is heavy and difficult to manage. Our guide could maneuver around physical things and interact with them without difficulty, but the rest of us required assistance to do the same.

The "vision" is of a plain around a city. Partially toppled buildings lie between rusted-out machines of war. My understanding is that this is a view of the future result of a war.

After seeing all this I come back to my body and wake up. The dream was more "real" than anything I've experienced while awake. Throughout the entire dream I was perfectly aware of the fact that my body slept while my spirit was free, active, and conscious.

This dream shows how information in a precognitive dream may be acquired. While sleeping, a lebengeist goes to this location in the mundus alo. Once there, a servo spiritus directs their attention to this or that event in the future. Some remember clearly, others remember only fragments, but regardless, more than one person will wake with a dream about the same subject.

When I think back on the sensation of what "matter" was, heaviness was its most striking quality. That, and the fact that absolutely everything in the mundus limus was made out of it. It is this dream that inspired me to use the term "mundus limus" to describe the entirety of the physical universe.

So far, we have seen that dreamers meet up with one another in the mundus alo while their bodies sleep. In the Texas dream, it seemed like a random collection of unacquainted, uninterested parties. In the dream of the African woman with a message, it was just the two of us. With the wayfarer's tent and this last dream, the specific identities of individual lebengeists were irrelevant because they weren't present together to converse among themselves, but to meet one or more servo spiritii who could only be found in the mundus alo. The meetings, though not random, may appear casual, but this is not the case.

DB16/104, 9/2/04

I think of some people I met at the 1994 SIGGRAPH conference in Orlando, and wonder where they are now. As soon as I have this question in my mind, it is answered. I see that we all have appointments to keep, like at the conference, and then to move on, like so many individual trains going their own way. We always have someone with us for a part of the journey, but who that is may change often.

The schedule is relentless, with no time to rest. I see one section where I have the camera debt (a reference to an expensive lease I had). I see the debt, and then right on schedule it is turned off and I have to meet another train. The station is reached by passing out of the mundus limus to the mundus alo.

When I get to the train, I pick up an assignment. Once I have the assignment, I have to go back to my life and accomplish it. When finished, I meet the next train and am given something else to do. It is important to always pick up the assignment, to meet the train on time, complete the assignment, and to catch the next train. This requires split second timing and an all out effort. Each task is urgent because I have to finish in the right place and the right time to meet my next train.

Here I am told that my assignment is done and that I have to pick up the next one from the train. Beside the train are some boxes full of art supplies, some portfolios, and an easel. I understand that I am to use them to get to the next train at some distant point in the future.

At the time of the dream, I had just left a career in the CG animation industry, and had just started showing my paintings in galleries. When the time came for me to meet my next "train," I found myself teaching art in Europe. Looking back on these career switches, it is clear that each of my activities led from one to the next. If I hadn't done the things I did, I wouldn't have found myself here now, or in several of the other places necessary to get me here. In the context of the Satterwhite dream, where split-second timing was necessary, this dream is credible. It is more than that though, because it clarifies a question I've had for a long time: are our meetings in the mundus limus pre-arranged? According to this, they are.

DB21/27, 11/17/07

I am on my way somewhere when I come across a number of large mushrooms growing in front of a narrow slit between two enormous rocks. There are beautiful woods all around me, while this crevice between the rocks is overrun with thorny brambles, but for some reason I want to go through. How to do it is beyond me, because the opening cannot be more than a hands-breadth wide at the widest. I give it a try regardless and get through.

On the other side, I became instantly aware that I am dreaming. Other lebengeists are here too, and we all know we are dreaming. There is a train platform before us, and a train is due to arrive soon.

I recognize some people from when I am awake, and others from here in the mundus alo. I have a continuous memory of running into these people on a regular basis while dreaming. We all do whatever we are supposed to do in the mundus limus while we are awake, and then are sometimes called together here when we sleep. I remember all of this in a rush, at the same time remembering specific meetings, in the mundus limus or the mundus alo, with many of the lebengeists I see around me. Some of them I meet in one place or the other exclusively, others I meet in both. Some I haven't met in the mundus limus yet, but will later.

While waiting for the train, I see someone who I want to talk with. The train comes before I reach him and we both have to get aboard. He gets into one car, I board another. Nina and I board together, but do not sit together. It feels great to have my memory back and to remember not only previous visits with these people while we slept, but why we do it.

We get information on the train, all of it useful, and coordinate our waking lives here also. This is so exciting that I start talking with other passengers about it, "Isn't it amazing that we came here while our bodies sleep, all together, all for the same reason, and then we all get something valuable from it and separate?" I was amazed, but happy too because I had forgotten about this place for a short time.

Then a servo spiritus starts talking. Everyone immediately knows they are supposed to be quiet, prompting them to cease their conversations and listen. He asks all of us to look at a piece of paper, a copy of which appears simultaneously in everyone's wallet, or pocket, or whatever they had. We are supposed to look at a part of the little paper or ticket, the part its owner is meant to fill in. He said something very specific about this that I thought was very interesting. Just as I tried to remember what it was so that I wouldn't forget when I woke, the train stopped and we all had to get out.

Unfortunately, I didn't do a very good job of remembering the important message. For me, the dream was interesting enough without the message. It explained several things I hadn't understood, one of which was *how* do we arrange our meetings in life? The simple answer is that we arrange them in the mundus alo, either on our own or acting on suggestions by others.

*Chapter Fourteen*

# Lessons and Teachers

In sleep, servo spiritii sometimes give me lessons. They can be private or group lessons, with other lebengeists participating with me. This happened for the first time in 1987.

DB1/7, 1987
Swami Satchidananda picks up my "meditation box," a box made of wood, like a cigar box. Light from inside escapes through gaps in the poorly made object. Unlike mine, Swami Satchidananda's meditation box is beautifully crafted. It has no avenue of escape for the light it contains other than the lid. He opens the lid as a demonstration. Light from inside emerges in a finely focused beam. He teaches me how to make one and then gives me his as an example to study.

This is a typical example of the role symbols play in dreams. Unlike literal dreams, which can be more difficult to interpret, the use of symbols makes them clearer. They are like logotypes, where, for instance, the concept of a friendly hamburger restaurant is represented by "the golden arches" of McDonald's. With that symbol, a building that might not otherwise be distinguishable from any other, suddenly becomes a familiar place with a history.

In a cipher, a message is reorganized and added to in a purposeful effort to destroy any hint of the original content of a message. The end result is a complex mess of characters. With a symbol in a dream, what would otherwise be complex is reduced to something simple, as here with the meditation box.

Until this dream, I didn't understand meditation. Closing my eyes was the part I managed the best, but after that I was lost.

"Think about peace, calm, serenity..." (to use a popular example). How? My mind wandered, without direction. Once I saw the two meditation boxes side-by-side, with my inattention represented by a leaky box, and Swami Satchidananda's ability to contain and control his thoughts represented by a secure one, I understood. The boxes and their meaning were in no way obscure. Almost anyone reading this would have grasped it right away, as if it had been a magazine advertisement.

The point is that if it is difficult to understand a symbol in a dream, then it isn't a good symbol. Another important point is that not everything in a dream is a symbol. I have not mentioned any dream symbols until this part of the book, but have described close to a hundred interesting dreams. Dream books tend to imagine symbols where there are none, or to assume that entire dreams are nothing more than a collection of symbols. In my experience, the use of a symbol or multiple symbols in a dream is a creative choice made by someone communicating a message. If you see something directly in the mundus limus, you won't run into any symbols because there aren't any. Nothing is being communicated to you, you see whatever is there.

In a visit, as long as the subject of the visit is awake and going about his business, you are also unlikely to run into any symbols. Todgeists will not use them to show you how they died, because it is so much easier to just show you. Symbols are a special type of language that is used primarily for higher order communications, the kind of thing you can expect from a servo spiritus. Even then they may not resort to using them if it isn't necessary. In my experience, when I hear others talk of "symbols," like falling, or a pack of dogs chasing them, these are poor reporting, nothing more. True symbols are rarer and tend to be easy, rather than difficult, to understand. Consider the following example:

DB9/39, 6/6/01
Someone gives me some allegorical advice in the form of

common dictums known to be ridiculous. One concerns the purity of metals. It says that only the most purified and exclusive of metals should be saved, and all other forms of it could be wasted.

The reason this doesn't make sense is that the purified form of the metal cannot exist without the raw form. If all the raw ore were discarded, there would be nothing to purify and therefore no pure form of the metal would exist either. The spirit who says this to me clearly desired that I understand the metaphor as it applies to humans.

He says there are four different steps to the refining process. They form a closed loop that renders the existence of any of the metals' purification stages impossible without the others. Without adulterated metals, there is nothing to clarify. Without raw metals, nothing to process. Without processed metals, there is nothing to make alloys from. Without alloys, there is nothing to temper. Without finished tempered metal, there is no example available to understand the value of ore.

This describes why earth has good, evil, and a gradient between them. It shouldn't be taken to mean that evil must be tolerated. Clearly, it is meant to be refined, obliterated in its present form and made into something better. This may be done by the influence of the good that exists in the same environment, or by the trials of life, culminating in successive incarnations, each of which is another stage of the refining process.

Not only is the meaning of the symbol apparent in this dream, it is actually pointed out by the servo spiritus who communicates it to me. The difference between a message that is communicated with symbols and one that isn't is stark:

DB21/7, 9/24/07
A Japanese man points to the stars above us and says, "In youth they twinkle with life, wonder, and inspiration of God. As we

age, we think we know better and forget. We watch movies that assume a different origin for the universe. Before we know it, we've not only forgotten God, we've become ashamed of our former knowledge. This is an evil thing.

All things that contribute to our loss of wonder at God's miracle have sinned. To restore knowledge and wonder is an obligation for those who can, and an obligation I accept. You lost your wonder at creation once, and are now only beginning to restore it. How much more alive the stars and other things of creation are when you see their origin. Look on them and do not be afraid of what they are or how they were made. Fear only the one who made them and be thankful you can see again."

The "Japanese man" comes across as earthbound in a way that is not true of most servo spiritii, leading me to believe he is a todgeist. The message is complex, and delivered almost entirely in words. It is clearly stated, but its length requires greater effort on my part to remember than if he had used symbols.

The "visit" dreams are also called "out of body experiences," or "OOBE's." An OOBE is when a person's body is unconscious but their lebengeist is free to act independently of its body. In this condition, it is possible to visit friends, family, strangers, and distant locations. It is also possible to visit the mundus alo, but this ordinarily would not be described as an OOBE because it cannot be verified by observations made within the mundus limus. My principal objection to the term "OOBE" is that it does not recognize that a lebengeist, when free of its body, is not constrained to the mundus limus, but does freely visit other non-physical locales as well. Despite this objection, it is sometimes the best term to use, because it so ably describes how the lebengeist is made free to roam:

DB1/9, 1988

Swami Satchidananda in a gothic church. He says, "It's time I showed you how to come out of your body." He then pulls my astral body loose from my physical body. The sensation is exhilarating. Then he says, "Maybe you aren't ready for this yet." I wake immediately.

DB2/14, 2/14/90

I am trying to sleep when a helper appears nearby to help me get out of my body. He first gets my legs free by bringing my astral knees up, and then I feel like I am in two places at once. At first my twin centers of consciousness are close together, but then they move farther apart until I can see my body lying on the bed.

The sensation of leaving my body is like an electric current followed by separation. Once free, I can go wherever I want, but if I think about it too much, I wake up instead. It was difficult to calmly allow the electric vibrations to wash over me, but I had to or the excitement alone would wake me. Calmness of mind and steady focus were required.

In other dreams, I noticed a servo spiritus present when exiting my body. Whether or not their presence is required to effect the separation described here, servo spiritii are with us all the time, or nearly so. When they are not present, they will come if a mental request is made.

What did Swami Satchidananda's mean when he said it was "...about time" he showed me how to leave my body? Just like the many dreams of the future, where I seemed to be putting each foot, one after the other, into pre-existing footprints, this statement made it seem that even in the mundus alo there was a carefully managed timeline.

Just as Swami Satchidananda shows me how to leave my body, in the next dream I am taught to do something practical:

DB1/129, 1/18/90

The spirit of someone who reminds me of the late clairvoyant Eileen Garrett takes me to see a 'Dr. Marini', who wants to conduct a few experiments. The object of one experiment is to disrupt the electricity to my apartment. I am very excited to have him teaching me in the use of my psychic skills, and would have liked it to continue much longer.

I woke immediately after this dream, in the early hours of morning, to the sound of our appliances suddenly turning on. I learned there had been a power outage for our entire block that night. When power was restored, our appliances turned on again, and the sound woke me up. I had to wonder if the outage was related to the challenge in the dream. Given some other things that have happened, like the healed thumb or the jumping painting, I can't rule out the possibility, though it may sound incredible. If true, it may be the only example in my journal of a physical effect that can be linked to something I did in a dream.

In one dream, I had an opportunity to hear the answer to a question about the nature of time. Here is the exchange:

DB14/103, 9/16/03

A servo spiritus is asked, "Is it possible for an event to take place before the instigating event?" He answers, "Yes. Because matter by its very nature has no knowledge of time. It is therefore not restricted by it." Knowledge of time is a device to prevent the impression of simultaneity.

Matter is not constrained by time because it has no knowledge of it. It is a queer paradox that knowledge of one thing can blind us to knowledge of another.

The theme of linear versus non-linear time comes up often in the dreams. Why is the illusion of linear time so important? What is it for? Do we understand things better, because we have seen each slice of its maturation over time? Is the illusion of free will caused by the illusion of linear time? Without it, we would be able to see the entire history of anything, from past to future. There would be no surprises, and perhaps we would learn less from the experience of being human.

The quality of "being human" is discussed in several dreams:

### DB5/442, 6/18/99

A servo spiritus appears and directs me to a magazine titled *Living*. Another servo spiritus asks me to read an article in it if I want to know how our spirits are bound to our bodies. The article shows the process happening, and it is more cooperative than expected, because the spirit influences aspects of the body it will occupy as it is formed.

The magazine is an invention of the two servo spiritii to help me remember the dream and to answer my question. It was like an encyclopedia of information about the process of becoming attached to, or associated with, a body.

### DB21/6, 9/23/07

Someone says, "Yes, a human body is indeed complex, but knowing this, and knowing that it is a complex machine of a kind does not mean that its secrets are available for sale like one of your machines. What secrets it has, will always be secrets to men."

### DB2/17, 2/16/90

The last thing I hear before I wake is a compassionate female voice saying, "Children sleep very hard in life." The "children" she refers to are the people of earth, "sleep" is what we would call our waking lives, "hard" is what it is because of our separation from God, and "life" refers to our incarnated existence. The statement implies the promise of something much better when our earthly trials are complete.

These words have stayed with me since I first "heard" them in this dream, reminding me of the challenge and reward of my experience in the mundus limus. Both previous dreams are what I call "waking messages" because they are delivered immediately before I wake, making them easy to remember. What I take from these dreams is that there is a purpose to our lives, and the purpose is worthwhile, or we wouldn't be willing to give up so much of our spiritual lives to undergo it.

At the same time as the teachers explain things to me about life in a body, they give me lessons as a lebengeist, to hone the abilities I posses in that state also:

DB3/78, 7/6/90

A beautiful girl and her brother swim nearby. She is training her second sight to see auric colors accurately. She keeps her eyes closed while creatures swim against her and she calls out, "These are violet, still several shades to go before black." She offers to include me in the training if I say "yes." I agree, but when she names colors, I have a hard time seeing what she is describing. To me it is all black.

This is the first of several dreams where I am taught to see auric colors. In later dreams, I see them quite clearly. At first I expected rays of light, like in Proto-Renaissance paintings of halos. Instead, they are a miasma of ever-changing colors that float around a person in three dimensions. Within them, all sorts of information may be found; scenes from that person's life, their health, emotions, and moral character. The colors can change fairly quickly. In one dream, a woman spotted some money lying on a sidewalk and bent to pick it up. As she did, her colors changed to reflect her avarice.

In this dream, the teacher described where each color began

and ended, and what the difference was between adjacent colors. This was all to help me discern the differences myself, but her sensitivity to these colors is greater than mine. The colors in question belonged to extremely low order spirits and were consequently so dark to me that I couldn't distinguish between them. Learning to see these differences was, however, good practice.

Just like any school in the mundus limus, there are exams in the mundus alo:

DB4/38, 8/14/90
Suddenly, the town I am in becomes all dry and dusty like a ghost town. As I walk around, I am told that everything in sight is an illusion and that I am about to experience proof of the difference between "objectified existence" and "reality."

I am chased out of town until I reach a desert-like beach. A bunch of attractive models cavort nearby. I think of a loosened swimsuit, and immediately one of the models' swimsuits slips and she has to catch it. In fact, anything I think of immediately happens. A voice continuously reminds me that everything I see is an illusion. At one end of the beach is a huge rectangular structure jutting fifty feet out of the sand. It is made of a smooth, flat material without handholds.

The voice tells me that my objective is to get to the top of the structure. This is an important test and a puzzle. To give me incentive, ocean waves start crashing up against the platform and me. I try to ride the waves to the top, but they don't even get close. Then the models in swimsuits start coming towards me and some bandits approach from the other side. The voice lets me know that I am supposed to solve the puzzle before they reach me. Then I figure it out. Because everything is an illusion and everything I imagine immediately becomes real, I imagine a flight of steps in front of the platform. They instantly appear and become part of the illusion. I then race up to the top and the test is over.

In "exam" dreams, I am given challenges designed to test many things, in this one, to trust the power of imagination in the mundus alo. In another, I was told to enter a castle and make my way to the top of a tower. Along the way, I encountered numerous distractions. I ignored them all until I happened to spot what looked like the profile of a beautiful woman. I continued going up the steps, but then my curiosity got the better of me and I went back. At that point the test was over, and I had failed. I hadn't even been told what the test was, just the goal: to reach the top of the tower.

This reminds me of the numerous "aiming" exercises I have had in dreams, and the exams that go with them. To succeed, I have to imagine the target struck by my projectile. No amount of aiming can accomplish the result. To get a strike, I have to "see" the desired result in my mind and then release the projectile. As if I needed to be reminded of how powerful imagination is, I had this dream:

DB16/90, 8/6/04

I try to explain something to someone else, but he doesn't get it, so I asked him to imagine that he doesn't have forearms. This was by way of example, so he would understand what I was saying. Unfortunately, because we are in the mundus alo, as soon as he thinks of it, it happens. I am then told that even in a dream I must be very cautious what I do, say, or think because the results are immediate, even if unintended.

In America, criminals are punished only *after* they have physically committed a crime, or have in some other way committed *to* the crime in a physically demonstrable manner. People are not punished for their intentions, but their actions only. Consider this dream in that context. In it, a careless suggestion had an immediate and shocking result. Imagine what would happen if it was the same in the mundus limus. The mundus limus, with all of its problems, suddenly looks like a kind of "safe" playpen, as spirits learn to control their thoughts by first learning to control their actions.

DB15/60, 1/27/04

I am at a "University" where the classes are all on spiritual subjects. A woman mentions an extensive database of information about me. I'm amazed that the school would go to the trouble to assemble so much information, so she points out exactly how many gopher holes are on the grounds, how many gophers live in the holes, which gopher holes have chipmunks or other creatures living in them, and what individual hopes and aspirations each gopher has. When I ask how she came by the information, she indirectly replies that the "University" is responsible for all the inhabitants of earth.

I thought the concept was interesting, but considered it a one-off, like so many other dreams that would describe some fascinating idea, and then I'd never dream about it again. This dream stuck in my mind as the "gopher" dream instead of the "database" dream. The error of this was highlighted in another dream about seven months later:

DB16/91, 8/7/04

Someone shows me around a part of my house that I'd never seen before. He shows me rooms, passages, and so many other things that I am amazed. He stops in a great library to show me the facility. He says I can come here any time to find information on anything I want to know.

There is a large "staff" to service those who need it, day or night. A man in an enormous kitchen offers to make me whatever I want. Near the kitchen is an enormous garden with giant vegetables. I eat there, while watching some rabbits munch on the greens.

Kitty and Nina are sleeping, but I want them to see this place, so I drag them out of bed. Kitty remains asleep as I take her and Nina around. This time, I discover even more, including a huge pool of totally pure water. Nina and Kitty fall asleep and disappear, leaving me alone.

Right about then my grandparents Paquette [both deceased] show up. My grandfather came first [died in 1998] and waited for my grandmother a while [died in 2003.] Now they are together and look wonderful. Both have brilliant auras that are beautiful to look at. I am then made aware that they will be leaving now, almost as if I won't see them anymore.

As I wake, I hear a voice say "My house has many mansions."

The dream started in my house, but then traveled from the mundus limus to the mundus alo. I didn't notice the transition, making it feel like the mundus alo library was contained within the mundus limus house. This was an error. Next, when I dragged Kitty and Nina into the dream, only Nina was "awake." This meant that Kitty could not wake within the mundus alo, at least not during this dream. Nina thought the environment was amazing for the time she could remain awake inside the mundus alo, but then she "fell asleep" also and disappeared.

I have "awakened" within dreams and "fallen asleep" within them as well, but this was the first time I'd ever seen it happen to someone else. What was the difference between Kitty sleeping in the mundus alo, and disappearing from it? Because she was there while sleeping, it is apparently possible to be brought to a location as a lebengeist *while unconscious*. This reminds me of other dreams where I've been asked to awaken within the dream, and have. Prior to that, was I there, but unconscious? Nina was asleep at first also, but it was much easier to wake her. When she could no longer sustain the effort to remain, she vanished, just like Kitty. My inclination is to believe they did not wake up physically then, but went back to whatever they were dreaming at the time.

The Servo spiritus who showed me around made it clear that the library and other facilities he showed me, were there for lebengeists during their body's sleeping hours. Lebengeists (and probably todgeists as well) were welcome and encouraged to visit at any time. He told me that if I ever wanted to know something, all I had to do was come to this library. It never closed, is always staffed, and happy to serve. More than that, the library was just a part of a much larger complex, the purpose of which was to support and nourish anyone who came here.

This was the last dream of my grandparents, who finally left the mundus alo, together.

The libraries described so far are strictly within the mundus alo. This next one could be considered part of the mundus limus, if you know how to look:

DB22/37, 11/15/08

A woman is asked to get some information by entering a small boat and traveling in it down some narrow, shallow, well-manicured canals. The information sought is something she can only see from the boat. On both sides, lush plants drip lazily into the water. Butterflies and other small creatures populate the air.

As the boat travels, I become its sole occupant. I travel through this fairytale landscape for a time, looking primarily at the small flying creatures, when the boat either enters a large marble building or the landscape becomes covered with so much architectural marble that I have the impression of being indoors. Either way, the space is vast, but I am now surrounded by carved marble banks covered with books in the middle of an enormous ancient library.

Looking more carefully, I see that the landscape is the library, and the library is the landscape. Each thing, each butterfly, each blade of grass, is like a book. All the information about each of these things, even transparent things like the air in the environment, is written out in a book-like form as part of the object itself. The information is comprehensive to a degree I'd never thought of before. How many books could be written about a blade of grass? In this environment, the creation and life of each blade is recorded, its statistics, the larger plant it is a limb of, most of which is beneath the soil, its relationship to its neighbors, what it looks like to the visual sensory organs of other creatures, everything that could be possibly known about it, is there. It was a matter of looking at the objects as information or as objects that allowed me to switch between seeing the library or the landscape.

# Chapter Fifteen

# Helping Others

Throughout the pages of my journal, I receive help. The dream in Amsterdam may have saved my life, the dream of being married to Kitty helped me through a rough part of our marriage, I got my art back in time to fix it for *The Atlantic Monthly*. and I even had a blister on my thumb heal right before my eyes, on request. My questions get answered, and I am shown wonderful things. Occasionally, there are hints that I might be of some utility to others, just as others have rendered assistance to me.

DB2/14, 2/14/90
...I keep feeling the presence of a servo spiritus named Michael from time to time, telling me if what I said was right or not, directing me where to go, etc. I begin to realize in the dream that I am asleep.

Now Michael wants me to go to a certain bar in a rundown part of town. I go in wondering if I am supposed to order a drink. I don't want to but consider doing it because that may be why Michael directed me into the bar. Finally I realize I just can't do it and instead tell the bartender that I am going to help ease his guilty conscience. He had been a bartender for ten or twenty years and during that time contributed to the corruption of many people by encouraging them to over-indulge in alcohol. Now that he is dead, he wants to make amends.

He agrees to let me help him, so I make his liquor stock disappear from the store and then direct him to seek out and aid, in whatever way he can, all the drunkards he can find. He is grateful for the advice and immediately leaves the building to begin his new work.

It is amazing to me how often I find myself doing exactly what I am supposed to be doing at the same time as I try to remember what it is that I am supposed to do. This dream is very much like the incident with Kitty's glasses in that respect. Just as I walked directly to our table in the living room and scanned the room from that location, wondering why I was there, I entered this bar without a clue. And yet, I must have known something or, just as when I looked down and noticed Kitty's glasses, I wouldn't have noticed this ghost who needed some help. Without knowing that I was being guided to do so, just as I retrieved Kitty's glasses, I gave this todgeist practical advice designed to assuage his conscience.

I imagine that he would have "haunted" any drunks he found, and made attempts to either frighten them away from drinking, or encouraged them to spend their time differently. I wonder if he's still doing it? Or maybe he's moved on since then? It would be interesting to know.

This is similar to the drowning man dream, where I also think I was trying to help a todgeist. Many of my todgeist dreams involve me helping them in some way, but usually it is to pass a message to someone in their family. This is unusual because it involves healing this todgeist's conscience.

## DB5/12, 5/14/91

I feel like a "family guest" at a house in the country. An old black woman, about eighty-five years old, is here, preparing to die. She walks outside and sits in the rays of the brilliant morning sun. After I observe her sitting there for a little while, I notice that her body lies inert on the grass, but she is standing beside her body looking very happy. I say, "There, it wasn't so bad, eh?" or something like that. I take her by the hand and we float over the countryside and talk about how no amount of money would have been enough to convince her to live in a city because the country is so beautiful.

This is a "moment of death" dream. I have had quite a few of these, and the script is always the same: someone dies, and I am there to help ease their passage from the mundus limus. In these dreams, I feel a bit like an aide at a nursing home. Instead of giving a tour of the recreational facilities, my job is to explain that the person has died and encourage them to leave the life behind. Whatever concerns they had are over and they need to concentrate on the next phase of their existence.

This message varies depending on the person, because sometimes, as with the bartender, the "next phase" requires that they remain in the mundus limus for at least a little while longer.

### DB5/64, 7/5/91

I am with a man in need of my assistance. His grave and tombstone are directly in front of me. He has occupied the grave since his death in the nineteen fifties. He was a criminal during his life and felt so guilty and ashamed that he stayed in his grave all this time as a todgeist. My help is necessary to get him out of the grave so that he can move on with his spiritual journey.

He tells me that he operated a forge in his last life, but wants to be an artist now. This may be why he attracted my attention, because I am an artist. Whatever the reason is, we talk as I try to get him to leave his grave behind so that he can do something productive with his existence.

After this scene, there is another where I say good night to, and tuck in, several persons. Of the dozen or so people involved here, most are children. One girl complains about nightmares, "I've had bad dreams, but I don't remember them," she says. One of these dreams is of her future.

My exact impression of the second scene is that I am helping these people back into their bodies, just as other servo spiritii have helped me into mine when it is time to wake. At the same time, I give them some encouragement just before they wake, which happens to be the time they are most likely to remember anything they've seen or heard in a dream.

The criminal in the first scene is a bit different. I don't know what his crime was, maybe I misheard him and he was trying to tell me he was a forger. Maybe it was worse. Whatever it was, it makes me think of the death penalty. The irony of the death penalty is that it could just as easily be called "the reincarnation penalty." It does solve the immediate problem, but because it is only the body that dies while the spirit lives on, it's a bit like removing warts without killing the virus that causes them. With the criminal in this dream, whatever his crime was, it was appalling enough that his todgeist had spent about fifty years haunting his own grave. This could not be allowed to continue. Just like Kitty's glasses and my assistance to the bartender though, I didn't know *why* it couldn't continue. From my point of view, I was there and there was a service to be rendered, so I gave it. How I happened to be in a position to notice is a question that never crossed my mind.

### DB4/4, 7/11/90

I am to receive psychic instructions regarding something I am supposed to do for a certain person. The instructions mention reincarnation and the idea that I have been prevented from taking notes until "the appropriate time." There is something about a skill dormant from a past life that will be exercised soon.

A voice talks almost nonstop and I am supposed to write everything it says. A man will be healed by following the instructions taken down in my notes. Unfortunately, although I carefully wrote it all down in the dream, when I woke, I had forgotten the details.

In this dream I am told that I have been "prevented" from taking notes about something for a period of time. This implies that information interesting enough to record was known to me, but I wasn't allowed to write it. Like the question of *why* must todgeists move on, both imply a larger order or design that dictates what must be done, and *when*. The *why*, if it is ever explained, is less important than completing the work when it is meant to be completed.

DB5/551, 11/1/99

It seems like I'm in a very real game where I enter a world (this one) but it is an illusion, even though it is a completely convincing one. We all have missions to fulfill in the game. In my case, there comes a point where I have to take a gun from someone to prevent something bad from happening, but I do it as a spiritual helper.

I cannot literally take the weapon because I am a lebengeist, unable to touch material things. This is not such a great limitation as it may sound, because I can give the man plenty of hints as he goes on about his life, giving him a simple, straight-forward set of instructions for the accomplishment of his goals, but he doesn't hear me very well, or maybe he just doesn't want to listen. Everything I say is designed to improve his life and to keep him away from the gun incident in his future, but he doesn't pay attention and misses some of my cues. The result is that he becomes a participant in a shootout. An Uzi machine pistol is involved and a man is shot in the abdomen many times by this weapon.

This dream makes me think of the illustration for *The Atlantic*, because another spirit could have used an identical method to accomplish that goal for me. In this example, I am reminded of how much we lose because of human insensitivity to the generous invisible support that surrounds everyone at all times. In my case, I was somewhat aware of it, and it has come to my aid on many occasions. With others, particularly those who purposely turn a deaf ear to their "conscience," they earn only trouble.

DB15, 10/2/03

I meet up with a very pleasant older woman, like the English servo spiritus from the wayfarer's tent dream. She asks me to accompany her to a little cafe for some tea. When we arrive, she gets our tea and sits down. She asks me about a troubled young man she expects to find here. She is worried about him and wants to help. He works at the cafe but hasn't been seen in a few days.

Finally he comes in, but he doesn't look well. He talks with the woman briefly, telling her he'd been treated badly so he was hiding from his boss. He says a few things about his life that make me feel a profound sympathy for him. At that moment, the woman and I simultaneously reach out to embrace him. As we do, he breaks down emotionally and sobs. He wants the protection of Christ, the love of God, and asks Jesus for his protection and love to shine on him too. It is a beautiful moment.

Every time I see this particular servo spiritus, some kind of drink is involved. There are at least five dreams with her in them, and at the beginning of each one, I am offered a drink. Usually it is tea, but once it was sake. On each occasion, I wasn't aware that I was in the mundus alo until I had the drink. The drink itself operated like a post-hypnotic suggestion by causing me to wake up within the dream. My perceptions became unclouded, I could see that I was asleep, and recognized those around me as spirits.

I didn't feel like I was all that helpful on this little excursion. It felt like a training mission, where I was allowed to accompany this woman as she rendered assistance to the young man. Because he was able to see us and interact with us, my first instinct was to conclude that he is a todgeist, but the things he had to say make me wonder about that. As a todgeist, I would not expect him to be asking for "the protection of Christ." This is the kind of thing a living person would say. For this reason, I think he is a lebengeist that we contacted while his body slept.

To the boy, he would have had a dream of two servo spiritii, a young man and an older woman (with an English accent), who expressed compassion for his plight and gave him some spiritual sustenance and encouragement.

## DB12/75, 1/31/03

I am at an airport on my way back to the US. A government contact comes up to me and tells me that we are both sleeping and he wants me to go with him somewhere. He brings me to some rundown buildings in Afghanistan. My guide enters a building with a large courtyard and I follow him inside. He stands in a hallway examining numerous jars. I go over and see they are filled with brightly colored soaps, perfumes, and other things with pleasant odors. He suggests I smell one, which I do. Smelling the spices has the effect of waking me up inside the dream, just like the small drinks offered to me by the British servo spiritus.

Now the man asks me to follow him to a poignant scene: a rundown room with a small group of people in it. There is a doctor, a sick girl on a bed, and her mother. The doctor says something about changing the girl's diet to help her, but I can tell by looking at her that this will not help. The man, who I now know is a servo spiritus, invites me to enter. As I do, I know what must be done.

I put my hands on the girls' shoulder. A strong green light comes from my hands and flows into the girl. As it does, the signs of her sickness vanish bit by bit until they are gone. Afterwards, she is standing and well again.

Next, we are in a large building somewhere else. There is a large population of sick young people here. There are two in particular that I am supposed to heal. One is here because he knows of me, the other was here to begin with. I go to the latter first. He is quite sickly, possibly with a serious skin disorder. Again, I put my hands on him and talk in a soothing manner on all sorts of distracting topics. I talk about anything but the healing. Again the green light comes from me, through my hands, and into the boy. Before my eyes and those assembled here, he is restored.

After finishing with him, I walk over to my next subject. He is watching television, but when he sees me, he moves away from the TV and the others who are also watching it. He is aware of who I am and why I am here. He is very nervous. I put my hand on his shoulder to help calm him, but he knows this is how my cures are effected, so it tends to make him more excitable, not less. I can see the green light moving into him, so I decide to leave my hand where it is and not worry that his mental excitement may interfere with the cure. I keep him engaged in light conversation, but all the while he is keenly aware of the bit-by-bit destruction of his sickness.

I've had between six and twelve of these healing dreams where I see green light flowing through my hands and into the person who is sick. It is never any other color, and it always works the same way. I also had a dream that I didn't understand at the time, where the green light was put *into* my hands. In it, a servo spiritus massaged what I thought was a green dye into my hands until it was completely absorbed as she talked about healing.

DB18/111, 6/9/06

During a conversation with a man, I am told that in a later stage of my life I am meant to perform many healings. The time he speaks of is "nearer than you think," he says. I see my own aura, and it is bright.

There is something else I am supposed to do besides healing, another type of action that will be considered equally amazing, but because I am so surprised to be told that I would heal people, and the other item was more or less expected (by me), I've forgotten what it is.

My overall impression from the dreams in this chapter is that I am serving a spiritual apprenticeship in the mundus alo, where servo spiritii, both lebengeists and freigeists, either show me how to do things, or bring me to places and people to test out what I've learned. They stand by to observe, possibly to intervene, though I don't recall that ever happening.

The statement that the time when I will heal people is "nearer than you think" means almost nothing to me. I've had many dreams reveal themselves as true visions of future events, but sometimes the time lag is so great, over a decade in some cases, that I am not going to hold my breath waiting for this to happen.

It is intriguing to see how often I perform "work" as a servo spiritus while I dream. On those occasions, it is difficult to see how the person or todgeist I come in aid of would see me as anything other than a servo spiritus myself, just as I see Swami Satchidananda as one also. How often, I wonder, is a person referring to a lebengeist acting as a servo spiritus when the words angel, spirit helper, guardian angel, or spirit guide are used?

*Chapter Sixteen*

# Guided Future

The difference between a literal dream of the future and one where a guide is present is huge. In one, I must struggle to determine what I saw and heard, and in the other, everything is explained clearly. Most of the best correlations contained in my journal come from dreams where a servo spiritus brings me to a place and shows me something that will happen later.

DB0/12, May 1, 1988
I walk down a wooded path with Swami Satchidananda, founder of the Integral Yoga Institute. I want permission to live at his ashram in Charlottesville, Virginia. I have been studying yoga at the IYI center in New York City and want to get better by studying at his ashram.

Swami Satchidananda listens to my request politely but says that his ashram isn't appropriate for me. He says "Here, I will take you to the ashram of a friend of mine. If you enjoy it you may stay. If not, you won't like my ashram either." After he says this I have the feeling that the Swami expects me to last about two weeks before leaving. Right about then I notice that I am standing on the driveway leading to this ashram he spoke of, and Swami Satchidananda is gone. I walk up the driveway with the intention of moving in and then later moving on to the IYI ashram in Virginia.

I pay some money for the stay and then proceed to settle in to the routine at the ashram. I experienced everything, from brushing my teeth to sleeping, chores, and conversations. On one day, I cleaned toilets and then looked out a second floor window at laundry being hung, mundane in many ways, but very real. I have good days and bad days at the ashram, but the overall impression is that I don't want to stay here. After two weeks, I leave.

Swami Satchidananda waits for me at the gate. I beg him to let me live at his Virginia ashram. He smiles but indicates a 'no'. He looks in the direction of Chicago and then New York. He said I was from the former and belong to the latter. I get the impression he thinks I will start a successful career in New York City and will have no time for ashrams and yoga before long. He says that if, when I am fifty and my career over I still want to live at his ashram, then I am welcome to. At the same time he expects that I will never take advantage of the offer because I will be too busy with other things.

After waking from this dream I refused to believe that I wouldn't be able to live at the IYI ashram in Virginia. I wrote a letter to them, requesting residency. They replied with a letter describing requirements I couldn't satisfy. About two weeks later, I was checking out a new yoga studio in Chelsea. On my way out after a class, I saw a picture of their ashram on a wall. It was the ashram from my dream.

The ashram wasn't too far away, in Woodbourne, New York. A couple days before I left to go there, I dreamed of someone who told me that we were good friends from another life, and I would be meeting him soon. He said he had lived in Alaska.

Within a week I was at the ashram, and two weeks after that I was desperate to get out. The experience of living there reminded me strongly of my dream, but it's hard to say for sure because I didn't write it down.

I do remember one scene in particular that happened; I was washing toilets in an upstairs bathroom when I looked out the window and had a conversation with a woman hanging out the laundry below. Simple, but the sense of déjà vu was uncanny. I felt it the whole time I was there, but my memory of specific events from the dream was fuzzy, so it never went beyond feeling 'familiar'. I decided to end my stay because I spent more time bagging sprouts than practicing my yoga postures.

A week before I went home, The swami of the ashram had a big audience with everyone. He made several pointed remarks in the direction of one person in particular, a physicist named Richard, who was at the ashram for the weekend. On the following day, I ran into him lacing his boots just before he caught his ride back to New York City. We talked for a few minutes, and discovered that we lived only a few blocks apart. With that, we exchanged numbers and agreed to meet for chess when I got back. We became friends, and sometime later, I learned that he had lived in Alaska for a short while.

As Swami Satchidananda suggested, I did leave the ashram and stopped practicing yoga. I focused on my career, got married, and had a family. If someone asked me to live in an ashram now, I wouldn't want to.

The differences between this dream and any of the literal dreams of the future from earlier chapters should be obvious. Unlike those dreams, I did not have to fumble my way through the scene trying to figure it out. Every step of the way, I understood what was going on. Not once did I have to look at some object and try to figure out what it was. The key is in the context. Swami Satchidananda told me before I went in that it was an ashram belonging to a friend of his. With that information alone, I could figure out the rest. As soon as I know it is an ashram, I know what to expect from the building and all the activities there make sense. Somehow, the presence of a guide is enough to restore my knowledge of *what things are*. Without one, a dream is like looking at an example of Modern Art and wondering if it is meant to be a cow, a refrigerator with legs, or an automobile with an especially large hood ornament.

The only trick to knowing the difference between an ordinary dream of the future and a guided tour of it, is identifying that there is a guide. With Swami Satchidananda, it is easy, but it isn't always that way.

DB4/238, 3/3/91

I go through something like a tollbooth with a woman. After we pass through, we are in a totally different place. We come to a very hilly landscape covered with extremely beautiful gardens. Now I see that this woman is British. She points to her part of the garden. It has blue and white flowers set off by an abundance of green. She points out a stand of what appears to be an example of every tree variety on earth.

After the garden, two men bring me to the British woman's home. One of the men is an officer; the other is a Chinese helper. One of these men pours me a small glass of what I assume is either sake or strong beer. I take a sip but it is very strong, so I hand the remainder to one of the men. After drinking from the glass, I am aware that it is a special dream and it is important to remain alert to remember any valuable information.

Next, I am brought to the kindly British woman again. She looks between fifty-five and sixty years old and has white hair. She gives me some advice regarding my talents and gifts. She explains that I should focus on these abilities for maximum benefit and exploitation.

She says that I am gifted in painting with oils (fine art) but that my efforts in comic books will be blessed. She says that my pay will be "doubled and doubled." For this reason, she says I should focus on comics entirely for the time being and worry about painting later in life.

She had nine points, blessings, or pieces of advice, but I feel myself waking just as she is giving them to me. Then, as I am supposed to leave (along with some other lebengeists that are with me) she instructs the Chinese manservant to give me a copy of a comic titled *Wildflower #1*, to ensure that I remember the dream. He then leads me and two or three others down a flight of stairs to a little mudroom where he and his son prepare to take each of us to where our physical bodies are sleeping.

I did not become a successful comic book artist, but my work in comics helped me get a job at Epic Games as a 3D artist and I was successful at that. At the time I had the dream, the most I'd ever earned in a single year was $15,000, not a sum that many would brag about. My next job paid double that, the job after that paid more than double the previous one, and a few years later, I'd more than doubled that figure again.

I identified the British woman as a guide based on her behavior. At first, there isn't much to arouse my suspicions, though the toll booth, or barrier, is something that occurs in many dreams when I pass from the mundus limus to the mundus alo. Without any other information, it can be ignored. The next item of interest is the drink. After drinking it, my awareness is enhanced, specifically in relation to the dream. Anytime I notice an awareness enhancement, I start thinking in terms of the mundus alo. The next thing that happens is that the British woman speaks to me directly without any prompting. I only get this kind of direct communication from spirits. If this were a visit to someone who was awake, she wouldn't have been able to see me. She isn't a todgeist, because if she was, she would be too self-involved to pay attention to my concerns. Once I know this is a "guided" dream, I know it is probably true, as it turned out to be.

In the dream of the ashram, I was shown a series of events, as I would literally experience them. In the dream where I am told that my income would "double and double," I am given a fact, described verbally. No symbols are used in either dream. This is better than an unguided dream, but dreams that do include symbols can say much more with much less, and this can make them more interesting.

DB5/125, 9/8/91

I am shown a "fiasco" involving visiting Soviet officials and their US counterparts.

The American representative is seated, greeting a short line of representatives from the Soviet Union. When the American reaches out to greet the first Soviet in·line, he discovers that instead of a hand, the Soviet man proffers a monstrous several foot long claw. When he shakes this in lieu of a hand, he is dismayed to discover the fragility of the claw, which proceeds to break off. Underneath, an even more hideous appendage is revealed in its place. When he tries to shake the Soviet's remaining "hand," the second appendage is likewise broken off and falls away, revealing an even more hideously deformed claw. After going through this spectacle three times with the first Soviet official, it then happens again, also three times, with the next official in line.

The Soviet Union was in the news often around the time of this dream, thanks to Mikhail Gorbachev and Boris Yeltsin, both of whom were vying for control of their country. In the United States, the news portrayed the difficulties of the USSR as the result of democratization efforts, the inevitable birth pangs of a fledgling democracy. Overall, the coverage was friendly to the Soviet Union. My dream on the other hand, showed menace behind the friendly gestures.

Recent years have shown, with events like the assassinations of political reporter Anna Politkovskaya and FSB officer Alexander Litvinenko in London, that the Cold War is still on, albeit in a new form. Large-scale military incursions into former republics like Chechnya and Georgia, and the attempted assassination of Ukrainian president Victor Yushchenko make clear that, at the very least, the new Russia isn't a great deal different from the old.

This dream didn't say anything about a specific incident;

instead, it provided a little play in symbolic form that expressed skepticism of Russian claims at the time. Based on later events, this skepticism appears to have been warranted. It is included with other "guided" dreams because it is symbolic. For a symbol to be present, it has to be made by someone. If I see something as it literally is, there is no need for another party. A symbol, however, is an explanation left by an absent author. This implied presence is assumed to be a guide because the nature of the message is to inform. Another thing I have to keep in mind is that when servo spiritii show me information, they make an effort to get out of the way of whatever they are showing. This makes it difficult to remember that they were present, even if they were.

The three primary types of guided dreams are: a tour, a statement, or a symbol. The ashram dream was a "tour," the "doubled and doubled" dream was a "statement," and the Russian claw dream is a "symbol." In the next dream, although no guide is present, it also, like symbolic dreams, has all the hallmarks of being a constructed message.

## DB4/65, 9/10/90
On a beach. Kitty and a female relative are nearby, but not near enough to see. I look up into the sky and see an amazing vision.

It is a sign of some kind, like when people saw ghost armies in the sky over battlefields during World War I and World War II. It's a military group of Native Americans dressed in ceremonial clothes. Some stand to the left of the sun, while others lie prone to the right of it, hundreds of them, eyes closed, as if dead. The vision is in vivid color and richly detailed, leaving nothing to the imagination. The patterns on their clothes, the texture of their skin, the many grey and black hairs on their heads are all distinct. The vision is connected to the current conflict with Iraq.
I want Kitty to come see it, but when she comes over, the image

fogs over and rain begins to fall. The vision vanishes behind all this weather, leaving nothing for her to see.

My impression from the dream was that US and coalition forces would quickly overtake the Iraqi army, despite frequently stated fears to the contrary that were common in the press at that time. This came to pass. Four months later, on January 16, 1991, the air offensive Desert Storm was initiated. By February 26, Iraqi troops withdrew from Kuwait. Only 100 hours after the ground campaign was initiated, a cease-fire was declared and Kuwait had been liberated.

I interpreted the dream as an indicator of success for US troops because that was the result, however tragic, almost two hundred years ago, when they warred against the native tribes of North America. This dream is what I call a "vision" because it is a single static image of epic scale. Visions like this are very rare for me, occurring perhaps two dozen times in the last twenty years.

More recently, I had another dream that compared American troops and the native peoples of America. That dream was different:

DB22/63, 2/25/09

An old man talks to a group as if we are children. He shows the Indians driven away by European colonization in America, then the wars raged against them by the fledgling US Army. "They thought the wind that drove their enemy before them was raised by them, was powerful because of them, and was for their glory. But the inheritors of that generation will soon see that the wind sowed a different seed, not of glory, but of their own destruction. The wind is returning, it is the same wind, and they do not know it. I know this because I am Methuselah, and I have seen it."

Then I see similar scenes in Israel with the Arab conflict.

In this scene I don't see the vision that "Methuselah" is describing, but he saw something, and it does match my definition of a vision from the way it is described: a returning wind of destruction. The symbol is excellent and easy to understand. Its scope, typical for a vision, is epic. I call dreams like this "reports." They are not "statements" because they refer to a vision, or in other cases, an event experienced by the speaker.

The name "Methuselah" is in quotes because I have no way to verify who this dream character is. This is the name he gave for himself as I heard it, but perhaps he was giving the name of the Shawnee tribal leader Tecumseh and I misheard it, or maybe I heard him fine, but he isn't *the* Methuselah. I use this convention frequently in my journal. Unless I have good reason to think an identification is correct, I put any names in quotes. Sometimes they check out, often with some slight spelling variation, sometimes they don't.

In most dreams, I am not told why certain things are shown to me. Sometimes, I get a hint:

DB7/7, 5/31/00

A servo spiritus shows me some scenes as a privilege. The first scene is of a school for Asian kids. There is something special about the place. Next there is a battlefield. People are slaughtered all around me. The servo spiritus reminds me that I am seeing this as a "favor." Although I see Americans, the overwhelming sense of the place is that it is Asian. I sense traditional antagonists Japan and China all around me. A group of American soldiers is disciplined for bad behavior. I am amazed that I can traverse this territory unscathed, but as a lebengeist, I am safe.

There is a hillside covered with the bodies of the dead and the dying. I see spirits leave their bodies here and there as they die. Many of the bodies are civilians. The servo spiritus presses me to look around at the carnage, but I am distracted and don't pay attention.

By "distracted" I mean that the carnage around me is so horrifying that I don't want to look. Despite this, the servo spiritus encourages me to do so anyway. He says it is a privilege to see these events, and that I am seeing them as a "favor." What kind of privilege or favor could he be referring to? There are times when I have a question on my mind when I go to bed, and then I have a dream where a servo spiritus shows me the answer, telling me as he does that the dream is a direct response to my unspoken question. For this one, I do not remember having any question that these scenes would answer.

A "favor" implies that it is an exception, but of what kind? A "privilege" has the same implication, a peculiar benefit, especially when attached to one's job. There are tantalizing hints of this kind spread throughout my dream journals. Taken together, they suggest that my dreams are not an accidentally discovered faculty, as I once thought.

In one dream, I have just seen a powerful vision, but Kitty, who is there also, cannot see it. This is just like the dream earlier in this chapter where my vision of the Native Americans is covered over when Kitty approaches, blocking her view of it. A servo spiritus explains why:

DB4/200, 1/24/91
...because Kitty doesn't say anything [about the vision], I get into a conversation with the servo spiritus about why that would be. As an example, he puts Kitty in front of me and asks if I can see him. The answer is no because he is behind me and beyond the range of my peripheral vision. This is why Kitty didn't see the vision also. He says that her "peripheral vision," or second sight, isn't wide enough.

Just as the governance of a large country requires the coordinated activity of many people, the activities of servo spiritii are coordinated also. In the dream where I accepted this life, I was shown every event in the life, significant or otherwise, and every ripple cast out by every action I would take. To accomplish the many events of the life, I had the cooperation of a large crowd of others, who in turn, I aided also. From the point of view of someone who is living through the events of a lifetime, it is difficult to understand how the pieces fit together, but when I was present with a servo spiritus as my life played out, I saw that all of the minutiae of life contributed to many other things in such a way that a multiplicity of objectives were satisfied across many lives. We don't realize it ourselves because we are just living our lives, but as we do so, just as a worm fulfils its purpose by simply living, we accomplish far more than we realize.

The ranks of the servo spiritii, at least some of whom are lebengeists, are there to provide support and comfort when needed.

# Chapter Seventeen

# 9/11

In 1989, eleven years before the 9/11 attacks in the United States, I had four dreams that referred to the attacks in various ways. On August 25th, 2001, I had a premonition that it was nearly time for these dreams to be realized. The dreams are not of the same type or quality, but they provide a good example of a "dream cluster," where several different dreams are relevant to the same future event. The first dream is a direct warning:

DB0/7, February 1989
I am in New York City, near Trinity Church, trying to get out of town. Everything is covered with very small, closely spaced tombstones and graves. What I actually see, however, are rocks and stones, like a tremendous pile of rubble from buildings suddenly crashing down on their occupants, crushing them underneath.

I am careful as I walk, not wanting to disturb any spirits that might lie underfoot. It is impossible though because it seems there is a person buried under every square inch of the area I am walking in. The next thing I know, there is a ghost chasing me.

He looks like a skeleton and carries a sword. I assume that I stepped on the wrong grave somewhere and run. But, no matter where I go, another skeleton pops up. I try to get to the New Jersey side of the river, but just as I make a dash for it, another skeleton pops up and slashes me in half with a flaming sword.

To my astonishment, I remain standing, though confused. The skeleton unlocks his jaws and speaks to me in a voice like rusty chains being pulled against each other. "That was your astral body I cut with my sword," he says. "If you ever return to New

York City to live, your physical body will die as well, in the same fashion as all the others." The skeleton then glances over to New Jersey, indicating I will be safe there, and I wake up.

This dream frightened me on a scale close to that of the Porgy dream. It was so powerful that, although I thought it was silly to take it seriously, when Kitty and I were forced to return to the New York City area for financial reasons, I insisted that we live in New Jersey instead of Kitty's choice, Manhattan. This was close enough to our clients, but we wouldn't "live" in the city. I hoped that the distinction between frequent visits to the city and "living" there would be enough.

The dream is more literal than it is symbolic, but the "skeleton with a flaming sword" is a "symbol," regardless. My concern about ghosts probably flavored the appearance of what was a servo spiritus, there to give me a warning. Either that, or he wanted to be sure I remembered, and picked an excellent guise for that purpose. By telling me that he had cut my "astral body" but it was my physical body that would be in danger if I remained in New York, he made a distinction that at the time of the dream I hadn't considered. This statement also made it clear that this was not an ordinary dream.

## DB2/67, 4/3/90

I am in New Jersey getting gas, thinking how lucky it was, that I decided to live in New Jersey instead of Manhattan because some kind of disaster had demolished it. I remember my Reade Street loft near the World Trade Center and how it was destroyed. I think of my New York City skeleton dream and know it refers to the same incident as this one.

In the actual disaster on 9/11, my Reade street loft was not destroyed, but it was in the disaster zone of buildings that were roped off by police. Other buildings that I had business in nearby, like the loft of photographer Diane Blell on Church street, was destroyed, by an engine from one of the planes as it smashed through the building.

DB3/20, 5/17/90
A disaster has happened recently in Manhattan. I assumed it was an earthquake based on the type of damage. Others in the dream say it wasn't an earthquake. It was caused by bad people, explosions were involved, and there were captives or hostages somewhere. None of this made sense to me, so I continued to think it was an earthquake.

From the beginning, I am aware that: 1) A disaster like an earthquake has happened, 2) Disaster status is extended to the city, 3) Friends and relatives pour into the city to get their loved ones out if they can be found.

A disaster management committee deals with the crisis when I interject, "You mean it wasn't an earthquake? So those were explosions? It sure seemed like an earthquake to me, that's amazing how you were able to create that effect, how did you do it?" They don't answer, leaving me to my confused ruminations.

Next, I am on the street outside at the site of the disaster, which is well below forty-second street. Many buildings are only partially intact on the lower floors. Tremendous amounts of wreckage from fallen buildings, crushed cars, and just about anything else you can think of, litter the streets. Street lights are inoperative, only a few cars are in working order, the roads appear to be buckled and are cluttered with debris.

*Fig. 17.1, Ground level wreckage, from the journal, May 17, 1990*

I am near two men who discuss an engineering problem related to the disaster. Many of the neighboring shops are damaged and I can see frightened people clustered inside them. Many of the city's residents are now buried under some former skyscrapers. I don't see any intact windows near me, all were shattered in the disaster. While the two men talk, the older one suddenly yells a warning. I turn and see a massive wave full of water and debris coming from the West.

*Fig. 17.2, Wrecked buildings and a "flood," from the journal, May 17, 1990*

Everyone who had been milling about start running from the wave, which is truly huge. I hear many shouts of "Run! Run!" When the two men reach the corner, they see another wave coming up that street from the South. They had to run twice as fast now to get ahead of that wave before it cuts off their escape. The waves collide in the intersection, quelling some of their force, but not enough to prevent them from advancing further up the city's streets.

Many people and an incredible amount of debris are caught up in the waves. I assume that at least some were killed or injured by this devastating force, but pay more attention to survivors than the bodies I sense lying broken in the streets.

Most of the people I see seem cold and are shivering, as if it is winter. I don't see any vapor breath, ice, or snow, nor are the people dressed for cold weather, but it still seems like winter for some reason.

The images from this dream are clear and strong and resemble my skeleton dream from 1989, where a disaster occurs in the Trinity Church section of Manhattan. I believe the two are related.

From the day I woke up from this dream, just like the short one from the previous month, I connected it to the skeleton dream. This dream, though literal, was almost as powerful as the skeleton dream. I only rarely change my plans because of a dream, but I did in reaction to the skeleton dream by moving to

New Jersey. After this one, even though we were safe in New Jersey, I first bought earthquake insurance, then took Kitty on "vacation" in Virginia, just in case. When we came back and everything was the same as we left it, I was surprised. I remember this feeling washing over me quite strongly just after we came out of the Lincoln Tunnel and headed south towards our old apartment on Reade Street and I saw the World Trade Center and some of the other tall buildings in that neighborhood, all unmolested.

This dream, and the skeleton dream that was connected to it, convinced me that something would happen. For the first and only time in my life, I actually sent warnings to various people I knew. Two went to the New Jersey mentalist, The Amazing Kreskin, because we were conducting an experiment at the time. The first Kreskin letter is dated May 17, 1990, the same day as the dream. In it, I write, "I am also enclosing a dream that I had tonight which I feel very likely to be precognitive, it is one of a large body of dreams on the same subject, the first of which was experienced during the month of January of last year...." A copy of the dream was also sent by mail to Dr. David Ryback, with the code "A45" written on the envelope to identify it.

The second letter to Kreskin, and the dream it described, is less interesting than the dream of May 17th or the skeleton dream, but it did have one part that had the hairs of my neck tingling. It starts with a telepathic conversation between us, on the subject of one of my "disaster dreams." To my knowledge, the only two I had at that time are the skeleton dream and the one of May 17, so it is probable that these are the two he is referring to. He complains that my description is to too symbolic, and wants more details. I drift away after this and see the following: A group of billiard balls rests on a shelf. The shelf slopes a bit, causing two balls to roll off, the "9" and "11" balls, in that order.

Over the years, I occasionally thought of the two primary

dreams of this group, the skeleton warning and the earthquake/flood dream of May 17, 1990. Eleven years later I would see what they meant, but first, I had a premonition.

August 25, 2001

Kitty and I planned to take Nina to Legoland to celebrate her birthday, but I woke in a truly foul mood, like nothing I'd experienced before. I didn't know what was bothering me, but whatever it was didn't make me nice to be around. On top of that, I had a headache that was worse than anything I'd ever experienced. I didn't want to ruin Nina's birthday, so I explained to her and Kitty that they should just ignore me. I expected to feel better at Legoland, but my mood and the headache only got worse the closer we got.

At Legoland, I could barely stand the pain in my head. I took a couple of Motrin tablets, but they were ineffectual. I did my best to pretend that nothing was wrong, but was not successful. Luckily, Nina liked the park so much that she wasn't overly distracted by me.

Legoland has rides interspersed with many tableaus built of Lego bricks all over the grounds. One section resembles an African jungle. It has amazingly realistic gorillas, giraffes, monkeys, elephants, and other animals, all built out of Lego bricks. Another reproduces major sections of San Francisco, including the Golden Gate Bridge.

By the time we got to the "San Francisco" part of the park, I wanted to tell Kitty that she could meet me in the car when they were done, because I needed to lie down. I started to say it, but then I saw something that stopped me in my tracks: the New York City tableau. As soon as I saw it, I knew that my headache and my mood were related to my skeleton dream and the May 17, 1990 dream about a disaster in lower Manhattan.

"Where's the World Trade Center?" one of us asked, because Legoland had built everything but the World Trade Center.

"Maybe it was too big to build it to scale," I suggested. "You know what, Kitty?"

"What?"

"That dream I had in New York about the earthquake that isn't an earthquake, it's going to happen soon, I know it."

My headache left me then, and the oppressive feelings I'd had all day were gone. The rest of Nina's birthday went without a hitch. On the way back I said it a couple more times for good measure: "Kitty, remind me to look that dream up when we get home, because it's going to happen."

At home, I pawed through my journals until I found it. It was easy to locate because of the distinctive drawings on its pages. One drawing is of a pair of twin skyscrapers that have toppled, leaving only a few jagged walls at their base. Another showed a multi-story wave of debris rushing down the streets. I still didn't know what to make of the dream though. It clearly described an immense disaster, but nothing like it had happened yet.

September 11, 2001

Two commercial jets are purposely flown into New York's World Trade Center by terrorists. Within ninety minutes, both buildings have collapsed, in each case causing a huge wave of debris to race down nearby streets. Over the next few days, many surrounding buildings collapse and up to a hundred others are found to be unstable.

One item from the May 17 dream journal entry is inconsistent with the attack, and a few items are misleading but not inconsistent. In my journal I clearly describe "a flood." The description of this "flood" and the drawings of it closely resemble the debris cloud racing down the streets as each of the two towers collapsed. It looked like a tidal wave, exactly my impression in the dream, but the two "waves" of debris did not collide, because the two buildings they came from collapsed twenty-nine minutes apart.

In the dream, I was aware that others around me referred to the disaster as having been "caused" and that "explosions" were involved, but I did not believe that the destruction I witnessed in lower Manhattan could have been caused by bombs. An earthquake was a more likely cause, and that is what I wrote. I was careful to note that this was my surmise based on what I saw and that this opinion conflicted with what I overheard from others inside the dream. In all, I think that without knowledge of the planes, my confusion makes sense. The rubble strewn streets in lower Manhattan are far more reminiscent of earthquake damage than what I had seen of previous explosion damage, like the Oklahoma City bombing. That had a local effect on one building and a couple of shops across the street. Until the events of 9/11, buildings of this size had never been destroyed before.

As for the "explosions," each plane exploded on impact and have been described in the media as "flying bombs." Numerous sources compare the impacts with a 2.0 earthquake as measured on the Richter scale. My impression that "hostages" and a crime was involved is true of the hijack and intentional destruction of the buildings. I can easily see the impression of "winter" coming from the sight of people and rubble covered with white dust and ash.

There is one thing about the skeleton dream that I never wrote down, ("conveniently" a skeptic might say), but I'll share it regardless. It seemed insignificant at the time, not worth mentioning, but here it is: at the beginning of the dream, I could still hear in my ears the fading echoes of an airplane passing by overhead. The roar was like an echo, but powerful enough to permeate the environment so totally that I couldn't shake it free of the dream.

## Chapter Eighteen

# The University

The Mundus Alo is the primary location for higher quality dream interactions. It is staffed by responsible servo spiritii, who are on call at any hour, on any day, to help when we need it. The compassion and generosity expressed by this arrangement is truly beautiful.

Many of the servo spiritii are the lebengeists of people alive in the mundus limus at this very moment. The compassion and generosity so poignantly expressed in the mundus alo, is often expressed by people that populate our waking environment. How many of us participate in this kind of activity?

In our souls, we may be better than we know, but it is up to us to improve ourselves, to refine and temper our thoughts and actions, to learn how to outgrow selfishness and become not just compassionate, but able and willing to assist others. A baby that never matures will always be loved, but will never take over the family business when its parents retire. We are meant to learn how to look after each other, and one way we do that, is to enter the mundus alo while our bodies rest, and provide selfless service to others, according to our capabilities.

The servo spiritii are not perfect, that is if my own example is enough to judge this by. I tried to free a todgeist from unnecessarily reliving the death of his body by attempting to persuade him he was dead. I failed in this effort, and if I can fail, so can others. If I can say "I think you should have it," and a servo spiritus interprets that as an invitation to drop a painting on Kitty, then not everything is perfect in the mundus alo, just as not everything is perfect in the mundus limus. Just as we work in our physical bodies to improve ourselves, we do the same in the mundus alo also.

The mundus alo improves the clarity of our vision, if not our understanding of things. It is populated by servo spiritii who are available to answer our questions. As I was told in a couple of dreams, there is a library, with information on anything I could care to know. It is available to all spirits, at any time. If the lebengeists, todgeists, and servo spiritii already knew everything it contained, the library would be redundant. It is needed because there is so much to learn. If I can be a servo spiritus, or indistinguishable from one to the casual astral guest of the mundus alo, then who is to say that the very same spirits who guided me through the facility don't occasionally avail themselves of it? I don't need to know everything about the place to show someone around, just as a museum guard doesn't have to be a master artist to keep an eye on the paintings.

The mundus alo is like a college or university. Some training is required to gain admission, but enrollment is not equal to achieving perfection. Upperclassmen give assistance to underclassmen, but they haven't graduated yet either. Mistakes are made, but the students make fewer of them than before they were accomplished enough to enroll. Above the upperclassmen are the professors, who have a pretty good idea what the curriculum is for, how each student is performing, and what is required to help each person achieve his or her educational goals.

All of these grades are represented in my dreams of the mundus alo. From a student, like myself, to a professor, like Swami Satchidananda. In between, there are gradients, like the English woman and her tea, who may be an upperclassman, or the Indian guru, who might be like a research professor: he knows more than a lot of the other teachers, but because he has very little contact with students, his communication skills are weak. Todgeists, like the inevitable ne'er-do-wells that sometimes accrete near the boundaries of a university, wander the halls, dipping into classes every once in a while, unsure whether to stay or go. Some stay and become students in good standing, others wander back to the mundus limus as poltergeists or haunts.

The mundus alo university even has its equivalent to a mundus limus athletics program; death-defying obstacle courses that require the exercise of confidence and mental focus as if they are muscles. Ultimately, just as a university is designed to help a student achieve a goal, to get from here to there, it is a way station, a between-place, a place to nourish and educate and then to eject to the next phase of our careers as spirits. This next place is the mundus sublimis. Some call it Heaven.

*Part Three*

# Clarity

## Mundus Sublimis & Mundus Divinus

## Chapter Nineteen

# The Book

DB16/49, 4/29/04

Allen Ponziani brings me to a doorway that is a portal between worlds. I go through, and immediately lose track of him.

Now I am with Kitty and Nina. We are guests in a ramshackle apartment. I'm grateful we have shelter, but ungrateful because of its poor condition. I wear a monk's habit and sleep on a worn-out straw mat. I look out the window at the street below and see about twenty people, all dressed in costumes reminiscent of medieval clothing, playing soccer. They all look rich and happy. I want to be with them, not in this threadbare apartment in dreary clothes.

Even as I think it, my surroundings disappear and I am alone in a featureless place except for a large book on a podium. At first I think the book is blank, but when I drop it, I see there are words inside. When I pick it up, it levitates upwards, carrying me with it. When I shut the book, we are gently brought to the ground.

Some of the people I'd seen in the street (who had since become my friends) walked in on me now. I showed the book to them. "Why, it's blank." one man says, but then a very odd thing happens. He continues looking at the Book as if he understood there was something odd about it. Then, the pages filled with words, page after page after page of information on absolutely everything. The words overflowed the book and cascaded out of it like an unstoppable waterfall of information. It filled the room, the world, and the universe itself with all this information. But it wasn't just information.

The words *were* the things they described. They made the things they described at the same time as they recorded what they were, why they were there, how all these things behaved together, and what their histories were and their futures would be. The viewpoint wasn't limited to a small or large scale, subatomic or galactic, but included every scale, from every perspective. It didn't stop with simple descriptions of all these things, but went on to explain the workings of the world and universe itself at the very same time that it was the blueprints for the universe and all it contained. Intuitively I knew it was all correct.

There were records on every person who had ever lived, was living, or ever would live. I saw my own file and grabbed it to read later. Even the glimpse I had was enough to know that the file was total; nothing was missing. When I grabbed my file, I noticed another thing: Every person in this place was subject to the rules of He Who Wrote the Book. "The Book" might sound like a Bible to some, but it isn't even close. A Bible is written for mankind by other men. This book was written by the author of everything, and was written for his own purposes. It is his own record of things, some of which is in the Bible, but only a small part of the total is represented there.

Now that we had read it and somewhat understood what it was, we became bonded to the Writer, like servants. Now there were rules to live by and obligations to keep. We each had jobs designated by the Writer, as did all of his other subjects. The world wasn't worse off for all these rules, because the Writer, who I was very much afraid of, had made good rules. The basis for my fear was the total perfection of the Writer. Anyone who could make this book of everything, had power beyond my ability to understand.

I didn't like the idea of being subservient to the Writer, so I pretended he didn't exist. I knew he was there, and the people around me definitely knew it, but I ignored my obligations to him. I spent some time trying to enjoy myself while going around with a knot in my stomach because I knew that the

Writer was well aware of everything I did. I was surprised he hadn't taken notice, or done anything about it yet, because I knew from what I saw of his work in the book that he could very easily destroy me. I knew that he was benign, but he was also serious about his rules.

I ran into my friends at a modern but medieval-looking outdoor market, doing whatever it was they were supposed to do now that they were subjects of the Writer. I told them that they didn't have to be his mindless servants, that they were stupid to devote their lives to the jobs he assigned to them. I described how I did whatever I wanted, totally ignoring the Writer, having fun instead of slaving away for an invisible task master. I did not tell them how empty I felt, how lonely it was to "have fun," while knowing that I was violating my obligations, and the fear I felt because I knew I transgressed. Despite all this, I entreated my friends to drop what they were doing and go out in the world with me, free of their master's yoke.

As a body, they disagreed. They made it clear that they were afraid of the Writer also, probably more than me. They protest that they have to perform their obligations to him, that their entire lives are ordered and dictated by him, and that they don't mind. If anything, they derive pleasure from the service they perform. That surprised me. I thought they did their work out of fear alone, but they actually said they were happy to do it. In fact, they appeared to be happier than before they opened the book, when they played in their expensive clothes and hadn't a care in the world.

They went further and said that I should be afraid of the Writer also, and listen for my instructions because he is whispering them to me. They also said that if I didn't obey, I'd meet the Writer someday and he wouldn't be happy with my "job performance." The last thing they say is that I should not hesitate, but immediately "report for duty."

This is another big dream, in some ways, the biggest. To see all of the cosmos unfold in microscopic detail, its full history, its epic scale, the pattern of its making, its purpose, and to see that it is all contained by the single words used to describe each thing, outstripped all other dreams.

At first, it takes place in the mundus limus, when I see people playing soccer in a medieval street, but then, when I am in the space with the book, it resembles the mundus alo, and maybe it is, but I don't think so. Above the mundus alo is the *mundus sublimis*, or, "the world/universe of the lofty, raised, or sublime." Above or coincident with that is what I call the *mundus divinus*, or, "world/universe of the divine." The nature of this book and what it revealed is most consistent with the mundus divinus. Through the book, I witnessed the creation of the mundus limus, as if I was there to watch it when it first happened. It was sublime, but divine also.

I write "divine" and yet nowhere does the word "God" appear in the dream, nor should it. I did not see God, nor the Writer. The Writer is inferred from the existence of the book, which was clearly created by design, even if its author is not present. The Writer is, of course, "God." Despite this, and I knew it in the dream also, I thought of him as the author, instead of "creator," even though he is both. The reason is that he created everything out of words. These weren't ordinary words, but words of authority that commanded the things they described into existence. Within each were the means by which the commands could be accomplished.

My reaction to the book was total fear. It was like watching as the means of my obliteration approached, passed me by, and kept passing me by, near and yet not in contact, for so long that I had to wonder at my own insignificance. Why else would I be allowed the benefit of continued existence? I wondered this because I knew in my heart that I was not fulfilling my obligations to the writer. I saw him make me, just as he made everything else, and I saw the words of my life, words that described my duties, and knew that I wasn't following them. This is what I thought as I saw galaxies both created and crushed, *by words*.

Creation was organized and beautiful, but it was also powerful, fast, explosive, furious, and elegant. At any moment, by shifting my attention from one word to another, the entire vortex of blindingly fast expansion would stop, so that I could examine it in minute detail. Its music hung in the air, a fading memory of crashing waves and thunder organized by the most delicate musical principles, and then on they rushed again, released to continue until creation was complete, both in space and time. When it was complete, like the most perfectly crafted gem in existence, the book was done.

In the dream, my reluctance to follow the Writer's commands had nothing to do with whether I believed he existed, but that he was like an absentee landlord. He might show up and catch me goofing off when I am supposed to be on duty, but he was gone for much longer than he was present, so it looked like I could get away with shirking my duties. This was a false rationale, though, and I knew it. From the book, I knew that the Writer was aware of my every thought and deed, because they were all written in the book. There was no way to get away with avoiding my job, but I tried to anyway, even when my friends warned me of the ramifications. I didn't know what a poor performance review meant in the context of displeasing God, but it couldn't be pleasant, whatever it was.

Is it any wonder that I decided to go to church when I woke up from this dream? I was thirty-nine years old and might have been to church on about ten previous occasions that I could remember. My mother brought me to a few Catholic Christmas masses when I was a child, and Kitty talked me into a couple of boring trips to the protestant churches she liked. Once, Stella brought me to dinner at a church in Maine, where I learned that yams could be truly ruined by bad cooks.

After the dream of the book, I paid attention. I suddenly had a reason to reflect on all the old dreams I remembered writing down, but had ignored, that contained religious-themed information. Some of them described scenes from the mundus sublimis.

A little over two years after recording this dream, I had an unexpected surprise. When I wrote it down, I thought of the mundus limus material at the beginning as a junk dream. Then, when I came back into contact with my "friends" from the first section in the mundus limus, I paid attention to what they said without reflecting on the fact that they came from a part of the dream I had discarded as junk. Just as I hired the man I thought I would never be in a position to hire, in the month of July 2006, the mundus limus scenes from this dream became reality.

As an American, I had only seen examples of medieval architecture in person when Kitty and I traveled to Europe in 1985, shortly after we first met. The dream image of medieval and modern superimposed never made sense to me, so I discarded it. In the twenty years since that trip to Europe, the idea of moving there never seriously entered our minds. By 2006, however, with my career destroyed after becoming a whistleblower, I was willing to consider any opportunity to pay the bills. When an opportunity to teach in Europe came along, I took it. Soon after, I found myself in a rented house with borrowed furniture, sleeping on a threadbare mat (because the bed was too warm) in a medieval town founded in 1382. One day I looked at the street below, a medieval street, from my third floor window, and saw World Cup enthusiasts, in costume, playing soccer near a pub, it was the first scene from the dream.

As if the dream hadn't been scary enough, now I knew that the entire sequence of events that led to my arrival in Europe, were events that had to happen. I had been bitter and angry about what happened in Hollywood. I was the good guy but I lost the most. Now though, I saw that the events I was so bitter about, were the very things that brought me to Europe. Without them, my Hollywood salary and Hollywood ego would have prevented me from accepting any job as a teacher, let alone a job halfway across the world. The inconvenience alone argued against doing it. Indeed, when UCLA sent an email to Sony employees, trolling for teachers, I had turned them down flat. If I was willing to turn down UCLA, why would I go halfway around the world for less?

What it took were some extreme disruptions to my life, disruptions that simultaneously prepared me for my work as a teacher, work that I enjoy.

The last scene in a village market square hasn't happened yet, but I do have local friends here, and there are several village markets in medieval squares, so I expect it to occur someday.

A few months later, a loose end from the Book dream was cleared up:

DB16/114, 9/26/04

I am told of an apartment in a large brownstone that I may rent. I don't want to because it is too expensive. Someone insists that I look anyway. The brownstone is much more than it seems. A servo spiritus there shows me a layout of the house. Overlaid on this layout, he shows me that one may enter certain passages within the building to transit between the house and its counterpart in the mundus divinus.

They are different from traditional secret passages in at least two respects: they aren't concealed (though they aren't apparent either), and they don't allow passage from one discrete physical location to another. They are more like portals than passages because although either end of these tunnel-like sections does open on different places, they aren't connected physically.

I didn't understand this when the servo spiritus first said it, but figured it out later. He was really telling me that I had been brought here to go through one of these passages. I misunderstood and thought he was a realtor trying to explain the layout of the house. I did what he asked, but only because he asked.

He tells me to enter the passage alone. It feels quite natural to act on the suggestion, prompting me to do so as if it is my own idea. I barely notice any of the features of the brownstone itself apart from the clear fact that it is extremely large and there are some horses on a bridle path visible through a window on the ground floor.

Where the brownstone was a normal though inordinately large building, the passage was strange. It was both endless in length and so short the distance couldn't be measured. It was featureless, as if it didn't have any boundaries. I saw no floor, ceiling, or walls, but felt as if squeezed through a tiny opening. I had a sensation of time passing between entering and exiting the passage, but it was very brief.

There is an opening at the far end of the dimensionless tunnel. It is the interior portion of the house that exists in the mundus divinus. I am there as soon as I see it. Now I am at the top of the house. It is beautifully made and furnished. The decor is made of contrasting bits of handcrafted dark hardwoods polished to a shine. The building is larger than I could have ever imagined. Rooms extend away from me in every direction except up. The rooms themselves appear as if they may be further broken down into more rooms, as if each room is a mansion all its own, each in turn containing a mansion in each of its rooms, while all of them reside in the larger structure. A large chandelier hanging over the central stair provides light to the entire building in every direction, as bright as several galaxies full of stars. The stairs themselves descend farther than I can see, and the mansions within mansions go with them into obscurity.

One room attracts my attention. It is at the top of the stairs and is the highest room in the building. It isn't overly large for what it appears to be, a study of some kind. There is a heavy, permanent looking desk; books, and neatly organized papers stored here. It belongs to the Writer who owns the house, the same Writer from my dream of the book in April, 2004. In a cupboard I see a number of files.

Curious, I walk over to it. Inside, it is no ordinary cupboard, nor is there anything pedestrian about the contents. First, all the files within reach appear to be about me. For instance I see a packet of photos. Each is a photo of me, one per year for all of my school years. There are photos of me as I grow up. They are all labeled "Andy J. Paquette." There are objects that belonged to me when I was young, making me wonder how and why the Writer acquired them. I didn't check everything, but it looks like every physical object of any significance in my life is stored here.

The most amazing thing is the hundreds of thousands or millions of papers that document my life. Each document is written like a report that may as well be chapters of my life. They are labeled with my name (as are all the objects) and contain a tremendous quantity of information. It is not limited to physically observable events, but also includes an intimate knowledge of my emotional state at the time. Even this has layers of depth because bundled up in my emotional state is a description of my motivation, my goals, my fears, and anything else that contributed to any aspect of any given situation.

At one point I almost dropped a file. When I did, I saw that behind the shelves, there was endless space. There was no bottom to the cupboard, no sides, no back, and possibly no top (though I didn't look up). At the moment I saw this, it occurred to me that I wasn't the only person the Writer was interested in.

In fact, I had the faintest impression that there were many collections of documents like the ones I saw with my name, but that those files are related to other people. There is a limit to the number of people in the files, but it is a very large number. I also have the impression that the Writer could call any file up to the cupboard's opening by wishing it. In this case, mine had been called up for me, but it could just as easily have been anyone else.

In the dream, I thought the Writer was writing a book about me. I wondered at his surveillance, amazed by how complete it was. I couldn't have done it myself even if it had been my life's work. The CIA couldn't have done it even if they had assigned every agent to the job and had full permission from me. I couldn't figure out how this Writer managed to do it without my ever knowing of his existence or efforts.

There is a curious feature to the files on me that goes several steps beyond the curiosities I've already mentioned. Each "chapter heading" included the hidden purpose behind events in my life, things that even I didn't know but could recognize after reading the chapter heading. As an example, one might read something like this: "Andy J. Paquette loses many things he cannot bear to lose so that he may learn to bear loss." Or: "Andy J. Paquette learns the lesson of being a victim so that he may increase his sensitivity to others."

The Writer had somehow made clear in the way these files were written that certain themes are important. The strongest theme in the files I looked at is my early interest in science and arrogance connected to it. I wasn't aware of being arrogant, but the Writer certainly is.

No matter how many files I look at, there are always more, as if they multiplied by themselves but without taking up any more space than they did originally. If a stack had fifty documents and I took the top two, the stack would still have fifty documents.

After reviewing the documents to my satisfaction, I wake up.

This dream is also a big dream. Remember how I pulled out "my file" during the Book dream? This is it, my opportunity to examine that file at my leisure, in God's study no less. Again, he wasn't present, but his presence permeated everything in the dream. The passageway to the mundus divinus, the servo spiritii, the colossal scale of his house, the rooms containing mansions that contained mansions that all extended nearly to infinity, all lit by a chandelier of galaxies, and then the study itself, were all *his*. These were not the ordinary sights of the mundus alo, or even the mundus sublimis, but a realm of divine activity.

I remember thinking, as I looked through my file, how much the Writer cared about every one of his creations, that he followed them so closely. His closet contained a file on every living being, past or present, and each file was utterly complete, without any gaps in the narrative or errors of any kind.

These two dreams were my introduction to what became a completely new way of thinking about my dreams. At first, the dreams were odd, then interesting, then educational. Now, they had a purpose.

## Chapter Twenty

# Heaven

I have had several dozen dreams of visits to the *mundus sublimis*, only a few of which are included in this chapter. Others are in succeeding chapters according to their content. These dreams are almost always lucid, that is I am aware that my body is sleeping. When I dream of the mundus sublimis, I am always disappointed to leave and wake up here.

DB0/12, 1982
An immense and intensely beautiful city built straight out of an endless ocean of pure, clear water. The architecture is simple, but glorious because every building is a tribute to God, as if they are all cathedrals. Light bounces off of everything and sparkles in every corner. It is intensely bright, yet I can see details without causing pain to my eyes. Every shadow is filled with beautiful reflected light.

A woman who radiates compassion and mercy asks me to follow her. She is a servo spiritus, but of a superior order.

We swim to a large building in the distance. It has no door, so we swim right in. Inside, the building is a single room of great proportions that extends upwards about ten stories. Openings dot the walls to allow light. The rays stream in and bounce all over the walls and the water below. Music fills the building and the waterways outside. It fills the sky as far as it extends, like a choir of angels singing God's praises. Tears flow down my cheeks. I don't ever want to leave, but know I must.

This was my first glimpse of the *mundus sublimis*, or the "world/universe of the sublime and lofty." When I first dreamed it, I thought I'd been to Heaven. The specific purpose of bringing me here may been the same as the reason a parent would bring a child to a favored place, just to do something nice, something the child would remember fondly for the rest of its life. If that was the purpose, it completely succeeded.

The difference between this environment and the mundus alo, is that the mundus alo is empty, but the mundus sublimis is completely filled with light. Sometimes a section of the mundus alo has some light, but it is localized, like from a flashlight. In the same way, the mundus sublimis can have patches of shadow within the light, but they never approach the darkness experienced in the mundus alo.

In the stage analogy, the mundus limus is the stage and the mundus alo is the backstage area, where the support crew do most of their work. Relative to this, the mundus sublimis is a beautiful vacation spot far away from both the stage and backstage locales. The mundus sublimis is a place removed. It is a place of beauty, but more particularly, of refreshment. It is a place of rest, a kind of Sabbath for the soul.

Each of these three major locales occupies one of the "mansions" within the larger mansion that contained the Writer's study in the last chapter. This larger space is the mundus divinus. Thinking about it now, I don't recall an extension beyond the mundus divinus, as if it had fixed boundaries, but through it, one could go anywhere else.

DB4/179, 1/3/91
**This is an exceptionally clear dream segment**
I am on a bus traveling from New York City to New Jersey. We go around a corner and into a tunnel. On the other side we are literally in Heaven.

I don't remember getting out of the bus, but now I am in a room with a male angel. The whole time I am here, I think of the fact that I am dead, don't know how it happened, and am somewhat surprised but pleased to know I will go to Heaven.

The angel tells me that my dreams sometimes combine elements in an unrealistic way. For instance, he reminds me of a dream, this one, where I'd dreamed of a bowl with pictograms inside and on the bottom. He shows me the actual bowl and tells me the reason for dreaming that it had pictograms. My dream of the bowl and the source data it was made from are similar according to the angel, but not combined correctly.

In the dream I think I will be picking out my next life soon. I get nostalgic and sad when I think of people I know from this life. When I say this, the angel is joined by a female angel and then he says something about when I will die. He then says something else that reminds me that I will die after doing something specific. At this point both angels tell me that I am free to return to my body and take their leave of me.

After they leave, a bunch of low level spirits arrive. These creatures make me uncomfortable, so I leave and wake up here.

This dream was like delivering a parcel to the back entrance of the White House. I get to peek inside, but without meaningful interaction with the environment. The "bus" is my way of making sense of how several lebengeists were transported to the mundus sublimis together.

Supposedly, you can't know the time and place of your death. With this dream I've seen it twice and had it described once more, and still don't know what's going to happen. In the dream where I see my entire life from birth to death, there was too much detail to remember it all before it faded. In this dream, I do remember what the angel said, but he didn't tell me specifically what would happen. He told me what I would be doing just before I died, without clarifying if this activity was related to the cause of death. He also said something specific about when, but it wasn't specific enough. It was like having someone tell you that you will die on Tuesday, or two o'clock, or in February.

These times recur on a weekly, daily, and annual basis, respectively. Without more information, there is no way to know which Tuesday, which day at two o'clock, or in what year you will die in February. In the same way, you can be told that you will be reading a newspaper when you die and that the newspaper is the last thing you see when it happens. This may mean that you are hit by a truck on the street or die of a heart attack at home, or the ink on the paper is made of polonium-210 and you are killed by the newspaper itself in a bizarre assassination plot. Like other dreams, enough information is given to recognize the event after the fact, but not before.

## DB18/60, 2/3/06

There is a broad plateau below me. It is supported by a narrow column protruding from the earth, extending miles into the air. The diameter of this column, which appears natural, not a work of architecture, is narrower than that of the plateau. For this reason, it is impossible to walk, run, climb, or drive to the top of it. Because of its height, it cannot be flown to with any type of aircraft. Despite this, there are people on the plateau, myself among them, as lebengeists and todgeists.

To one side is a beautiful building, like a huge courthouse. In front of it is a large cross. The cross is unlike the sort found on churches, or the more realistic crosses used in the movie *The Passion*. Instead, it is like the cross made of a pair of freestanding sections of broken girder left in the remains of the World Trade Center after the two towers were destroyed. My impression is that it is a symbol of the relation between an earthly trial, death, and its reward.

When I wonder how people are supposed to get to this plateau, I am told that the cross is a step, the final step, that all who aspire to come here must pass. It is like a doorway from earth to the mundus sublimis, which is infinitely more beautiful than any place in the mundus limus. The cross is a final task that all must undergo before their job is done.

The cross is the same for everyone because they all have to pass through, narrow as it is. The trial each person had to pass, however, is individually suited to their exact situation. This is why I saw the cross as the one left at the World Trade Center, because that was a great trial for many people. It resulted in death, and in some cases, people passed through the trial and the cross to arrive here in the mundus sublimis.

An angel tells me that very few people manage to get within sight of the cross, or the final trial, whatever form it might take. Their level of awareness, or their performance of various obligations is so poor that they aren't in a position to attempt the challenge presented by the cross. Of those who do know of it, and are in a position to attempt passage through the trials represented by the cross, many will fail. Those who do pass through the cross, will have achieved a great thing.

The angel describes to me the types of challenges faced by those who enter through the cross, the only point of entry to the mundus sublimis, and one characteristic shared by all of the trials. They are all physical and required physical effort of some kind. A person cannot get through the cross simply from knowledge or understanding. He or she will have to do something with their life to put their knowledge into action. If they know charity is good, they have to practice charity, or the knowledge is wasted. If they merely know that to love one's neighbor as oneself is good, it is not enough. That person has to follow through and prove it by doing it in his life.

The angel brings me into the building. Inside, she tells me that I am asleep and my body is on earth. She shows me my sleeping body, separated from me by a kind of barrier. She tells me that my dreams are created here and then sent to me. This surprises me, because the way she describes it, many of my dreams are direct communication between this place, which I understand to be Heaven, and me on earth.

The angel stressed that what I considered "my" dreams are not actually mine. They were made for me, and given to me for a certain purpose, though I don't remember what that purpose is. She then says that when I pass "this trial of the cross" I will be fully awake and never dream again.

I didn't describe it in any detail in my notes, but what I saw about how my dreams are given to me is worth writing here. When the angel described how my dreams are "made" for me, I saw in her mind how this was done. When a message had to be given to me, it was assigned to a servo spiritus to deliver it. This servo spiritus chose how it would be delivered, very much as a craftsman might consider his options before deciding how best to approach a project.

If the servo spiritus decided to show a literal event, because that is all the communication consisted of, then he might pick me up when I am asleep and then bring me to the right point in time and suggest I take a look, as in the Ramstein dream. A different situation might require more interaction, as when Swami Satchidananda explained certain things to me before leading me to the Woodbourne ashram. Even more complicated are messages that are compressed into symbols. In my dream of a series of lives and their various inducements laid out as a video game, one servo spiritus made the symbol for me, but then handed off the explanation to the British woman I have seen in other dreams. This is because some servo spiritii are more adept at creating these symbols, just as others might be more adept at communicating with living people, possibly because they are currently lebengeists themselves, and more attuned to how communication is managed physically.

My impression is that no more than about thirty percent of my dreams are given to me in this way, meaning that the rest are "normal." Another dream not included in this book referenced a figure of about thirty percent, but when I compare it to my list of "solved" dreams, I get a much lower figure, closer to only ten percent. Admittedly, I haven't checked all of my dreams, so it is possible that the figure is different, but it is also true that I don't remember or record all of my dreams either, and it would be very difficult to account for that. Given those difficulties, I am inclined to accept the explanation given in this dream at face value.

I got into some trouble with a religious friend by mentioning this dream to her. She complained that "faith, not works" is the way to Heaven. By that, she meant that a positive declaration of faith in Jesus that included accepting him as a "personal savior," combined with sincere repentance for past misdeeds, is enough to gain entry. If this dream is anything to go by, that doctrine is mistaken, but it doesn't mean that people who believe it are out of luck. According to this dream, anyone who has done what they need to do to get within sight of this final challenge will be given the trial. This means that a person might be completely convinced that a few declarations are enough, but when the time comes, a situation will present itself that must be dealt with, and that person will deal with it, regardless of their beliefs, and through their actions prove whether they are worthy. A person might believe she understands the principles of swimming, but will know for sure when she is pushed into the water.

DB22/5, 6/10/08

I am told directly that certain things will happen, will be allowed, because Heaven cannot, will not, cannot ever be, sullied by allowing admission to impure things. In this case, it refers to the souls of people that carry impurities because they have not yet been purged of, not just actual committed sin, but sinful thoughts as well.

The principle that is explained in this dream is that Heaven isn't Heaven if it allows impurity. Therefore, no impurity is allowed.

## Chapter Twenty-one

# Angels

An angel in a dream is different from a servo spiritus. Angels possess authority, power, and righteousness to an almost painful degree. In one dream, an angel brought me to a stone where I became immediately aware of all my sins against God, and was humbled. In another dream, two angels offered to answer some questions. The beauty of the angels was so overpowering that I couldn't think of anything to ask. It isn't always like that, but angels are definitely a breed apart, regardless of any variety among them.

DB17/27, 12/6/04
(This dream starts in an odd way, so be prepared).

An overweight, crass-looking man, and a young girl scream as the elevator we are in falls. With us is an imperturbable woman. The man uses some profanity in his fright and immediately, a large, strange-looking thing like a giant womb drops low from the ceiling, swallows the man up in one gulp, and then retreats into the shadows above us.

Moments later, we arrive at the bottom of the trip and the doors open. The womb-thing reappears and disgorges the man onto the floor of the elevator. Now he is encased in a flexible sticky sac that forces him into a fetal pose, as if he is a newborn baby. The girl looks on, terrified, but silent.

I get out of the elevator car with the woman, who possesses poise to a degree I have never seen before. She makes me think of an angel, that she might be one. She warns me against taking the Lord's name in vain as the other man did, because the creature that took the man and caused him to be born in this place is but one of many who will instantly grab up anyone who abuses the name of the Lord. She then warns me to keep my thoughts serene. Other types of adverse consequences are to be feared if we fail in this charge.

The environment we are in, a place we descended a great distance to arrive at, is monstrous. The creatures here are horrible to see, and frighten me by their nearness. Luckily, they pay no attention to us.

I follow the woman around a bit, in awe at her constant poise in the face of an entirely adverse environment. There are a few despicable acts carried out before our eyes, making me worry she will become angry or fearful, but she doesn't. A normal-looking man approaches the woman. He wants her to lose her temper or give way to fear. If she does either, she will give herself over to this man, who I now see is in charge here. He is Satan.

His argument to her is simple. He says, "Listen to me, it is an effort and a strain to maintain your temper in these circumstances. Relax, give in to your desires to express yourself, to be yourself. Doing so will give me some power over you, but only so that I can make some difficult choices for you and relieve you of a great burden. Self-control isn't easy, and I am sympathetic. There is another price to pay besides my dominion of you, and that is that you will become ugly. It can be up to you in what way you become ugly and I can help you in those choices also. Many people have already made this bargain with me, so you won't be any different from them and your ugliness may not be noticeable to those around you."

Now I realize this is earth as it really is. The monsters around me are people who have given themselves to Satan. The land is broken, twisted, and ugly only because he controls it. At the same time I can perceive an illusion behind these things that looks very much like the earth I am familiar with when I am awake.

The angel, and I know she is an angel now, resists Satan's

entreaties, but it is an effort. At moments, her features deform slightly when Satan said certain things. When he is done, her face snaps back to normal and shines in her grace and beauty. She ignores Satan and takes me away with her. Her mission is done.

Satan was perfect in form and countenance. He spoke the truth but left out a great deal. Before I wake, the angel reminds me to take care with my thoughts.

The most important thing this angel wanted me to understand is that every thought prompts an immediate reaction, for good or ill. She showed me this in action, by stripping away the illusion we normally see in the mundus limus, so that I saw the spirits of the people there, and how disfigured they were. She showed that their disfigurement is of their own doing. Their sins, in thought and deed, modified their forms so much, like an endless accumulation of warts and pustules, that they were barely recognizable as human. Some of the most horrible-looking spirits were attached to what would be considered attractive bodies, but the spirits themselves were so hideous that if others could see them as they really are, they would be shunned.

I have had a few dreams of Satan, no more than five, and he always looks the same: like a completely normal, friendly man. He is good-looking in the sense that he isn't bad-looking, but not so much that his appearance draws undue attention. He comes across as genuinely interested in your well-being, but there's something off about how he does it. In this dream, he makes a compelling argument to slack off regarding all the things the angel is telling me to do. She says I have to watch my thoughts or become spiritually disfigured. He says, "What's the problem? If everyone is disfigured, then no one will notice. It's difficult to watch your thoughts all the time, relax. You don't need to have everything do you?" He can give you twenty percent of what you would get for working all the time to be righteous, but you don't have to work for it, how does that sound? The weird thing is that while everything he says is true, it doesn't result in anything good.

In another dream, an angel takes me and some others even further down this road, but I barely remember it. Maybe that's a good thing, I'm not sure. Regardless, sometime in 2004, I'm not even sure of the date, an angel picked me up and brought me to Hell, to show me that it "is a real place." The angel showed it to me three times, ironically, so I would remember it. What I remember is this: it was real, and it was far worse than anything I could have imagined. There had been times when I thought, with some conceit, that I would be righteous with my life as I conducted my own business, but would not concern myself with others. The way I looked at it, maybe that would be good enough, and if it wasn't, how bad could it be?

This is like thinking that you'll pay for your own ticket to a movie, but your date is on her own. The penalty sounds like it's not so bad, like having to pay double the price of her ticket, but this is only because you misunderstand what the penalty is. The real penalty is to be shredded in an industrial plastic shredder by Saddam Hussein. After seeing Hell three times in this dream, metaphorically speaking, I was scrambling for my wallet.

DB17/44, 2/12/05

An angel floats above a large city surrounded by water held at bay by manmade barriers. She has floated there for many years to protect it from disaster by creating a kind of dome above the city, to prevent the effects of severe weather. Then one day the dome is dropped and a deluge falls from the sky, destroying the city.

The angel is asked if she became too weak to continue holding back the destructive forces around the city. She replies that she is fine, but that she is no longer allowed to protect the city.

When I wrote this into my journal originally, I did not expect to see it happen. This is because I remembered very little detail in the dream. Then, on August 23, 2005, about six months after the dream, Hurricane Katrina made landfall in New Orleans and flooded eighty percent of the city. Although there were many levees built around New Orleans to protect it against exactly this kind of disaster, almost every one of them was breached. Many of the survivors rode out the hurricane at the Superdome, the most prominent structure mentioned in news coverage of the incident. New Orleans, one of America's largest cities, was effectively wiped out in this one event.

The angel said she was no longer "allowed" to protect the city. This is different from a servo spiritus who points up in the sky and says "look" just in time for me to see a mid-air crash between several planes. This isn't just an accident that happens to reside in a particular place at a certain time. This is something that happened as the result of a decision. The decision was that the city would no longer be protected, and it was almost totally destroyed.

By 2006, I was in very shaky condition financially. It was like a single engine plane diving into a fusillade of bullets. There wasn't much left to cushion the landing, and we were nosing into the ground too fast to stop. It was amazing that we'd lasted as long as we did on the tiny amounts of money we had coming our way after we left Hollywood. By April 10, we'd hit the wall. We hired a bankruptcy attorney. Then, like every other night, I had a dream:

DB18/87, 4/11/06
Everywhere I turn, there is good financial news. It is bizarre because for the past four years, there has been nonstop bad news. Any time something good looks like it will come along, it doesn't. Now, everything is good. I wonder how this can be. As soon as I ask the question in my mind, an angel answers it. She says that,

just as God can oppressively withhold his favors, once he decides to shower them on a person, there's no stopping them.

Within a half hour of recording the dream, I checked my email and found a job offer for the position I now hold. The next day I received a painting commission. A day after that, I discovered that there was a large mistake on my truck lease in my favor. These were just the first three items, and they were immediate. The good news kept rolling in, and still does. So far it isn't anything extravagant, but it's a lot better than the really bad situation we were in right up to the night before the dream.

The fact that this dream accurately predicted later events is less interesting than the reason given: "If God withholds his favors...if God releases them to you...." This is not simply an accident of the universe where glimpses of the future may be had. Like the New Orleans angel who is no longer allowed to protect the city, this is a future that is controlled.

Angels take on many forms. The angel in the previous dream was gentle, the New Orleans angel was powerful, but obedient. Some angels are hypnotically beautiful, others are so powerful that you can barely believe what you are seeing...

DB17/72, 5/18/05
The view from my bedroom window looking east: a row of distant mountains, and the narrow stripe of Highway 74 disappearing behind Black Mountain nine miles away. It is almost dawn. A small amount of light from behind the horizon feathers its way up from the ground, like a mist.

In the sky, the agony of what I see takes my breath away. Without limitation, the entire vault above me is filled with angels. They are God's servants, an army of ferociously devoted, massively powerful, creatures. They hover in the sky, naked, their skin exactly like burning coals. Some angels look like young men, some old, some like infants. All are male. Each and every one is so much more than a match for anything on earth that these physical distinctions make no difference one way or another. All of them have wings, but they are like symbols, not real wings at all. They do not flap to keep them aloft, but stick out to either side, fixed, unmoving. Their bodies shimmer as if on fire, but the light emanating from each one is far more powerful than any earthly fire. They are each like a sun.

I know that each angel is waiting for the same thing: a word. This word will release them all upon the earth, to destroy. Nothing will stand against them, because nothing can.

All that I have seen so far is understood in a single gasp of astonishment and recognition. I want to wake Kitty and Nina to show them this amazing vision, but it is impossible. The power of the angels is such that my entire life is blown away like a leaf in a firestorm and I remember who I am. I remember my life as a spirit and my earthly trials. Then my life comes back, resurrected, and every sin I have ever committed shames me. It is like shackles are thrown up from the ground to encircle my wrists and then to yank me to my knees, but the entire movement is voluntary and automatic. I cannot help myself, I remember God, and I worship him with all my might, head down, so that I do not offend the angels. I cannot stop myself.

While I worship, I see, and hear, that every angel is casting a whisper around the entire world, in millions of individual voices, and one voice. The message is in every language, and one language. All of them speak simultaneously to every person, each in its own language, in a whisper so low that an effort must be made to hear it, but so strong that if the effort is made, it will be heard.

As they say the terrible words, their countenances are beautiful, terrifying, and sad all at the same time. They are beautiful because the Lord is soon to return, terrifying because he comes in vengeance, and sad because he loves those who will be utterly destroyed. What they say is this: "Time is short.

Repentance at the hour of revelation is too late, for at that time, all will know and none will be spared. If you are wise, you will repent now and never do evil again."

When I woke from this dream at six o'clock in the morning, every nerve of my body felt alive with sensation. The power of it is well beyond every dream I'd ever had. I wanted to tell Kitty and Nina about it, but they were still asleep. To assuage my restless energy, I wrote some emails to friends, describing the dream.

It is now four years later. Clearly, "soon" either doesn't mean the same thing as it does in a dream, or it doesn't mean anything at all. I have had dreams take over a decade to happen even though they felt imminent, and this may be like that, but there is no way to know for sure. To me, this is like having a safety gate go down and the alarm bells go off at a railroad crossing. You might not be able to see the train, or the signal may be malfunctioning, but you don't want to ignore the warning only to find yourself on those tracks when the train punches through the intersection.

DB19/34, 8/17/06

I see powerful non-human beings on their way to earth. Their purpose is to destroy our bodies and give us new ones. The new bodies will differ from our current bodies because they won't require food, water, air, or sleep, nor can they procreate.

In the dream, this distressed me because I liked these things about my current body. The new bodies would make it totally impossible to enjoy physical pleasures because the bodies would not require the satisfaction of these desires as our physical bodies do.

I hope that readers can see, from the examples given, why angels are a class apart from a servo spiritus. I don't doubt that an angel could, would, or has intervened to save a person in dire circumstances, but I do think that if a servo spiritus can be as effective, that is who will do it instead. The angels of this chapter, some anyway, have a completely different agenda.

## DB17/17, 11/22/04

An angel says "There will be a great calamity as a sign that Jesus will soon return. I will show you the sign and then repeat this message three times, so that you know it is true."

Next, we are high in the sky, looking down at a huge swath of coastline. Thousands and thousands of people fill the beaches. Then, the people stand and run from the water. They are swept up in it and there is tremendous loss of life, unthinkable numbers of people are drowned.

The angel then says, "I have now shown you the sign. I will repeat the message two more times for a total of three times, so that you know this message is true. There will be a great calamity as a sign that Jesus will return soon. I will now show you the sign for the second time." Again I see the thousands of people at the coast. As before, they all get up and run, in sheer terror, as the water chases them down and drowns them en masse.

The angel looks at me and says, "Now you have heard the message and seen the sign two times. I will repeat the message again and show you the sign for the last time, so you may know this is true." I then see it again, every bit as devastating as the first two times.

And then I wake up.

On the night of this dream, I was sick and didn't feel like writing in the journal, so I wrote it down quickly and went back to sleep. When Nina got up, I remembered the dream and told her about it. Almost a month later, I had this dream:

DB17/29, 12/20/04

A Japanese seismology station. One of the machines records a magnitude seven earthquake, but one of the technicians says, "It's not that big." I can see the graph and there are dozens of quakes represented on it, of varying magnitudes. If anything, seven seemed to be at the low end of the scale for this group that topped out in the high eights.

I wonder why no one seems concerned, and a technician says to me, "It's not here," and then he looks to the Southwest and I can see on a globe that he is looking to a place to the south and west of China, in a great southern ocean.

Three days after I recorded this dream in my journal, I read online about a magnitude 8.2 earthquake between Australia and New Zealand. Over the course of the next twenty-four hours, the story updated several times to reflect large aftershocks. Then, after two days, the second-largest earthquake ever recorded, of a magnitude between 9.1 to 9.3, occurred near the island of Sumatra, and spawned the Boxing Day Tsunami. The tsunami killed approximately 300,000 people in twelve different countries, most of whom were vacationing on the coast when the tsunami waves hit. They tried to run, but with thirty meter tall waves that moved at five hundred miles an hour, they didn't have a chance.

I mentioned this to Nina, expecting her to remember that just a few days earlier, I had shown her the dream about the Japanese seismography station. She did, but then she surprised me by saying, "And the other one too, it's just like that one also." I had no idea what she was talking about. Somehow, I'd totally blanked out on the earlier dream, possibly because I'd been sick that day, but more likely because it was a dream from the middle of the night and I went back to sleep after writing it down. Nina insisted I look for it in my journal, and I found it, just about a month before the tsunami. It was one of the few occasions, possibly the only one, when I felt a cold chill up my spine as I read it. I remembered it as clearly as if I had just woken up, with the angel saying, "This will be a sign..." and then the people running in vain away from a hungry ocean.

It was clear that the dream of the repeating calamity was the Boxing Day tsunami, just as the earthquake dream from just a few days before the disaster was a literal view of one aspect of the event. What disturbed me about the dream, and disturbs me to this day, is that the angel said it was a sign, a sign that Jesus would return to earth soon. This was a first for me. I'd never had a dream like it.

Up until this dream, every precognitive dream I could remember was either a literal dream of an event, or a guide has simply shown me an event without comment. In both, the future event is neutral. Here, I was told that the calamity, the "sign," was in itself a proof of another, much greater event, one that has been awaited for a couple thousand years by Christians around the world.

Because this is my first dream of a "sign," and the second half of the dream has not happened yet, I am free to have some doubt about the second half of the dream. This makes me think about the Porgy dream, and how, when my dad told me Porgy was dead and how he died, I immediately knew I'd seen his ghost. I denied this for years, even to myself, but in my gut, I always knew that I had seen him. With this dream, it's a bit like that. A part of me doesn't want to admit that this dream was more than a simple precognitive dream, but what is traditionally called a prophecy.

When I first noticed that I was having dreams that appeared to correlate with future events, but before I started the journal and knew it for a fact, I also discovered the discomfort of knowing something that my peers didn't believe was possible. In 2004, fifteen years after the journal began, I had a large number of dreams that had powerful religious imagery. By then I was comfortable with my dreams of the future. With religious dreams, the things they suggested put me right back to 1989. I thought they looked solid, but until they happened, I wasn't comfortable.

## Chapter Twenty-two

# Prophecies

A prophecy, unlike a simple precognitive dream, is divinely inspired. Most of the future dreams in this book are not prophetic because their subject matter is mundane or the dream is the result of my own casual glimpses of the future. Some dreams, like the 9/11 dream with the skeleton, might be considered prophetic on the basis of their magnitude, but without a specific divine reference, I am unwilling to agree.

The New Orleans dream was prophetic because of two things. It contained enough information to recognize the Hurricane Katrina event, and the angel said that she was no longer "allowed" to protect the city, implying that divine oversight was involved. The fiery angels in the sky certainly appears to be prophetic from a subject matter point of view, but by the time it is proven, if ever, it will be irrelevant. That dream has to be taken at face value or not at all. The tsunami dream is also prophetic, for reasons already explained.

None of the dreams in this chapter have happened yet. They are presented regardless because they are intriguing. If they are prophetic, they may also prove useful to some readers.

DB17/28, 12/16/04

Jesus and two friends follow a path that leads into a valley between high cliffs in a desert. A large stone wall or building rises up from the valley below them. The path itself becomes a well traveled road that runs directly into the stone wall, where a large gate blocks the way. In front of this wall, and on either side of the road, are carefully tended olive trees.

Jesus explains a piece of ancient scripture to his two friends. It is not a part of the Bible. It is a short letter of some kind called (I think) "Micaneas." He points to verses 1:50-1:55 and compares them with verses 9:50-9:55. He says the two are related, though separated by many other verses. The first group of verses describes the taking of olives from a planted garden, the second is about a man in church being used for a pre-designated purpose.

The scripture he refers to is well-known to these men, though I've never heard of it. He takes pains to draw their attention to the relatedness of the two sections of this scripture, which he holds in his hands like a scroll. "You see how it says here in 1:50 and 1:55, 'The garden is planted, the olive is taken' and in 9:50 and 9:55 it says 'He is among men, and then he is gone.' These two verses are saying the same thing."

My impression is that Jesus and these men intend to meet others among the olive trees below, where certain olives that grow on certain trees will be taken, and then they will enter the city and certain inhabitants will be taken also, each according to their destiny.

I have had a few dreams of Jesus over the years, and he always has at least two friends with him. On the one occasion I referred to them as "disciples," Jesus corrected me by saying, "They are my friends." In other, earlier dreams, Jesus and his friends work on a large-scale project that they are all excited about. In this dream, they appear to be getting ready to carry out their plans, at least part of which involves a selection process by which people will be taken from their residences.

When Nina was twelve, she had a dream that reminded me strongly of this one. It was all the more striking because she almost never remembered her dreams. Here it is, as written by her:

In my dream, I felt that I was in a mansion but could only see one gigantic room. It was circular, with towering walls that ended in a domed ceiling painted like the night sky. The floor wasn't really a floor, but a gaping hole above a black void. This "floor" was divided into sections like a giant pie, and each section was filled with stars. There were billions and billions of colored stars, floating within the constraints of the sections as if held in by them.

Each section held a different color of stars. All the stars of the same color were grouped together in their section. I got the idea that each color corresponded to a class of people and each star corresponded to a specific person.

I was attached to the red stars and hung around them. It was really beautiful and I was happy to have all these red stars, but then I had the sense that white is the best color of all to have. But there were no white stars in the entire gigantic room.

Then a voice spoke to me, coming from the ceiling. I don't remember anything of what it said, though at the time I found it to be extremely interesting and the voice seemed very powerful.

When the voice finished, a gold teakettle fell from the ceiling into my hands. I took the lid off and looked into it, and saw a clear liquid that was too thick to be water. I poured it over some of the red stars, and they vanished.

I was sure the stars had not vanished into the void they were suspended over, but had been transported into another place. There was still a large number of red stars left.

At that point, I became involved in another dream—it was not important, but I became very involved in it. It went on for a while, and then suddenly I found myself back in the great room with the stars. Everything was as I'd left it; a portion of the red stars was still missing.

The voice began speaking to me for a long time, and when it finished, a shower of stars rained down from the ceiling like confetti. They were in all different colors. Whether they went to their respective sections in the pie or whether they disappeared in midair I don't know, but the focus of this event was on the last star to fall from the ceiling: a glittering, shining white star.

In the dream, I wanted that white star. I was entertaining a desire to have a section full of white stars, and I figured that the one white star—the first one I'd seen in the dream thus far— would help me reach that goal. As luck would have it, the white star landed in "my" section—the red section. When the white star touched my red stars, it made a large number of stars disappear, and then it vanished.

The voice spoke again for a short time. When he finished, a second gold teakettle fell into my hands. This teakettle was full of the same liquid as the first, and when poured over my stars, they vanished, just as before. More than half of the red stars were gone at this point, but many remained.

At this point I wanted to tell Daddy about my dream, so I went away to find him, and woke up shortly after.

When I've told people about my dreams, they sometimes tell me theirs. Usually, they are ordinary dreams. Only a small number of dreams has been genuinely interesting, and only two had me riveted to my seat. One was told to me by a friend in Phoenix, and the other is this one. To my ears, I'd just heard a dream that, had it been mine, would have ranked high above many other dreams in my journal.

It is a symbolic dream, but like all good symbolic dreams, it isn't that difficult to work out. Also like good symbolic dreams, if you try to imagine how the same information could be conveyed *without* symbols, it is easy to see that this is the better way to do it.

Each star represents a spirit. The "pie" as Nina calls it, is the mundus limus. The different colors differentiate the spirits based on an unknown quality. It is enough to know that they are differentiated and that they are numerous. The kettle is a lamp of oil for anointing, which is exactly what Nina accomplishes by pouring it on some of the stars. Anointing is done to identify, or consecrate, something for a holy purpose. By anointing these spirits, they are made to leave the mundus limus, presumably to the mundus sublimis. The "white star" is Jesus, who has a much more powerful anointing effect than the small lamp given to Nina, and takes away a proportionately greater number of spirits. Despite all this activity, many more are left behind than are taken away. The repetition of dropping the teakettle into Nina's hand twice is not done to increase the number of anointed spirits, but to remind Nina of the events of the dream, so that she remembers when she wakes.

This correlates with the "Micaneus" dream. The large orchard of olive trees is analogous to both the walled city and the "pie" of Nina's dream. The individual olives are likewise analogous to the anointed among the city's residents and the anointed stars from Nina's dream. Jesus appears in both, so no interpretation or symbol substitution is required.

Both of these dreams are saying that Jesus will come and take some spirits away, and leave many behind. The implication is that this is good for the ones who are taken, less good for those who remain.


DB22/15, 7/22/08

A semi-darkened room containing two side-by-side wooden thrones. To either side of each throne, there is a niche built into heavily ornamented wood paneling.

The first throne is for a great bishop, the other for a king. The niches are empty, but then I see some small sculptures taken out of a storage place, of bishops and kings. These are placed, in alternating order, starting with a bishop in the first of the niches.

By placing the small figure in the niche, the throne is made ready for the man who will occupy it. There are two of these thrones, the last of a long succession. In the past, a great number of these small figures were placed in niches leading up to the thrones by a caretaker.

At the end, there is no niche for another king after the last bishop, leaving me to wonder who would occupy the final, and empty, throne. Beside it I see the last bishop, but know that his reign will be supplanted by another. Beside the throne there is no niche for a figure, nor a figurine to place there.

It is here that someone shows me an intricately written document made of a thick but flexible material, like an animal's skin. The writing is beautiful and complex, but I do not understand it. Despite this handicap, I somehow have the impression that the last king is being held as a ransom and that a penalty will be paid for his return.

Again, the symbols in this dream are good quality, and explain what might otherwise be complex in an easily remembered series of images. The small figurines are of men who hold positions of power in both secular government and religious administration. I don't see any earlier thrones because there aren't any. Until the ransomed king is returned, all of these positions will be held by men. The "bishop" who is returned will be more than a man, and this is why he has a throne waiting for him instead of a niche in the wall. The "penalty" may be something along the line of the destruction described in other dreams. There is no throne for a last king, because the last bishop will rule over all things.

DB19/1, 6/13/06

There is a large pool in front of a large cathedral. I resist the urge to have a swim. Instead, I walk to the cathedral. Inside, it has vaulted ceilings, stone floors, and wooden furniture. There are chairs set up like thrones in niches on either side of the long main hall. Each niche is extraordinarily large to accommodate the size of the chairs themselves, which appear to have been designed for giants to sit upon. The seats of each chair are taller than a tall man, an indication that anyone who could sit comfortably on one of these would be about six meters tall, or eighteen feet. There are as many as twenty-four of these chairs in total, with one at the far end of the room.

An old man stands near the farthest chair. He is tough, strong, in perfect health, kindly, moral, intelligent, and the guest of honor. A large crowd of people wait to see him, but he beckons me over. I pass through the crowd to get to him, marveling as I do at the large scale of the ancient furniture in this room. These large chairs are important in a way that escapes me now, but at the time I was aware of their history and how important they were.

When I am near him, the old man tells the crowd how modern people live so differently from people in biblical times that the meaning of many parts of the Bible have become distorted. He tells how he lived in exactly the way the ancients did when he lived in the holy land. I can see him sleeping outside under the stars at night as he tells us of his life there.

As an example of how things were done he describes how he had to make a small bag to carry seeds for a journey. It is made of rough cloth, and sewn together with twisted vegetable fiber used as thread, and a thorn as a needle. To open it, he had to partly unravel the "thread." To close it again, he had to sew it shut. I assumed the seeds were food for traveling, but don't remember if he said so.

Whatever their purpose, it is a rough job to make these things compared to simply buying a bag at a modern shop. The man wants everyone in the cathedral to make one and then fill them with seeds. I don't want to because it is pretty clear my hands would be hurt in the process. Even though he had brought sufficient supplies for everyone to make one of these seed bags (and I was first in line), I said "No thanks, I can understand by what you've shown how difficult it is, and don't need to make one of my own." After that, I left.

On my way out, the old man complains that I haven't made my bag. He says there is a spiritual benefit to making it or having it, or both. Even so, I keep walking. As I walk, I listen to the various conversations of the people around me. They are all excited about an imminent great work, the return of Jesus to the earth. Everyone is talking about it, and of the preparations they are making to get ready, this present gathering among them.

Near the exit, I see ten young girls just like in the parable of the virgins. They carry unlit lamps and appear ready to be married. I exit the building, see the pool again, and jump in. After that, I wake up.

Here is the parable of the 10 virgins, to provide an inkling of what I meant just before exiting that dream:

From Matthew 25:1-13 (NIV version):
[1]"At that time the kingdom of Heaven will be like ten virgins who took their lamps and went out to meet the bridegroom. [2]Five of them were foolish and five were wise. [3]The foolish ones took their lamps but did not take any oil with them. [4]The wise, however, took oil in jars along with their lamps. [5]The bridegroom was a long time in coming, and they all became drowsy and fell asleep.

[6]"At midnight the cry rang out: 'Here's the bridegroom! Come out to meet him!' [7]"Then all the virgins woke up and trimmed their lamps. [8]The foolish ones said to the wise, 'Give us some of your oil; our lamps are going out.' [9]" 'No,' they replied, 'there may not be enough for both us and you. Instead, go to those who sell oil and buy some for yourselves.'

[10]"But while they were on their way to buy the oil, the bridegroom arrived. The virgins who were ready went in with him to the wedding banquet. And the door was shut. [11]"Later the others also came. 'Sir! Sir!' they said. 'Open the door for us!' [12]"But he

replied, 'I tell you the truth, I don't know you.'

13"Therefore keep watch, because you do not know the day or the hour.

For years after I first had this dream, I wondered what it meant. It seemed important, but the idea of making little bags for a handful of seeds seemed silly, and the meaning of the dream escaped me. Looking at it now, it is obvious. The seed bags are equivalent to the lamps, and the seeds to the oil. Both are made in readiness for the same thing: in one, the return of the bridegroom, in the other, the return of Jesus, who is acknowledged to be the "bridegroom" referred to in Matthew. So the parable of the virgins, and this dream, both describe an activity in preparation for a journey. With the virgins, they needed light to see their way, with the man in my dream, food for the journey. In either case, failure to prepare equals failure overall.

Most of the dreams in this chapter make explicit references to Jesus. Those that do not, strongly imply that he is their subject. I am made uncomfortable by these dreams. The reason is not simply that he is a controversial figure, but that I have come to no strong conclusions about him myself.

I have not read or seen any good argument to disbelieve that Jesus existed. I have no problem with the miracles claimed for him in the Bible. I've had smaller scale "miracles" in my own life, so there is no bar to them on the grounds that they are impossible. Indeed, when I said, "I think you should have it" and the painting jumped on Kitty, I was reminded strongly of the saying by Jesus that "if you have faith the size of a mustard seed, you will say to this mountain, 'move from here to there' and it will move." I enjoy the parables of Jesus a great deal. The teaching stories have real merit, making it very difficult to fault them. I disagree when Christians claim that Jesus is God, and that there is a Holy Trinity.

The book *Misquoting Jesus* by Bart Ehrman does an excellent job of tracking down errors and omissions in Bibles, modern and ancient. Many of the worst errors center around attempts to incorporate pagan traditions into what became Christianity, among them, the idea of a holy trinity. But this book is about my dreams, and it is there that my strongest objections, and my confusion, reside.

I have dreamed of Jesus and of God. They are so far from being the same, there is no comparison between the two. If there is any truth to my dreams, and there is some evidence to support the idea that there is, then there is no such thing as a "holy trinity," and Jesus is not God. That is my objection. On the other hand, I have dreams about Jesus that clearly match Messianic and Apocalyptic expectations. Most of the traditions regarding these things were unknown to me until *after* a friend would point out that a dream matched up with some passage in the Torah or the Bible. I did not know about the Bible until after I found that many of my dreams contained references that matched sections of it that I'd never seen before.

Based on my dreams alone, Jesus is an important figure, but where exactly he fits, and what exactly he *is*, is a mystery to me. If I look at them with a critical eye, some of the references in this book that appear to refer to Jesus are references to the return of an unnamed powerful figure of great religious significance. The description of this figure happens to match Christian expectations, but he is not named, leaving the question open. The problem is that he is clearly named in the only dream that has provided any amount of proof so far: the tsunami dream.

It is easy enough to discount Nina's identification of Jesus because of her youth and much greater exposure to the Bible (Kitty took her to church regularly). The dream of the thrones may well describe a throne for God, not Jesus, and the "bridegroom" dream is allegorical enough that it could refer to an event instead of a person, or to God instead of Jesus. This leaves my three dreams of Jesus himself, in which he is organizing a great work with his friends. In these, he can be assigned servo spiritus status without any difficulty, despite the fact that he is apparently directing this great project. Then we are left with the tsunami dream, and all by itself, it is a formidable obstacle.

Without the tsunami itself, I wouldn't have to pay attention to it, but there *was* the tsunami, and this dream didn't show it to me just once, but three times, and I heard the message three times also: "This is a sign of Jesus' return." I may dislike some major aspects of Christian doctrine, I may not understand religion at all, but I do know what I wrote in my journal that day, and I do remember the dream itself. I have to take Jesus seriously, and do, exceptions noted.

# Chapter Twenty-three

# God

DB21/40, 1/3/08

I meet a man in the desert. He has colored lights dancing around in front of his face. It is a weird effect, but looks natural, like light passing through the colored panes of a stained glass window. The colors are distinct and pretty; blues and yellows. They move slightly when he moves his head or speaks. He tells me I have colors in front of my face also, but they are all greens.

Next, I'm in a large mansion as a guest. Several people come up to me and ask me to do things related to selling an artifact that is called something like "Templar Knight," but I don't think it is an entire man in armor. It is something else.

I get the idea it might be an ancient chronograph, or timepiece. The people here say that it has all been arranged, that this thing is coming. A woman comes to get me, and then introduces me to a couple of men. They ask me to follow them outside to see something they have in their vehicle.

They open a locker in their trunk to reveal all sorts of catalogs and brochures, not one of which has one of these gadgets that everyone is talking about. Now I remember that I have agreed to market the templar knight thing (whatever it is). So when it arrives, though it isn't mine, I will present it to potential customers.

One of the men asks me if I know what the knight is. I start to answer, but then admit I have no idea. These men, like everyone else, are excited about the scheduled arrival of the knight, and want me to know what it is so I can do my job better.

After admitting that I don't know what it is, I am suddenly in a different room in the mundus sublimis. It is an enormous room, with a smooth, black floor. The two men and I are at one end of the room, and on the other, brilliant light projects outwards from a light source that might be twenty feet tall. There is someone else present, but I can't see him because he is inside of this brilliant light and a screen partly blocks my view. He is very powerful and authoritative. The servo spiritii wait patiently as their superior tells me what they brought me here to know.

The voice from within the light totally fills the room, telling as it does, about the imminent arrival of the knight. The voice says that he has judged something and found it wanting, so the judgment is against this entity, which is comprised of many people, like a company going out of business. The company is the entity judged, but it is the company's many employees who are terminated.

So I'm listening to all this, wondering what it all has to do with me, despite being invited to witness the meeting. Next, I'm back on earth. A servo spiritus is there with a document to show me. He opens it up and starts reading. It all has to do with time, God, the nature and relationship of time and God, and God to time.

What I see on the paper is a fixed schedule of events that even God will not alter. It does appear to have some flexibility, but only because this is God's schedule. One section of the paper describes a series of events that will take place at God's command. Shortly afterwards, he will personally arrive on earth. Then the spirit says something like, "This is because Time is not relative to God, but God is relative to Time."

The spirit explains that God's schedule for the events has been fixed since the beginning of time, but his actions at these appointed times may vary, depending on circumstances.

It is frustrating that I was so out of it in this dream that while I was dragged around, I had barely any notion of what was going on. The good news is that I remembered enough details to make sense of the dream afterwards, even though I was in no condition to understand it at the time.

The first man with the colored lights in front of his face is a servo spiritus. The green color he sees around me is the dominant color of my aura. I hope it is more related to health than avarice, both of which I associate with green. This servo spiritus brings me to a mansion as a guest. It is unclear from the description or my memory in which mundus it is located.

The "people" who come up to me to discuss the "Templar Knight" have to be spirits of some kind, simply because they have knowledge of the Templar Knight and they can talk to me while I am sleeping. They are servo spiritii. At first I think they will be selling the Templar Knight, making me immediately classify it as an "it" instead of a "who." This is why I think it is an object. I wonder if it might be an ancient and valuable timepiece, probably because of a misinterpreted reference to the schedule. It is at this point that a woman comes to get me, like a hostess ushering a drunk guest outside for some fresh air, to meet two men. Naturally, these are servo spiritii also.

They show me a trunk full of catalogs and brochures. Together, they contain images and descriptions of every object I could possibly imagine being for sale, but none contains a Templar Knight. The point they are trying to make with this example is that the Templar Knight is not an object, nor is it to be sold as a commodity. I don't understand, but these servo spiritii know I'll be able to figure it out when I wake up, provided I remember what they show me.

Here I make a slight, but crucial, breakthrough. I will be *marketing* the Templar Knight, not *selling* it. I still don't know what it is they want, but am closer to the idea. Marketing isn't right either though, because what they really expect is some publicity. Because I started with the idea of a product, I have a hard time shaking it. Both servo spiritii know that something is wrong, *but I don't*. To snap me out of it, one of them asks if I know what the Templar Knight is. I'm all set to answer, but as soon as the first words roll out of my mouth, it hits me: I don't have a clue.

Now they take me to the mundus sublimis, possibly even the mundus divinus, and even this isn't enough to wake me up. I'm like a completely dumb human recording device. Someone else has to push all the buttons, and I record whether I know it or not.

God is the source of the bright light, and the "superior" of these two servo spiritii. He explains to me why the Templar Knight is being sent to earth and that he will be dispatched soon.

I return to earth and then I know that something is up because to return, I must have been somewhere else. I pay closer attention now and the rest is pretty straightforward. What this dream is telling me is that some being that has been given the symbol of a Templar Knight will be sent to earth by God as a consequence of a judgment he has made that went against many people. The timetable explanation is given to me so that I understand that this is an event with a fixed time attached to it. It is scheduled, and God will not alter it. My part is to help prepare the way for the arrival of the knight with publicity of some kind. Shortly after the arrival of the knight, God himself will arrive on earth as well. This is why everyone is so excited by all these preparations.

If I had to guess at the identity of the Templar Knight, I would say it is Jesus. If so, then Jesus comes with the fiery angels seen before, and God follows. If it isn't Jesus, then we're back to the symbol of the knight. Speaking of that, as a symbol, it isn't a bad one. The Templar Knights were named after the Temple of Solomon in Jerusalem, which they used as a headquarters starting soon after the city was captured by European powers in 1077. Their duty was to protect pilgrims to the holy city, as well as the temple itself. What better way to protect the innocent and the righteous than by destroying the unrighteous?

DB17/82, 6/21/05

I wake up to find my bed in a large and ancient chamber. God himself is at my bedside, and has been since before I woke. Intense light projects outwards from him in all directions, but it only illuminates our figures and the immediate area we occupy. He looks like an old man, but an intensely powerful, robust, old man. There isn't a shred of infirmity in the lines of his face, his posture, or his speech. Just the sight of him is enough to know he wields world-crushing power. He was already speaking before I woke, and continues without pause.

At first, I am overwhelmed to see him so close, but have no time to collect myself because he is saying important things to me, and I have already missed some of them. His voice is strong, but he speaks in a whisper, his words uttered one after the other, precisely timed, without hesitation or correction. I want to take notes, but cannot because he does not pause. One word after the other, swift, like trying to catch the current of a powerful river. I must listen attentively, and do my best to remember. He continues, and I pay attention. The first thing I remember him saying is this:

"I speak to you so that you may hear. These words are spoken directly to you for a purpose. I have chosen you to hear these things." There was more, but the point was, he wanted me to know why he was speaking to me. Next, came the message:

"These things will shortly come to pass: We are in a holy place. The relics in this place are holy and will soon be recovered to man."

When he says this, I see that the cave we are in is stuffed with ancient artifacts. I also understand that when God says they are "holy," he means that he has imbued them with holy qualities that make the objects truly holy, like nothing else on earth. He goes on to say,

"There is a poor place in the world, not unknown to local inhabitants, but whose holy nature has been concealed for centuries. It is by the sea in another country. Divers will enter the water. The water is filthy around the entrance to the secret, and this is what keeps people away. When the discovery is made, this city, which is fallen and corrupt, will be restored and sanctified to its former state."

As he says this line, I see the corruption of the city built into the land above and around this cave. I see prostitution, thieves, corrupt officials, and tradesmen selling mass-produced religious idols. Then I see all of them destroyed. The people of the city run and scream; none escape. God continues speaking:

"At that time, the city will be known by its true name instead of the false name it has borne for so many years."

"This ground is holy, but unknown to man. Above us is an unrighteous city. When the discovery of this place is made, I will be known to all. This city will be holy again."

I see everything he describes as it happens in the future. The holy relics are not just recognized for what they are, but some aspect of their holiness exerts a powerful influence on those who see them, forcing them to be humble and repentant. They fall to their knees and worship God. God comes back to them, and to the world.

In the next instant, I am alone. My first thought is to tell Nina what I have seen. I find her in a crowded restaurant, where I excitedly tell her of the discovery to come. I speak in a loud voice that attracts the attention of some neighboring diners. I tell one woman that when the name of this town is changed, that will be a sign for her so that she will know I have spoken the truth.

I take Nina out of the restaurant to show her the secret place. To get there, we first enter an antechamber with rough rock walls. The hidden relics are nearby, but there is no entrance in sight. Instead, there is a single lamp stand with an old-fashioned oil burning lamp upon it. Determined to find the hidden chamber, I walk through the center of this space, passing the lamp as I do so. When I am level with it, it is miraculously filled to overflowing with anointing oil. Flaming jets of burning oil shoot out in every direction, filling the room with a bright light. It lands on everything in sight, but as Nina points out to me, it consumes nothing. Then I see the oil somehow projected outside, arcing over the entire city, and striking every single item within it, making it holy.

God did pronounce the "true name" of the city several times, but because it is a foreign word and I was unfamiliar with how to spell the sounds he used, I was forced to write it phonetically into the journal, knowing it was wrong, but retaining some qualities of the correct word. It reminded me of the Navajo word "Chielly," pronounced "Shay-ee," but there is more to it than that. I was surprised about a month afterwards when I heard an Israeli exchange student behind me say what sounded like "shay-ee" while I was talking with someone else. I turned around and introduced myself, then asked her to repeat the word, which sounded like "yay-roo-shay-eem." She had to say it a few times before I figured out that she was saying "Jerusalem."

Jerusalem does not match the other characteristics of the city however, at least not without stretching the imagination, so I am not satisfied with this identification. Jerusalem is not on the coast, is not "poor," and its "holy nature," whether real or imagined, is not "concealed."

The scene with the burning anointing oil is an excellent symbol to represent the primary elements of the main dream. The lamp stand and lamp are holy relics, the anointing oil consecrates other things as holy, the oil is on fire because it will not be painless, and it covers the entire city because it will be purified in its entirety.

The dream of the coming knight shows the action as it is projected from the mundus sublimis to the mundus limus. This dream of a cavern filled with holy objects shows the same thing from the point of view of the mundus limus. Within the mundus limus, holiness is recovered for the people of a poor and corrupt seaside town. It is humbled, destroyed, and restored. The destruction aboveground, it may be assumed, is related to either the knight or the army of angels, or both. When it is over, holiness on earth is a reality once more.

In one dream of mine, I couldn't stop crying. It was because, everywhere I looked, there were either people who were far from God who I wept for out of pity, or whose nearness to God made me weep for joy. In the dream of the cavern, when I spoke with Nina in the restaurant, I wept there also, because I could feel in my soul the beauty of an entire city of truth and righteousness. Its proximity, as conveyed in these dreams, was so near that, like a mirage in the distance that was no longer a mirage, I was ready to knock on the door and ask to be let inside.

The price of entry was simple: remember God, repent, and sin no more.

## Chapter Twenty-four

# Awake

In the summer of 1985, at three in the morning, I found myself sitting up on a thirty-guilder cot. My room was lit by a pink and blue neon Marlboro sign hanging in front of my window. It illuminated my open eyes, eyes that were open when I was asleep and then when I was awake, unblinking, unseeing, but remembering a mugging three weeks in the future. I woke up when I recognized the sign in front of my window, but not when I opened my eyes. They were already open, they could already see what was there. Only when I understood my environment, could I resume my life within it. Only then could I "click in" and be a part of it again.

That night in Amsterdam, I had no idea who I was. I thought I was a random collection of molecules, assembled by various unpredictable forces of nature and evolution into a thing that cannot help but grow at the end of a string of DNA, because that was all there was to a human being. The dream gave me the first clue that it wasn't true, but I didn't accept it at first.

When the journal first produced results, I saw each event individually, without any idea how they connected, or if they ever would. I didn't even consider the question. The pieces were interesting enough on their own to keep my mind busy. I experienced the dreams as if each individual event were one domino in a row of thousands. As each domino fell, I only watched the domino that was falling at that moment. I had no appreciation for the pattern they made until they had all fallen and I ceased to be distracted by their movement.

Now that I have a better perspective, I am amazed by what these dreams turned out to be. For one thing, they weren't

271

dreams at all, at least not by the common meaning of the word. Instead, they are memories of real events. Sometimes the "event" is a common fantasy, given life by the plasticity of thought. Other events are genuine interactions between spirits of all varieties, in various non-physical locations, some of which are not bound by linear time. To describe all this as a "dream" is like describing the history of the universe as a "car." Cars are involved, but they are a very tiny part of the story.

The part of a "dream" experience that is described as being a dream, is the remembered event, whatever it is. The part that comes closest to a modern definition of the word is the act of remembering the event, but this doesn't differentiate between a memory from our waking experience and one from our *other*, non-physical, waking experience. The word "dream" does distinguish between sleep and wakefulness, but implies much that is false without including enough of what is true. Without an acknowledgement that a dream is a memory from our permanent non-physical existence, the word is misleading.

Sometimes our memories of this other life are so polluted by our own poorly controlled thoughts that it can seem incomprehensible. Even without that stumbling block, carrying memories into our bodies from a non-physical state is difficult, and results in a confusing puzzle made of imagination and reality. The puzzle is incomplete and contains elements that at first don't seem to belong, and yet they do. Even the junk dreams are legitimate, because they show how great an impediment our desires and prejudices can be when trying to observe or understand something clearly.

One of my earliest theories was that everyone had dreams like mine, but forgot them. Enlarging on that, I suspected they were purely natural side effects of unknown powers of the mind. Then I tried to categorize them. This is precognition over here, that is an OOBE, this other thing is an after death communication, there isn't a name for that one yet, but it's like a near-death experience, and so on. All of these pieces of odd events were just so many pieces. They were connected by their weirdness, and a few similarities in the way they behaved, but beyond that, they were a mystery.

When I started this book, I thought I understood my dreams, but I didn't. What I didn't realize was that there was more than one way to look at the information. My problem was that, just like the Spanish Spider-man comic, I was trying to read the dreams in the wrong language. I thought they were "dreams," but they were *life*. A "dream" as it is defined today, is a myth.

The end result of this project is not what I expected, but it is also better than expected, because answering the questions I asked of myself while writing it taught me more than I thought could possibly be squeezed out of the subject. I found myself looking at dreams like I'd never seen them before, with fresh eyes, newly awake to what they meant. Even more than that, I have recovered some of my wonder at the immensity of creation and all that exists beyond it. I now believe in God, and accept that our world and all it contains was made by him. This is a step in the right direction, if for no other reason but that this is where the evidence leads.

Andrew Paquette
- *Mundus Limus, 2009*

# BOOKS

mySpiritRadio